IRONCLAW

IRONCLAW

A Navy Carrier Pilot's Gulf War Experience

Sherman Baldwin

William Morrow and Company, Inc. New York

Library of Congress Cataloging-in-Publication Data

Baldwin, Sherman.
 Ironclaw : a Navy carrier pilot's war experience / Sherman
Baldwin.
  p. cm.
 ISBN 0-688-14303-2
 1. Persian Gulf War, 1991—Personal narratives, Americans.
2. Persian Gulf War, 1991—Aerial operations, American. 3. Baldwin,
Sherman. I. Title.
DS79.724.U6B35 1996
956.7044'2—dc20   96–2287
                     CIP

Printed in the United States of America

First Edition

1 2 3 4 5 6 7 8 9 10

BOOK DESIGN BY LEAH CARLSON

For Alice, my strongest supporter, my most honest critic,
my best friend, and my greatest love

PREFACE

Naval aviation is an inherently dangerous business. This book is about that business and my personal experiences as a naval aviator on the USS *Midway* just before, during, and after the Persian Gulf War in 1991. The book represents a personal account and offers my opinions, insights, and feelings about what life is like serving in a squadron on an aircraft carrier at war. The people in the book are all real, but I have used only call signs so as to preserve an "everyman" flavor to the writing. I believe that although my squadron was special, it was also representative of the character of modern carrier aviation. The stories I have selected and dialogue I have reconstructed are based primarily on my memory and my logbook. I have also relied heavily on daily letters that I wrote home, the recollections of my squadron mates, and the experiences of other friends from the *Midway*'s air wing. The events described herein are forthrightly portrayed, and are, to the best of my knowledge, historically accurate.

ACKNOWLEDGMENTS

I wish to express, first and foremost, my thanks to my family for their love, friendship, and patience during the lengthy process of writing this book. My wife, Alice, and my son, Henry, were supportive above and beyond the call of duty. Without their love, this book would never have been possible.

My mother, father, and brother also provided strong encouragement throughout this project as they have throughout my life. Their unfailing love is my foundation. Alice's family is also a great source of strength for me. I am truly fortunate to have such a wonderful family.

There are many friends whose knowledge, expertise, and judgment have had a significant impact on this book. I offer my sincere thanks to: Andrew Auchincloss, Scott Bush, Lieutenant Brett Carroll, Sandy Coburn, Randy Castleman, Dr. George Denniston, Niel Golightly, Captain William Harlow, Lieutenant Commander Randy "Viktor" Mahr, Commander Terry Pierce, Lieutenant Commander Steve Recca, Lieutenant Commander Matt "Gucci" Scassero, Chris Schroeder, Jim Townsend, Commander Sam Tangredi, and Lieutenant Jeff Trent.

The jacket photograph was taken by Terry A. Cosgrove, who in his minimal spare time helped me get the right shot. The other photographs in the book are courtesy of the United States Navy.

Some of these photographs were originally contributed to our squadron yearbook by members of VAQ-136.

I also want to thank Mary Clement, who was kind enough to introduce my writing to William Morrow and Company. Without that introduction this book might never have been written. It has been a pleasure working with the staff at William Morrow throughout the publishing process. I am most fortunate that Larry Hughes convinced Zachary Schisgal, my editor, to take on the project. These two men have been generous with both their time and their wisdom.

CONTENTS

GULF WAR

CHRONOLOGY

August 2, 1990   Iraq invades Kuwait.

August 5, 1990   President George Bush states, "This will not
                     stand. This will not stand, this aggression
                     against Kuwait."

August 7, 1990   Operation Desert Shield begins as President
                     Bush directs the deployment of US forces in
                     response to a request for assistance from the
                     government of Saudi Arabia.

November 29, 1990   United Nations Security Council authorizes
                     "all means necessary" to enforce previous UN
                     resolutions, if Iraq does not completely with-
                     draw from Kuwait by January 15, 1991.

January 16, 1991   Coalition air forces conduct the first strikes of
                     Operation Desert Storm.

January 29, 1991   Iraqi forces capture the Saudi city of Khafji,
                     seven miles south of the Kuwait border on the
                     Persian Gulf coast.

January 31, 1991   Coalition forces liberate Khafji.

February 24, 1991   Coalition forces start the offensive ground
                     campaign. By this time most of Kuwait's
                     1,330 oil wells have been sabotaged.

February 28, 1991   Iraq surrenders, bringing an end to Operation
                     Desert Storm.

If a man hasn't discovered something that he will die for, he isn't fit to live.

—Dr. Martin Luther King, Jr.

THE PERSIAN GULF REGION

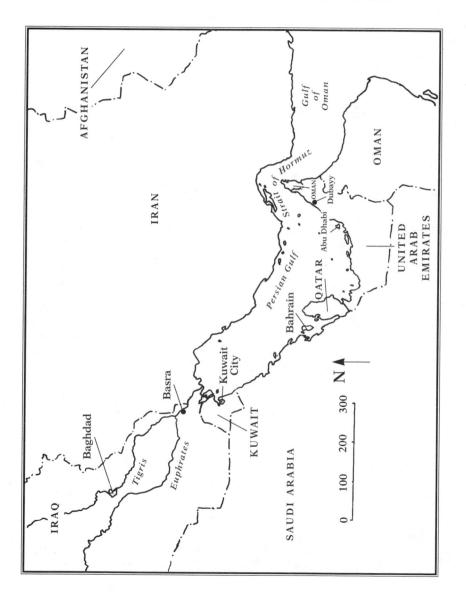

CHAPTER ONE

The Iron Maiden

The jet blast deflector began to lower as the steam from the freshly fired catapult swirled around outside the cockpit. My eyes strained in the blackness of the night to watch the vanishing glow of the F/A-18 Hornet's (see Glossary, page 259) engines, which just seconds ago had been on the catapult only a few feet in front of us. Now it was our turn. I slammed the parking brake handle in to free the wheels of the 57,000-pound EA-6B Prowler, allowing it to roll toward one of the USS *Midway*'s two steam-powered catapults. The steel wall that had protected us from the blast of the Hornet's engines was now being lowered by six sturdy hydraulically powered steel arms. As soon as it was flush with the flight deck, the Prowler's nosewheel tentatively rolled across it toward the catapult's shuttle. The steam still obscured my view of the yellow-shirted aircraft director. Unable to see his signals, I stopped the jet and swore under my breath.

"They're showing me a fifty-seven-thousand-pound weight board, and I'm rogering it," said Cave as he made a circular signal with his flashlight, informing the blue-shirted sailor ten feet below us on the flight deck that he had correctly guessed our jet's gross weight. *Cave* was short for "Caveman," which seemed to be an appropriate call sign for the man sitting next to me. His dark hair was closely cropped in a traditional crew cut, and his square jaw seemed to pull his ruddy skin tightly over his face. His medium build was muscular but not excessively so. Most important, he was an experienced and competent Electronic Countermeasures Officer (ECMO) trained extensively in the arts of navigation and electronic combat. ECMOs did not have pilot training, but Cave had the calm temperament necessary to help a first-cruise pilot like myself, known in the air wing as a "nugget," adjust to the intensity of fleet carrier operations.

The catapult's billowing white steam cloud finally subsided and the yellowshirt reappeared like a magician from the midst of a cloud of smoke. He gave us the wingspread signal followed by a frantic hand signal for me to start taxiing the jet faster toward the catapult. I felt rushed and my brain was reaching task saturation. Simply stated, my bucket was full.

"Spread the wings," I said over the intercom system, but Cave was way ahead of me. I glanced in the rearview mirror and saw the wings unfolding and spreading to the extended and locked position.

"Spread and locked, no flag on the right," said Cave. "Go dirty."

"No flag on the left," I responded as my hand moved the flap lever. I could barely see the flaps and slats moving in the darkness. "Going dirty."

"Call 'em when you got 'em," said Cave.

"Flaps thirty, stab shifted, slats out, and boards are in. Checks complete," I said. My breathing was labored and sweat was cascading down my face into my eyes.

Like a blind man following his long tapping cane, I maneuvered the Prowler forward as its nosewheel launch bar searched for its home in the shuttle that would connect the jet to the catapult. The yellowshirt's motions became slower and more precise as the launch bar approached the shuttle. I followed his hand signals explicitly, and now instead of a full arm signal, he signaled me with just a nod of his head. A nod to the left and then a nod to the right was all it took before I felt the comforting thump of the launch bar sliding into the shuttle. The yellowshirt now backed away from the jet to a safe distance and signaled me to continue my forward progress. I advanced the throttles so that the Prowler was straining slightly against the holdback fitting of the catapult. The holdback was designed to keep the Prowler stationary until the catapult generated 53,000 pounds of force. At that magical moment the holdback would snap and the jet would accelerate from a standstill to 150 miles per hour in less than two seconds. With approval from the catapult officer, the yellowshirt jumped in the air and flung his left arm forward parallel to the deck and cocked his bent right arm toward the pitch-black night. He looked just like a quarterback preparing to throw a deep pass.

In response to the yellowshirt's signal, my left arm jammed the throttles forward to full power. "I'm in tension," my ritual litany began, "my feet are to the deck, I have a visual on the stab, the controls are free and easy, engine instruments are good, no warning lights. My lights are coming on." My left thumb flicked the external lights master switch, and instantly the Prowler was transformed from a dark-gray machine into an eerie glowing mixture of red and green lights. The jet was straining against the holdback fitting that restrained the two powerful Pratt & Whitney engines roaring at full power beneath me. As soon as the lights came on, the catapult officer knelt down and touched the flight deck, giving the signal to the catapult shooter. The final safety check was done and the launch button was pushed. Our fate was sealed.

My head slammed against the ejection seat's headrest, and I groaned audibly over the intercom as I strained against the rapid onset of G forces from the catapult shot. The instruments looked fuzzy as my eyeballs compressed into the back of their sockets, and the jet shook violently as it rattled down the catapult track toward the pitch-black abyss. By the end of the catapult stroke I was able to focus again. The numbers *130* and *120* were ingrained in my brain. My eyes began to search for them in fear of the actions these numbers represented. Before the catapult shot I had set a marker on the airspeed indicator at 130 knots. If the indicator's needle pointed at an airspeed less than 130 knots at the end of the stroke, I would be forced to jettison all of my external stores, lightening the jet by 7,400 pounds, enabling it to fly away safely. If I saw less than 120 knots, I would instantly command eject the Prowler's four-man crew out of the jet, because no matter what happened, we did not have sufficient airspeed to fly. Thankfully, I saw the indicator's needle passing through 145 knots and said over the intercom, "Good airspeed, good shot," as the blackness of the night engulfed us. My instruments showed us climbing, and I hoped they were right. There was no horizon and I could not see anything outside of the cockpit. My left arm was locked at the elbow, and my entire body was tensed against the throttles, squeezing every last bit of thrust out of the two large engines that lay only a few feet below me.

"You can raise the gear now," chuckled Cave.

"Roger," I gasped as we passed 1,500 feet. I should have raised the gear immediately after the cat shot in order to reduce drag, but my eyes were locked onto the instruments and shaken by the violence and uncertainty of the night catapult shot. I quickly lifted the landing gear handle and waited for the proper indication. "I've got three up and locked, waiting for one eighty-five," I announced, letting my crew know that I would not raise the flaps until the Prowler had accelerated past 185 knots, the minimum flap retraction speed for the aircraft. "Passing one eighty-five, flaps are moving on the left," I said as I watched the slats retract in one of the cockpit's rearview mirrors.

"Moving on the right," said Cave.

"I'm up, clean, and isolated," I said, referring to the aircraft's configuration and the status of the hydraulic system isolation valve.

What pilots hate about night catapult shots is the lack of control. You are launched into the night, praying that the catapult has given the jet enough airspeed to fly when it reaches the end of the deck. In the daytime your eyes can see the acceleration and they signal your brain, saying that this catapult shot looks good. However, at night all the visual cues are gone and all that you have are your instruments. You still feel the violent onset of G forces, yet there are no visual cues, so you focus on your airspeed indicator and pray that it does not lie.

"Ironclaw 605 is passing 2.5," said Cave, referring to our altitude as he followed the departure procedures to the letter. Each squadron had a radio call sign; for our squadron it was *Ironclaw*. I liked our call sign because it sounded tough, and on an aircraft carrier, tough is good. Cave had several cruises under his belt and so did his flight boots. They were so old and worn that you could see the faint white salt stains on the tongues of the boots where his sweat had permeated the once-shiny and supple black leather. As a "nug-get" pilot it was comforting for me to be with an experienced ECMO like Cave.

At seven miles I turned to intercept a ten-mile arc around the *Midway*. I circled the carrier until we were flying on a northwesterly heading of 330 degrees. "Departure, Ironclaw 605 is kilo, switch-ing," said Cave telling the *Midway*'s departure controller that we were mission capable and switching to the strike-control frequency. We needed to switch radio frequencies from the departure con-troller to the strike controller before eventually starting our mis-sion. Each controller was responsible for different air space around the carrier. "Strike, Ironclaw 605 is up for Parrot India checks." Cave was ensuring that strike's air traffic controllers had an accurate readout of our jet's position on their radar scopes. The Prowler's Identification Friend or Foe system would reply to the carrier's radar interrogation with a discrete signal and altitude readout. In peacetime this discrete signal would allow the controllers to mon-itor our mission and tell us of any conflicting traffic. In wartime this system helped the carrier's controllers tell the good guys from the bad guys.

"Ironclaw 605, Strike holds you sweet and sweet, you are cleared to proceed."

"Switching," said Cave as he quickly twisted the knob on the radio to give us the proper radio frequency for the E-2C Hawkeye, an aircraft that acted as an airborne controller monitoring our mis-sion and keeping us clear of any conflicting air traffic. The Hawkeye had launched fifteen minutes earlier in order to establish an air "picture" of the entire operating area for the mission.

"Liberty, Ironclaw 605 is up for ESM."

"Ironclaw 605, Liberty, roger," said the voice of the Hawkeye controller, acknowledging our jet's presence on his radar scope.

"One thousand to go," I said over the intercom, announcing the fact that we had just passed 19,000 feet climbing toward our final altitude of 20,000 feet. I gradually reduced the jet's rate of climb, pulling back on the throttles and lowering the nose slightly. The level-off was smooth, and I smiled under my oxygen mask. I des-perately wanted to give the ECMOs confidence in my airmanship.

Tonight Cave was in the front seat with me, while Face and Bhag-wan were the two ECMOs in the backseat of our Prowler. Face was called *Face* because he liked women and believed they liked him. He had a deep, dark, permanent Mediterranean tan which was fitting for his image. Bhagwan, in contrast, was a short, stocky, and feisty bulldog of a man. His call sign was *Bhagwan* because we thought that if you wrapped a turban around his head, he would look convincingly like a Bedouin with a name like Bhagwan.

Our mission tonight was officially Electronic Surveillance Measures, and we would use the Prowler's sophisticated electronic receivers to detect and locate possible hostile radar emitters in the Gulf of Oman. Face and Bhagwan would search for electronic signals that could be linked to enemy radars that, in turn, would identify an enemy position. The *Midway* was sailing several hundred miles south of the Strait of Hormuz, the narrow body of water that connects the Persian Gulf with the Gulf of Oman, so we did not expect to identify any threats tonight. Actually, the real but unstated mission of the flight was to update the currency of my night-landing qualification, and to see how I would stack up in the constant competition among my fellow pilots that surrounds carrier landings.

It had been fifty-three days since my last night carrier landing in training and I was more than a little nervous. The navy's regulation stated that nugget pilots were allowed a maximum of twenty days between their last night trap in training and their first night trap in their new squadron, if their squadron was at sea. However, the political situation was tense in the Persian Gulf and my squadron needed a new pilot, so the commander of Air Wing Five (known as the CAG, a holdover from when his title was Commander of the Air Group) on the *Midway* had waived this regulation for me. I was glad to be trusted, but that did not make me any less nervous.

Only ten days ago I had completed my shore-based training at Naval Air Station Whidbey Island, Washington, just north of Seattle. Now, on December 10, 1990, I found myself at Saddam Hussein's doorstep four months after the Iraqi Army had invaded Kuwait on August 2. I faced an incredibly steep learning curve. Knowing that the *Midway* would be in the thick of any combat action, I had requested this assignment, but now I was feeling overwhelmed and unsure of myself. At the completion of my two and a half years of flight training I had made a total of twenty daytime carrier landings and only six at night. Not only did I feel inexperienced and awkward in the fast-paced environment of fleet-carrier operations, but there now existed a high probability of combat in the near future. In order to be "combat ready," I knew I needed to increase my pilot proficiency level rapidly, if I hoped to survive. In aviation a pilot's proficiency is perishable over time, meaning that if a pilot does not fly frequently, his skills quickly deteriorate. The great pilots are always a step ahead of every situation in the cockpit and use good judgment to choose among various courses of action. They are proactive, rather than reactive. Being ahead of the aircraft comes from experience and practice. Tonight, being inexperienced and out of practice, I felt slow and reactive, behind the aircraft rather than ahead of it. It was not a good feeling.

"Nav is tight," said Cave as he diligently updated the navigation solution using the Prowler's ground-mapping radar to send position updates to the jet's Inertial Navigation System.

"Roger that," I said. "Hydraulics are good, oil is good, and we're looking at fifteen thousand pounds of gas." We had another forty-five minutes to go until our recovery, when my rusty landing skills would be put to the test. Right now I felt comfortably above my fuel ladder calculations. Projecting forward at the current fuel-flow setting that I had chosen, we would have 11,400 pounds of fuel when the recovery began. That was ample. The Prowler was limited by structural design to a maximum of 8,800 pounds for a carrier landing, so I figured that we might even have to dump some fuel. Fuel is every navy pilot's major worry when the only place to land is on a ship in the middle of the ocean. I began to feel more relaxed. I realized that I was finally starting to think ahead of the aircraft, anticipating the possible sequence of events.

Fortunately, tonight we were within range of a small airfield called Seeb in the United Arab Emirates. The UAE had given the *Midway* permission to use the field for emergencies only. We had been briefed that Seeb was a last-ditch divert airfield because it was a short field without arresting gear to stop our jet, and we were all unfamiliar with it. Since we were roughly one hundred miles from

Seeb, it would be a 3.5 bingo. This meant that if we had not landed on the carrier by the time we reached 3,500 pounds of fuel, then we would immediately turn toward Seeb, and commit ourselves to landing with a low fuel caution light at an unfamiliar field. This was a thought that nobody in the crew was excited about. The three ECMOs in my crew all realized that this was my first night trap in the squadron. I'm sure they hoped that I would be able to get aboard without any difficulty, but they also knew that nuggets were unpredictable and often had a rough time with night landings when they first arrived in a fleet squadron. In turn, my crew was ready for anything. During the preflight brief Bhagwan had produced his toothbrush and a clean pair of underwear as testament to the fact that he was prepared in case I was unable to land back aboard the carrier tonight and we were forced to divert to Seeb.

We had flown north for thirty minutes toward the Iranian coast, trying to identify any signals of interest that were being emitted by the Iranian air defense forces. Face and Bhagwan were operating the Prowler's ALQ-99 surveillance system, which had extremely sensitive receivers able to identify a vast range of electronic signals. The ESM mission was focused primarily on the backseaters. Cave and I were responsible for navigating a specific course that would place us in the optimum position to receive signals intelligence, while Face and Bhagwan worked the system to pick up as many signals as possible. They were probably chatting back and forth about what they were seeing on the system, but I could not hear a word of it because they had the front seat deselected from the intercom so as not to disturb my dialogue with Cave in the front seat regarding the navigation of the mission.

The Prowler's Internal Communications System (ICS) was quite complicated. Usually on missions the backseaters would do most of their talking to each other about the electronic countermeasures (jamming enemy radars) or electronic surveillance (listening to enemy radars) that they were doing. They would normally set up their ICS in the backseat so that they could also hear everything that the frontseaters were saying, but they would need to press a switch to talk to us in the front seat. This created an environment where an insecure pilot might always be wondering what his backseaters were saying about the way he was flying. It did not usually even cross my mind, but I was now the new guy in the squadron, hoping to make a good impression. I could not help wondering what Face and Bhagwan might be saying about me in the backseat. Perhaps they were betting on the odds of my being able to land back onboard the *Midway* tonight. I tried to push such thoughts out of my head and keep my confidence up as we continued to fly through the darkness. "We are showing hardly any activity on the system," said Face.

"Well, keep looking," said Cave. We flew our preplanned route without incident, and about twenty minutes later, I finally heard Cave's voice say in my ear, "We might as well head back to the ship." I nodded in agreement and turned inbound to the ship as Cave began to orchestrate our return. The Tactical Air Navigation (TACAN) system indicated that we were ninety-five miles northeast of the *Midway*. I immediately began to think about the upcoming landing. On our departure from the carrier, we had flown through several layers of clouds at lower altitudes that would be extremely disorienting during the approach to the carrier. Flying in and out of clouds at night was never fun and I was not looking forward to it. After a few minutes of flight toward the carrier, Cave made the first of many standard radio calls. "Strike, Ironclaw 605 is fifty miles to the northeast, state is base plus 8.6." By using the base number from the kneeboard card of the day, which today was four, the ship would know that we had 12,600 pounds of gas.

"Ironclaw 605, Strike, roger. Case III recovery marshal radial is the 090. You're cleared inbound and cleared to switch marshal." I still found the radio dance somewhat confusing and was glad to have Cave, who quickly switched to the marshal frequency where we would be given our holding instructions and other pertinent information about the recovery from the controller aboard the *Midway*. As soon as the frequency was dialed into our radio, we heard some familiar chatter from the other air wing aircraft airborne, preparing for this recovery. There were eight squadrons in the *Midway*'s air wing: three Hornet, two Intruder, one Prowler, one Hawkeye, and one helicopter squadron, for a total of more than sixty aircraft. Because of the small size of the *Midway*'s deck we did not have any F-14 Tomcats or S-3 Vikings in our air wing. We liked to think that our air wing's composition of predominantly Hornets, Intruders, and Prowlers made us the premier attack air wing in the US Navy.

"Marshal, Eagle 510 is checking in, state is 9.0," said the A-6 Intruder's bombardier/navigator (BN), meaning he had nine thousand pounds of gas.

"Eagle 510, marshal, you're cleared to marshal on the 090 radial, angels 13, expect approach time 59, altimeter 30.10." As soon as the BN had read back his aircraft's holding instructions Cave jumped on the frequency. "Marshal, Ironclaw 605 is checking in; state is 12.6."

"Ironclaw 605, marshal, you're cleared to marshal on the 090 radial, angels 14, expect approach time 00, altimeter 30.10."

Cave read back the instructions verbatim as I started a descending turn toward our assigned holding point 29 miles due east of the carrier at 14,000 feet. Before long, nine aircraft were stacked neatly from 6,000 feet all the way up to 14,000 feet due east of the *Midway*. Each aircraft was separated by 1,000 feet and the holding points were determined by adding the number 15 to the given holding altitude. I was holding at angels 14, or 14,000 feet, so my holding point was 29 miles away from the ship. The lowest aircraft in the stack would fly the first approach starting at time 2152, followed by the aircraft 1,000 feet above him at time 2153, and so on. The aircraft in the marshal stack would continue to fly approaches to the carrier in this way until those of us at the top of the stack had trapped on the carrier's deck.

"Time in fifteen seconds will be 46," said the marshal controller. There was a brief pause and then his voice returned. "Five, four, three, two, one, mark time 46," said the voice of the marshal controller, ensuring that each of the nine aircraft in the marshal holding stack had the correct time so that their approaches would be synchronized. As each aircraft checked in the marshal controller would give them their assigned position in the stack.

Each aircraft was expected to commence its approach from the holding point plus or minus five seconds of the given approach time. If you started your approach either earlier or later than five seconds either side of the given time, you were expected to confess over the radio and publicly embarrass yourself. The confession helped the controllers to sequence the jets and ensure that the minimum amount of separation was maintained. The confession also served as a severe form of motivation to the pilots who, to a man, feared nothing more than looking bad in front of their fellow aviators.

Tonight the recovery started out smoothly. The lowest jet in the stack was an F/A-18 Hornet at 6,000 feet. At 2152 I heard, "Dragon 307, commencing, altimeter 30.10." We had eight minutes to go until we would commence our approach to the carrier. The Prowler's holding speed was 250 knots. The technique I used in order to hit the holding point on time was to fly the jet in a six-minute racetrack pattern. At 250 knots and 22 degrees angle of bank, it took the Prowler two minutes to turn 180 degrees. So if I could set myself up heading inbound at the holding point with six minutes to go, then I could fly a two-minute outboard turn, a one-minute outbound leg, a two-minute turn inbound, and then a final one-minute inbound leg, which would place the jet at the holding point exactly on time. The length of the outbound leg could easily be adjusted, depending how much time was remaining. There were now six minutes and thirty-five seconds remaining until the approach time of 2200, and I was on the 090 radial at thirty-two miles. Aside from the timing problem there was also a fuel concern; I still had 11,500 pounds of gas. Flying the approach would require about 800 pounds of gas, so when I commenced my approach in seven minutes, I wanted to have no more than 9,600 pounds in order to land with the maximum allowable limit of 8,800, according to the stress limits of the jet's fuel tanks. I needed to dump gas quickly. "I'm going to dump about two thousand pounds," I announced to my crew, letting them know that I was ahead of the jet. I turned the dumps on as the DME (mileage) indicator in the TACAN read twenty-nine miles, and I commenced my 22-degree angle of bank outbound turn. The clock showed that there were five minutes and forty seconds remaining until my approach time. That translated into a fifty-second outbound leg in order to hit the holding point on time. Cave led me through the challenge-and-reply descent and approach to landing checklists. He turned on the Automatic Carrier Landing System (ACLS) and the Instrument Landing System (ILS), testing each one for proper operation. Both systems seemed to be operating normally, but we would not really know until we were on our final approach.

The word *automatic* in the ACLS system was truly a misnomer. For the Prowler, there was nothing automatic about landing on the *Midway*. On the larger nuclear-powered carriers, some fleet aircraft could be landed, using this system without the pilot touching the controls throughout the approach. However, the combination of the Prowler's older automatic flight-control system, the *Midway*'s small deck, and its minimal hook to ramp clearance of only ten feet made it a completely manual process for the pilot. Even if it was not truly automatic, the ACLS was still invaluable to all of the *Midway*'s pilots. ACLS was an interactive system between the *Midway* and each aircraft as it flew its approach. The ACLS radar on the carrier could lock on to a jet's radar beacon and then send continuously updated azimuth and glide-slope information to the jet's cockpit. The information was then displayed to the pilot in the form of a vertical and horizontal needle as a background to a small-aircraft symbol. The horizontal needle displayed glide slope and the vertical needle azimuth. The pilot's job was to fly the jet so that the small-aircraft symbol was directly superimposed on the cross-hairs formed by the two needles.

"Checks are complete and I'm securing the dumps. One minute to push and we've got 9,600 pounds of gas. We're in good shape," I said as I smiled under my mask. Everything was going smoothly.

"Delta, delta, all aircraft stand by for new approach times," said the voice of the marshal controller.

"Shit," said Cave. The delta call signaled a delay in the recovery and as a result, a delay in our approach time. I wished there were a way to bring back the gas I had just so carefully dumped. The controller now started asking each aircraft its fuel state. "Eagle 510, say your state."

"Eagle 510 is level angels eleven, state is 7.0," said the Intruder BN ahead of us at 11,000 feet. He had already started his approach to the ship when the delta had been called, so according to procedures, he had leveled off at the next odd altitude after he heard the delta call.

"Ironclaw 605, say your state," said the controller.

"605, state 9.6," came Cave's terse response. Everyone's thoughts turned to gas. For the moment we were fine, but one could never tell how long the delay might be. "There's no Texaco tonight, but there is an Iron Maiden. Its call sign is Mako 12, at angels twenty-four," said Cave. I cringed. Texaco was the navy term for the carrier-based A-6 tankers which I had learned to tank from in-flight training. Many A-6 pilots on the *Midway* wore Texaco patches on their flight jackets because they provided the air wing with gas. Iron Maiden, on the other hand, was our squadron's nickname for an air force KC-135 tanker. The KC-135 was a converted air force cargo plane that was truly a gas station in the sky. The tanker had earned its nickname because tanking off it was a cruel form of torture that had already broken dozens of our air wing's refueling probes.

"We still have lots of gas to play with," I said cheerfully.

"Yeah, we should be fine," Cave replied. "Don't break out your toothbrush yet, Bhagwan."

It had now been six minutes since the marshal controller had given us the delta call and we were back at our holding point. The weather was disorienting at our holding altitude. There was no discernible horizon, yet I could tell that we were flying in and out of the clouds because of the varying intensity of the reflection of the Prowler's anticollision strobe lights. Delays in a recovery could be caused by a number of different situations. The frustrating aspect of it was that the carrier never seemed to tell you the nature of the delay. *It could be that a few jets had boltered, missing all three of the* Midway's *wires, and the landing pattern around the carrier was now full. Or it could be that a jet has just crashed into the back end of the boat,* I said to myself. I smiled under my oxygen mask, realizing that I had already adopted the naval aviator's habit of referring to the ship as a boat, the stern as the back end, and the bow as the pointy end. It was language used by aviators to annoy the officers in the Surface Warfare community who were cut from the more traditional naval cloth.

The back end of the boat was also called the ramp. When an aircraft crashed into the ramp, it was called a ramp strike. They were rare, but everyone had heard stories of the massive fireballs that would light up the dark night. The ramp at night became the type of a monster that lived in every pilot's nightmares. All navy pilots have had at least one close call with the ramp that they would prefer to forget. The pilots who learned from the encounter forevermore flew on the high side of the glide slope—and those who didn't learn—well, it was just a matter of time. The ramp monster began to creep into my thoughts as we waited to learn our new approach time. My eyes glanced repeatedly at our fuel gauge as it kept getting lower and lower.

Once again the marshal controller asked each aircraft to say his fuel state. And once again we heard, "Eagle 510, state 5.5."

"Ironclaw 605, state 8.0," said Cave. In another ten minutes we would be below our ramp fuel of 7.0, which was the target fuel that Prowlers were expected to land with, according to our air wing's standard operating procedure. As long as we stayed above 4,700 pounds, I would be happy. At 4,700 pounds or less we would be sent to the Iron Maiden, and I really wanted to avoid that at all costs.

After what seemed an eternity, we heard the controllers voice again: "Standby for expected approach times."

"Great," I said. We would be fine if we pushed in the next ten minutes. The time was now 2210.

The controller's voice came over the radio: "Acknowledge your approach time with fuel states. Eagle 510, expect approach time 16."

"510, approach time 16, state is 4.5," repeated the Intruder's BN, who was now getting quite low on gas. It was time to land. Time was becoming critical.

"Ironclaw 605, expect approach time 17."

"Ironclaw 605, approach time 17, state is 7.0" said Cave. "Another six minutes to our approach time. We should call the ball with about 5.8. That's plenty, no problem," said Cave.

"Calling the ball" happened at three quarters of a mile behind the carrier when the pilot transitioned from an instrument approach to a visual approach. It was the most critical part of a night carrier landing. It would take about twenty seconds to fly that final three quarters of a mile. Those twenty seconds were infused with the purest form of survival instinct. Night carrier landings were the practice of overcoming the fear of death that lingered in the back of every pilot's mind.

"The ball" or "meatball" was the nickname given to the navy's Fresnel lens system that offered pilots a visual reference to help them fly a constant glide slope from three quarters of a mile all the way to landing. Five specially cut rectangular lenses of light were stacked vertically in the middle of a horizontal row of green circular lights. The vertical stack of cells projected a yellow "meatball" of light toward an incoming jet. The top four cells were yellow and the bottom cell was red. If a pilot saw the yellow "meatball" higher than the horizontal row of green lights, then his jet was high. If the yellow "meatball" appeared below the row of green lights, then his jet was low. If the "meatball" turned red, then the pilot knew he was dangerously below glide slope and would hit the ramp if he did not make an aggressive power addition. Flying the ball was more of a philosophy or an art than a science. Pilots attached a Zen-like aura to those few who had truly mastered the art.

Tonight I did not feel as if I had the requisite Zen. I was nervous and I prayed that I would not bolter. Bolters were embarrassing, and I was determined not to be embarrassed tonight. However, I realized that boltering was a distinct possibility, and I wanted to have enough gas so that if I did bolter, I could go around again without being forced to go to the Iron Maiden. Bottom line: I needed to land before my jet's fuel gauge indicated 4,700 pounds. As my mind wandered and worried, our expected approach time drew closer. I needed to focus on the job at hand, which was to hit my holding point on time so that I would get a good start to my approach.

"Two minutes to go," said Cave, as we both closely monitored our progress in the holding pattern. We had ninety degrees of turn left and then we would have a fifty-second inbound leg. The timing problem seemed on track, but I continued to focus on our fuel situation. The gauge indicated about 6,600 pounds, which was about 3,000 pounds less than what I would have liked to have. It would have to be enough. *No bolter tonight,* I told myself.

At time 2216 we heard, "Eagle 510, pushing, altimeter 30.10." The Intruder below us was on his way and we would soon follow in less than a minute. As I rolled out wings level on the inbound course, the timing looked good. The INS indicated a ground speed of 240 knots, and there were four miles to go. I was going to be right on time.

"Ironclaw 605, pushing, altimeter 30.10," said Cave as the second hand passed through the twelve.

"Ironclaw 605, I show you at 29 DME switch button 18," said the marshal controller.

"Switching," said Cave, as I eased back on the throttles to 75 percent RPM, lowered the Prowler's nose ten degrees below the horizon, and extended the speed brakes, which increased the drag on the aircraft and enabled a rapid descent. This maneuver quickly gave the Prowler a 5,000-feet-per-minute rate of descent toward the water below. I felt the rush of speed when I saw with my peripheral vision layers of clouds whipping by the cockpit as we plunged downward. The analog hand of the altimeter unwound quickly as I scanned my instruments to ensure that all systems were normal.

"Approach, Ironclaw 605, checking in at twenty-seven miles."

"Ironclaw 605, continue CV1 approach, cleared to angels 1.2," said the new voice on the radio. The large heavy nose of the Prowler naturally sought the water. The altimeter kept spinning at a quick rate until we passed 5,000 feet and the preset radar altimeter started beeping, warning me to reduce my rate of descent. My thumb pushed the speed-brake switch in, and the Prowler's wingtip speed brakes on both sides closed flush like hands joined at the palms closing together. I then pulled back on the stick in order to reduce my closure with the ocean below.

"Ironclaw 605, platform," said Cave, making the next mandatory radio call as our jet passed through 5,000. Having adjusted my rate of descent, I started to concentrate on the level off.

"One thousand to go," I said over the intercom as I gradually added power and pulled the nose up even farther, easing the descent to 1,200 feet. At fourteen miles from the *Midway* we were now flying straight and level toward the ramp at 250 knots.

"Ironclaw 605, stay clean through ten, I'll call your dirty up," said the approach controller.

"605," said Cave, acknowledging the call. The normal procedure was to transition to the landing configuration at ten miles, but because the Intruder ahead of us had pushed from a lower altitude than normal, there was a bigger gap between us. The controller wanted me to keep my speed up until eight miles so as to close this gap and expedite the recovery. The transition from 250 knots clean to 130 knots with the landing gear down and the flaps down was a major transition. Eight miles was considered the minimum distance to make a smooth transition.

"Delta, delta," said the voice of the approach controller. "Ironclaw 605, discontinue your approach. Take angels two and continue inbound." Our fuel gauge now indicated 6,000 and it seemed to be decreasing as I glanced at it.

"We have a foul deck for at least ten minutes. Ironclaw 605 estimate state on the ball at time 2230," said the controller.

"Stand by," said Cave.

"Ten minutes at this altitude will be about eight hundred pounds plus the fuel for the approach another eight hundred. We will be at 4.6." I grimaced as I said this figure because it was below 4.7.

"Approach, Ironclaw 605, estimating 4.6 on the ball at time 2230," said Cave matter of factly.

"Ironclaw 605, approach, copy 4.6. Your signal is tank. Mako 12 is overhead at angels 24."

"Damn," I said, as I rammed the throttles to full power to give me the most fuel efficient climb to 24,000 feet. The two Pratt & Whitney P408A engines roared, and the Prowler responded as if it were an angry horse that I had just kicked with the spurs on my boots. We quickly accelerated to .7 indicated mach airspeed, the Prowler's most efficient climb airspeed. *That damned Intruder ahead of us must have broken down in the landing area*, I said to myself. At 16,000 feet the haze layer disappeared below us and visibility drastically improved. The stars were out, and I struggled to pick out the tanker's white light amid the field of constellations. "One thousand feet to go," I said as the altimeter passed through 22,500. "I'll level off at 23,500 until we have the tanker in sight, and then I'll climb to rendezvous."

"Traffic at two o'clock a little high," said Cave. I cranked the jet around to the right to put the nose onto the possible tanker. Off to the right of the nose I saw a white strobe and agreed that it must be the tanker. The trick to any rendezvous is figuring out the aspect and closure rate with the other aircraft. At night, without a fighter's sophisticated air-to-air radar, the Prowler was at a distinct disadvantage. By turning nose to the tanker, I hoped to be able to develop a picture of the relative motion of the tanker to my jet. The white strobe began slowly to track from right to left across my windscreen. That was good. It was best to join up on the tanker from the inside of its left-hand racetrack pattern. I let the nose of my jet lag behind the white strobe light. This lag increased the rate at which the light passed across my windscreen. I then added power and climbed the final 500 feet to be co-altitude with the Iron Maiden. My airspeed was 350 knots and I expected Mako to be at the standard rendezvous speed of 250.

I was now facing the common tanking dilemma; if the rendezvous was not expeditious, then the length of time would run me short on fuel. Yet, if I was too aggressive in expediting the rendezvous, that too might run us out of fuel because of the high power settings required for maneuvering. I did not want to divert, so I needed to time the rendezvous just right. I now held an aggressive 100 knots of closure on the tanker and knew that I had to be careful. Such a high closure rate at night could easily get out of control. I increased my angle of bank to the left, now putting my jet's nose in front of the tanker. By leading the tanker in this way I was also increasing my closure rate. Afraid of too high a closure rate, I began to ease back on the throttles and decelerate. Now, with a slower airspeed of 300 knots, I felt much more comfortable, yet a left-turn rendezvous was never truly comfortable in the Prowler. The jet's side-by-side seating design, with the pilot on the left, made it incredibly difficult for me to see the tanker on my right side while I was in a left-hand turn. I strained my neck to see the KC-135 over the Prowler's canopy rail on Cave's side of the cockpit.

"Too much closure," said Cave anxiously. The tanker was getting very large very quickly. I pulled the throttles to idle, extended the speed brakes, and lowered the nose to make sure that we did not have a collision. I arrested the closure rate just in time, and, even though it was not a pretty rendezvous, we were now flying off the tanker's left wing.

"Ironclaw 605, port observation, nose cold, switches safe, looking for 5.0," said Cave, who had tanked off the KC-135s many times before and knew what to expect. We ran through the refueling checklist quickly and I selected air-to-air on the Prowler's refueling panel.

"Ironclaw 605, you're cleared in for 5.0," said the tanker pilot.

"Do you want to lower your seat?" asked Cave, knowing that every other pilot in the squadron had learned through experience that it made tanking off the Iron Maiden a lot easier if you lowered your seat.

"No, I'll just leave it like it is," I said with a mild tone of resentment. *Who does he think he is anyway? I'm the pilot, damn it*, I said to myself. I pulled the throttles back and maneuvered the Prowler behind the tanker and took a look at the Iron Maiden's basket for the first time. Our gas gauge now read 4.8, and my flight gloves were soaked with sweat. The leather palms of the Nomex flight gloves felt slippery on the stick's hard black plastic grip. My fingers were clenched around the grip, squeezing it tightly. I needed to relax, but too many things were happening tonight that I had never seen before. I was feeling the stress and knew my crew could tell that I was. If I could not tank successfully, we would have to fly to Seeb. What a nightmare; the embarrassment of not being able to hack it was too great to contemplate. I could imagine Face and Bhagwan taking out their approach plates and control frequencies for the divert field in anticipation of my failure. As a nugget, my every move was watched by everyone in the squadron. If I were to fly in combat, then I would have to be able to tank off these KC-135s at night routinely. I needed to prove myself reliable. I needed to hack it.

The KC-135's refueling basket had a hard steel rim illuminated by small orange lights. The basket was only thirty-six inches in diameter and was connected to a stiff nine-foot reinforced rubber hose by a metal ball joint that swiveled, depending on the position of the basket. The only "night" tanking I had ever done was off an A-6 tanker in training at Naval Air Station Whidbey Island. It had been done one minute after official sunset, and at twenty thousand feet it was still quite light out. At that time my instructor said, "I guarantee you that the first time you tank at night in the fleet it will be pitch black and you will really need the gas." I smiled wryly as I realized how right he had been. From talking to the other pilots in the squadron I knew that there were two obstacles I needed to overcome to tank successfully off the Iron Maiden. The first was the boom operator and the second was bending the hose.

The KC-135, being an air force aircraft, was designed to refuel air force tactical jets and had to be reconfigured to fuel navy jets. In the infinite wisdom of the Department of Defense, the navy and air force accomplish air-to-air refueling with completely contradictory philosophies. In the navy, the receiving aircraft positions itself aft of the tanker's refueling basket and the receiving aircraft's pilot then maneuvers his aircraft's refueling probe into the tanker's basket. In the air force, the receiving aircraft positions itself aft of the tanker and the tanker extends its refueling probe. While the receiving aircraft maintains its position, the tanker's boom operator will fly the tanker's refueling probe into a small basket that is located on the top of the receiving aircraft. On a KC-135 tanker reconfigured for use with navy jets, the tanker's refueling probe is replaced by a basket so that the navy jets can use their refueling probe to "plug" the basket. Problems arise when a navy pilot tries to "plug" the basket and a well-intentioned air force boom operator attempts to guide the basket onto the jet's refueling probe. The result is similar to what happens when one person in a group drops a coin on the floor and two people bend over to pick it up and smack their heads together. Even though both people are trying to accomplish the same thing, they are not coordinated. In the end, one person will bend over and pick up the coin. I hoped that the boom operator would simply let me "pick up the coin" and plug the basket without trying to be too helpful.

The second obstacle was staying in the basket long enough to receive five thousand pounds of gas. The A-6 tanker package had a much longer and more flexible hose that allowed the receiving aircraft to maneuver more freely behind the tanker. The other pilots in the squadron had described how it was necessary to bend the KC-135's hose into an S shape that would allow the pilot to control the swiveling ball joint of the basket. If the hose was not bent properly, then the swiveling ball joint could violently twist around the jet's refueling probe and possibly damage it so that further refueling was impossible. If the hose twisted quickly, then the best course of action was to disengage. However, on disengagement there was always the possibility that the basket's large steel rim could slam down on the nose of the receiving aircraft. With these thoughts swirling in my brain and my palms drenched with sweat, my stomach knotted with fear, I started my approach toward the thirty-six-inch basket.

The Prowler's refueling probe was illuminated by a small red light that was directed upward from the base of the jet's windscreen. My hands felt as if they were shaking, but they were simply making the minute movements necessary to keep the probe moving slowly toward the basket. The basket was now ten feet in front of the probe's tip, and as the distance decreased I watched the basket start to move. Was it my own poor technique or was it the friendly boom operator trying to be helpful? I couldn't tell. I added more power and continued to close on the basket. It began to move to the left and I made the necessary correction. I was almost there when the basket suddenly moved down. The probe tip hit the basket just inside the top of its rim and bent the swivel joint upward. Instead of sliding into the basket, the probe slipped over the top of its rim and the steel basket snapped down and smashed into the nose of the Prowler. "Damn it," I swore over the intercom system. I pulled back on the throttles and winced. I slid back twenty feet behind the Iron Maiden and looked at the nose of my jet.

"No harm done," I said.

"The probe looks all right," said Cave. "Well, let's give it another try." His calm voice belied the fact that our fuel gauge now indicated 4.2. I needed to get in the basket and stay in the basket. After a deep breath and unclenching my fingers several times, I began my second approach. My left hand gently pushed the throttles forward, creating the necessary closure on the basket. Once again the basket stayed steady until the probe was only a few feet away. Now I began to doubt myself. The boom operator was probably doing nothing. Was it just my poor technique that was preventing me from getting into the basket? The frenetic minor corrections I was making to chase the basket were getting smaller and smaller as the probe got closer and closer. At the last instant, the basket started to move down again. I added a handful of power and lowered the nose. The probe slammed home in the center of the basket and the swivel joint whipped the hose around the top of the probe. *Bend the hose, bend the hose,* I told myself. The hose turned and twisted wildly as I tried to stabilize my position and create the bend in the hose that was required. My hands jerked crazily as if I were being electrocuted.

The problem was that I could barely see the basket. The Prowler's canopy has almost as much steel as glass. Since I hadn't lowered my seat, I was forced to lean forward and awkwardly stretch my neck and roll my eyes upward in order to keep sight of the basket and the probe tip. I was leaning so far forward that my chest was right on top of the stick, so it was difficult to make the necessary corrections to keep the probe in the basket. The KC-135 had just reached the end of its holding pattern's straightaway and it started to turn. The angle of bank swung the boom out to the side, and as I tried to make the necessary recorrection my chest got in the way. The oscillations started to become too great. As I leaned back to allow more room for stick movement, I lost sight of the basket behind the canopy's steel frame. I pulled back on the throttles too quickly and could not recorrect in time. The Iron Maiden spit out the probe, and once again I found myself with more sweat and less fuel than I had had a few minutes earlier.

"Let's give it one more try and then we'll divert to Seeb. Our bingo fuel from here is 3.5 and right now we've got 3.8," said Cave.

"Concur. I'm going to lower my seat," I said, recalling Cave's sage advice given fifteen minutes earlier. I could just imagine the twinkle in Cave's eye and the grin on his lips.

The boom swung gently as the lumbering KC-135 continued its

turn. I rested and breathed deeply as the tanker turned. It would be much easier to plug and stay plugged once the tanker rolled out of the turn, so I decided to wait. As the tanker rolled out I looked at the gas gage; the needle wavered at 3.7. This was definitely the last chance I would have. The perspective was different now that I had lowered my seat. I felt my neck muscles relax as I was now able to look up comfortably at the basket while I added power and began to close the gap. The new seat position also gave me renewed confidence. The basket started to move again as I closed within ten feet. I pulled some power and stopped the closure. My hands kept moving and I wiggled my toes, which had always helped to relax me in the past. A warm rush of adrenaline pulsed through my veins as I added power. The basket stabilized and the probe struck the center of the basket. The hose quickly bent into an *S* shape, and now that I could see the basket easily, I knew that I could maintain this position.

"We've got good flow," said Cave. My hands kept up the frenetic pace of correction and recorrection. Each power addition would bend the hose more, and each power reduction would bring me closer to losing control of the bend and having the hose wrap wildly around my refueling probe and possibly spit me out again. Finally, after several minutes of torture, the fuel gauge indicated 8.5. "We've got all we need. Great job," said Cave. I knew he was trying to build my confidence because he knew as well as I did that the hard part of the flight was still ahead. I now had to land on the smallest carrier in the fleet.

CHAPTER TWO

Welcome to
the Fleet

"Mako 12, Ironclaw 605, thanks for the gas, we're switching," said Cave.

"605, you're cleared to detach. Have a good night," said the cheerfully relaxed voice of the air force tanker pilot, who knew he would be landing on a ten-thousand-foot-long stationary runway at the end of his mission. In contrast, I was planning to land on the pitching and rolling deck of an aircraft carrier that was less than a thousand feet long. As I turned the Prowler toward the *Midway*, I wondered how much the deck would be moving tonight. This carrier was infamous for rocking and rolling, and every *Midway* pilot had a good story about a scary night landing.

Her keel was laid in 1943, during the height of World War II, and for the first decade of the *Midway*'s service she was the largest warship in the world. Forty-seven years later, the *Midway* was now the oldest and smallest carrier in the US Navy. Her hull was originally designed for a cruiser, which made the *Midway* a nimble ship compared with the newer and larger aircraft carriers. In the late 1960s the *Midway* was decommissioned and brought into the yards for extensive renovations in order to extend the ship's service life and enable it to handle the navy's new high-performance jets. One major aspect of the renovation was the addition of an enlarged steel, angled flight deck. The new larger deck surface, combined with the ship's small cruiser-type hull, made the ship top heavy and therefore extremely unstable in heavy seas. Not being pilots, the naval engineers did not appreciate the importance of having a stable deck on which to land high-performance jet aircraft. The navy made several attempts to stabilize the *Midway*, but she quickly developed a reputation as being the toughest ship to land on in the fleet. The *Midway*'s roll angle occasionally exceeded twenty-four degrees, and the pitch angle was so bad that pilots on final approach had seen the ship's propellers breach the surface of the water. Another part of the problem was that the larger, more modern aircraft carriers in the fleet had four arresting wires to catch their jets, whereas the *Midway* had only three.

My mind was brought back to flying by Cave's voice. "Marshal, Ironclaw 605 is tank complete, state 8.5."

"Ironclaw 605, Marshal, we have a ready deck. These will be vectors to a manual push. Take heading 090, descend and maintain angels 1.2, altimeter 30.10."

"Marshal, Ironclaw 605 heading 090, descending to angels 1.2, altimeter 30.10," said Cave. Cave quickly reviewed the approach to landing checklist and tested the ILS and ACLS boxes, ensuring these instrument landing aids would be working properly. Everything seemed to be operating normally.

The good news about a manual push and a ready deck was that I would get spoon-fed the approach information and would not have to go through the hassle of setting up a holding pattern in order to hit my holding point on time. The bad news was that because it had taken me so long to tank, all the other jets had already recovered. Now the entire air wing was sitting comfortably in their ready room chairs waiting to watch me fly my approach on the carrier's closed-circuit television. The Pilot Landing Aid Television (PLAT) was on channel seven, and it was probably the most watched channel of the four or five channels available, which included a movie channel, a news channel offering taped delay CNN, a weather channel, and an educational channel. The PLAT picture on the screen was produced by a small flush-mounted video camera lens installed on the centerline of the carrier's landing area. The PLAT recorded every approach and landing made on the carrier.

Superimposed on the lens were crosshairs that projected a rough estimation of the proper glide slope and lineup that a jet needed to fly in order to land safely. The favorite pastime for aviators who were not flying was being a "PLAT LSO." LSO stood for Landing Signals Officer, and they were the pilots onboard the carrier who were responsible for the safe and expeditious recovery of the air wing's aircraft. They controlled the recoveries and also evaluated every pilot by grading every landing made on the *Midway*. The expression "Everyone's a critic" was probably developed on an aircraft carrier. Every night the squadron ready rooms around the ship were packed with aviators criticizing their comrades' approaches. The banter was always fast and furious.

"He came down like a ton of shit," one aviator would say.

"If I were the LSO, I would have waved him off," another would respond.

"That was really ugly," would say the first and then they both would nod and prepare to critique the next approach on the TV, knowing full well that the next night it would be their turn to fly the approach and someone else would be criticizing their performance. The PLAT offered everyone on board the carrier a chance to tease a pilot if he boltered or flew a particularly poor approach.

The professional critics, the air wing's LSOs, were actually on the flight deck only a few feet away from the jets as they landed. Teams of five or six LSOs would write down descriptive comments concerning the deviations from glide slope, lineup, and airspeed on every approach and then assign a grade. The meticulous grading of each landing allowed the air wing to monitor its pilots' performance. The consequences of poor performance were too severe to let substandard landings continue for very long. As a result, any pilot with consistently poor landing grades would face a board of inquiry and risk losing his wings. The pressure to make safe landings was real and intense, especially for the nuggets, like myself, who were being watched very closely.

Thinking about the several thousand eyeballs that were going to be watching my approach did not help me relax as the altimeter unwound past five thousand feet. The radalt started beeping and I retracted the speed brakes and pulled back on the stick to reduce my rate of descent.

"Marshal, Ironclaw six zero five, platform," said Cave.

"Radalt is reset to three thousand feet," I said.

"New final bearing one seven five," said the approach controller. The radar altimeter started beeping again as we descended through three thousand feet.

"Radalt is reset at a thousand feet." The TACAN indicated that the ship was only twelve miles away.

"Ironclaw 605, stay clean through ten, I'll call your dirty," said the approach controller. A minute passed. "Ironclaw 605, at eight miles, dirty up," said the approach controller.

My left hand pulled back on the throttles and then lowered the landing gear handle and moved the flap lever to the down position. As the Prowler started the clumsy transition to the slower airspeed, my right hand pulled the hook release lever, lowering the tailhook. As soon as I could see all the proper indications, I blurted out the landing checklist: "Gear one, two three down and locked, flaps thirty degrees, stab shifted, slats out, hook's down, harness set, holding the boards, pressure's normal and on speed will be one twenty-eight knots with 7.8 on the gas." My thumb began to move at a feverish pace adjusting the electric trim button on top of the control stick in an attempt to "trim out" any extraneous stick forces so that the jet would fly smoothly through the night down the glide slope once we hit the tipover point at three miles. Night carrier landings are like nightmares—but worse. At least in nightmares one has the luxury of being able to escape one's fate simply by waking up. During a night landing, one's eyes are wide open and one's senses are on full alert, as the jet approaches the stern of the pitching and rolling carrier. During those last twenty seconds of the approach as the deck gets closer and closer, it is a pure survival instinct that guides the pilot's hands through the wakeful nightmare.

"Ironclaw 605, at four and one half miles, ACLS lock on, call your needles."

"Fly up and right," I said, hoping that the controller would concur.

"Concur, 605, this will be a Mode II approach," said the approach controller, meaning that I would get voice calls from the controller from three miles to three quarters of a mile, telling me my glide slope and azimuth status. Inside the cockpit I would listen to these calls but would be focused primarily on my ACLS needles, which would give me the same information in a more timely fashion. The first call had confirmed that the needles on my instrument panel's gyro were giving me accurate azimuth and glide-slope information. I was not flying the jet precisely enough. Fortunately, there was still time to correct. My instrument scan felt slow. My eyes were sluggish with exhaustion and were not darting around the cockpit's instruments quickly enough. Every pilot develops his own personal instrument scan pattern, his own way of looking at his instruments and absorbing all of the information presented by them. The quicker the instrument scan, the better the pilot.

The miniature aircraft symbol on the gyro was to the left of the vertical needle, so I needed to fly to the right. Maintaining twelve hundred feet, I turned to the right until the vertical needle was centered on the aircraft symbol. The horizontal needle now started down rapidly, indicating that the jet had intercepted the glide slope and that I needed to begin my descent. "Boards are out, landing checks complete," I stated, as I nervously squirmed in my ejection seat.

After establishing a steady rate of descent, I looked up over the instrument panel and saw a faint yellow light in the distance, which was all I could see of the *Midway*. *Great, I'm going to land on a faint yellow light*, I said to myself. Immediately, my eyes were back inside the cockpit scanning the instruments, my hands twitching as they made minor movements with the stick and throttles. The toughest aspect of a night carrier landing was the visual transition that occurred at three quarters of a mile. At that point, I would transition from an instrument scan inside the cockpit to a visual scan outside the cockpit for the last twenty seconds before landing. I would have to leave my instruments and refocus my eyes outside the cockpit on three critical parameters: the "meatball" for glide-slope information; the deck's lighted centerline for lineup information; and the jet's angle of attack (AOA) for airspeed information. Controlling these three parameters was the juggling act that I needed to perform in order to land safely.

If I flew low I would hit the ramp and would be swallowed instantly by the ensuing fireball. If I flew high I would miss all the wires and bolter. If I drifted right my wingtip might slice the nose of a parked jet on the crowded deck, and if I drifted left I might go over the edge for an unwanted swim. I would also need to maintain a constant airspeed so that my tailhook would be in the proper position to catch one of the three arresting wires when I landed. The jet's AOA indicator was located on the far left side of the cockpit above the instrument panel. Its location allowed me to use peripheral vision to see it as I scanned the meatball and centerline outside the cockpit. The AOA indicator would display an amber circle or "doughnut" if I maintained the proper airspeed for the jet's given gross weight, plus or minus one knot. If the jet accelerated, the indicator would display a red chevron, and it would make the jet prone to bolter because of the nose down, hook up, landing attitude of the aircraft. If the jet decelerated, the indicator would display a green chevron, telling me that the jet was close to stall airspeed. These instrument lights in the cockpit were wired to and repeated on the external nosewheel landing gear door, which was clearly visible to the LSOs standing near the ramp, telling them whether the jet was fast, slow, or on speed. Each one of the three parameters of the approach was critical, and all three needed to be within strict limits in order to make a safe landing. If there was any significant deviation to any one of these three parameters, the LSOs would turn on the red waveoff lights, and I would be forced to abort the approach.

"Ironclaw 605, you're lined up left and on glide slope at three quarters of a mile, call the ball," said the controller.

"605, Prowler ball, 7.5," said Cave. My eyes now came up from the instruments and I shifted my focus to the landing area and the meatball which was now less than three quarters of a mile away. I dipped the right wing to correct for the lineup deviation, but did not add enough power to compensate for the wing movement.

"Don't settle," came the call from the LSO. I added power but the "meatball" still appeared to be centered, so I went back to looking at lineup. Lineup was now good. My heart was pounding, and I was hyperventilating. The faint yellow light in the distance was now a huge floating piece of steel. Only a few more seconds to go.

"You're low," said the annoyed voice of the LSO. "Power." My eyes flashed back to the meatball and I saw that he was right. The meatball was now below the horizontal datum lights. My left hand shot forward adding lots of power. It was too big a correction, and the meatball began to rise rapidly.

"Easy with it," said the LSO in a softer voice. "You're overpowered." In the periphery I saw the red chevron of the AOA indicator and knew that I was now high and fast. I pulled back on the throttles and the engines started to spool down. "Right for lineup," said the LSO, then followed quickly by a crescendoing call, "Power! *Power!*"

I had drifted to the left and gave a big right-wing dip to correct, but I neglected to add power for the lineup correction. I was horrified to see the meatball start a rapid descent and within an instant it changed colors to red. Ramp strike was all I could think as I rammed the throttles to the stops. Terror coursing through my veins, I was unsure whether or not I would clear the ramp. The Prowler careened onto the carrier's flight deck. My body was hurled forward violently as the tailhook grabbed the *Midway*'s first wire. After two seconds and 195 feet of roll out on the flight deck, the jet had gone from 128 knots to a standstill. My left arm was locked at the elbow and my knees were trembling. Above the sound of my heart pounding in my chest and my hyperventilating I heard a calm voice, that of the air boss looking down at me from the tower, say, "It's OK, 605, we've got you now, throttle back, and turn off your lights." We had made it. Bhagwan wouldn't need his toothbrush after all, but I smiled with the thought that he might need that clean pair of underwear.

I quickly pulled the throttles to idle, turned off my lights, and raised the flaps and slats lever. The terror of seeing the meatball turn red still had me shaking. Once the flaps and slats were retracted, Cave was able to fold the wings so that we could taxi around the crowded flight deck. The outboard ten feet of each wing was raised and folded across the jet's back in order to reduce the Prowler's wingspan, making it easier to avoid the many obstacles around the carrier's flight deck. I taxied toward the bow, following the signals of the yellowshirt. My legs were still shaking from the combination of utter fear and adrenaline from the landing. Pilots called it "sewing machine leg," and it was actually humorous to look down and see my legs bobbing up and down uncontrollably on the rudder pedals.

"It looks like we're going to do the bow dance," said Cave. I reluctantly followed the yellowshirt's signals toward the bow of the carrier. If the engineers at Grumman had ever done a "bow dance" on a carrier at night, they would have designed the Prowler differently. The two front seats in the Prowler are six feet in front of the nosewheel. As a result, it is possible for the nosewheel to be within inches of the edge of the deck and the two aircrew in the front cockpit actually to be sitting over the water. In my mind, it was reminiscent of the pirate's tradition of forcing people to "walk the plank." After a stressful night landing, doing the bow dance is an absolutely awful way to end a flight. I taxied up the starboard side feeling helpless. We were completely at the mercy of the yellowshirt. It was a black night and I could barely see the edge of the deck. The yellowshirt was now slightly behind my left shoulder, still signaling me to taxi forward. I knew that the nosewheel must have been within a foot of the edge of the deck. If I stopped the momentum of the jet then it would be much harder to make the left turn into the parking spot they had reserved for me, but if I kept rolling, I was sure that I would go right over the edge of the deck. Finally, the yellowshirt signaled me to turn left and my shaky left leg pushed the rudder pedal to the floorboard. Since my right thumb had engaged the nosewheel steering switch on the stick, the nosewheel started to swing to the left. Soon my body was back over the deck and I started to relax. Moments later I pulled out the parking brake and our mission was complete. "They're tying us down here. Let's safe our seats," I said over the intercom, reminding my crew of the importance of securing the two ejection handles on each seat before leaving the aircraft.

The yellowshirt passed control of the jet to my squadron's plane captain, who signaled me to shut down the engines. As the second engine spooled down, I asked Cave if he was clear of the canopy. Cave responded with a thumbs up, and I raised the canopy.

The cool sea air rushed into the cockpit, and all of the tension and stress began to ebb. A feeling of exhilaration took hold of me and I smiled, realizing that even though it had not been pretty, I had gotten the job done.

In the darkness, my hands instinctively reached for the fittings that bound me to the ejection seat. Within seconds I released all six fittings and began to pull myself out of the jet. The salty breeze felt refreshing on my sweaty face as I grabbed the familiar handgrip that was welded to the inside of the canopy's frame. The Prowler's forward cockpit was extremely difficult to access and it required the flexibility of a contortionist to make the awkward motions necessary to enter and exit the jet. Once out of the cockpit, I perched on the small boarding platform waiting for Bhagwan to clear the ladder that would take me down to the flight deck. Face had already exited on the other side.

Once my feet touched the deck I was surrounded by the maintenance crew. The first face was a young third-class petty officer named Clement. The face of this young avionics technician was smeared with oil and grease that had been baked into his skin after a long day on the flight deck, working next to the burning-hot jet exhaust. He was a slender kid who wore a permanent smile that some might call a smirk. He had probably been far too bright for his high school and his boredom had helped him develop his mischievous smirk.

"How'd she fly, sir?" he asked. He was starting the standard interrogation of the pilot to discover any serious problems with the jet so that they could start working on it right away, in the hope that the problem could be corrected before the first morning launch.

"Just fine, I don't have any major gripes," I said.

"Did you tank?" asked Clement.

"Yes, we took about five thousand pounds of gas."

After asking me several more specific systems questions, he finally released me. "Great, sir, thanks a lot." Clement turned to Chief

Ross, our squadron's flight deck coordinator, and gave him a thumb's up, meaning that the jet was good to go for the first launch of the next day. I saw the chief start talking on his headset microphone built into his protective helmet, telling flight deck control that they could park this Prowler in a "go spot" tonight. Clement and the other maintenance experts who had gathered around me all dispersed and started working on the routine maintenance and checks that needed to be done after every flight. The oldest one among them was probably twenty-five. They were all good, but Clement had been selected to be the troubleshooter, the one maintenance man who would interact with the pilots when there were problems. He had an excellent knowledge of the aircraft and more important, a calm and friendly personality. Without fail, he knew how to reassure even the most senior pilots that their aircraft looked good and was ready to fly. He was special and our squadron was lucky to have such a good troubleshooter. He seemed to have endless energy, which is exactly what he needed.

The normally hectic pace of the flight deck was now more relaxed. The deafening noise of jet engines was gone and, now that flight operations for the night were finished, the troops on the deck seemed to work at a calmer pace. The flight deck at night was like a field filled with fireflies. All of the yellowshirts were now using their flashlights to signal to the blueshirts who were driving the tractors that towed the jets around the flight deck. The jets were being pushed and pulled around the deck, being respotted for the first launch of the next day. The Aircraft Handling Officer, otherwise known as "The Handler," was the man responsible for all of the jets' movement on the flight and hangar deck. His job was to solve this complex jigsaw puzzle every day, so that the carrier could launch and recover aircraft in the most efficient manner. The tight spaces on the flight deck forced the jets to be parked within inches of each other all over the deck. Moving so many jets in such a tight space was a mishap waiting to happen, but fortunately, the *Midway*'s handler was a puzzle master.

I joined the ranks of the fireflies by taking my flashlight from my survival vest and using it to make my presence known to others so that no tractor would run me over in the darkness. My crew was already off the deck not waiting for me to finish the maintenance debrief. It did not bother me that they did not wait. I would do the same thing in their shoes. The flight deck was not a place to linger. The flight deck always made me nervous. There were simply too many things that could go wrong, too many ways to get injured. My flashlight illuminated the dark ladder that led off the carrier's deck onto the catwalk that lined most of the carrier's deck edge. The steps led me to a large watertight hatch that needed a strong shove to loosen the lever that bolted the hatch shut. Once through the hatch, I entered into the midst of our maintenance control office, the heart and soul of every squadron.

"So, did you break my jet, lieutenant?" asked the senior chief, a bear of a man with a bushy black mustache, who ran our squadron's maintenance effort.

"Not tonight, senior chief, the jet flew well. I have no gripes."

"Well, that's good," he said, happy to know that there weren't lots of complaints about the jet that would keep his people working throughout the night.

"It looked like you were trying to get some extra flight time tonight," said another voice from the other side of the small office. It was the voice of our Maintenance Material Control Officer, who had the endearing nickname of Beast. His barrel chest and two sinewy arms said, "Don't tread on me," but his gruff exterior belied the warmth of the man. If one looked closely, one could see an irreverent twinkle in his eyes. He was teasing me about my approach and informing me that the PLAT LSOs in maintenance control thought I had been lucky not to bolter on my approach, because I had gotten so high in the middle.

"No, thanks, I had plenty of flight time tonight," I said, grateful that I had been able to catch a wire. The senior chief would have come up with another sarcastic comment, but I did not give him the chance, as I walked through maintenance control and into the equipment room where all of our flight gear was kept. Upon my arrival, our entire crew of four was standing in the cramped space trying to shed the forty-plus pounds of personal survival gear that we wore on every flight.

"That was a pretty big settle at the ramp," said Cave, a master of understatement.

"Yeah, I took off too much power to correct for the high in close," I said, grudgingly, accepting Cave's unsolicited comments. It had not been a great approach, but I hoped that people would refrain from commenting on my efforts. It had been a long night, and my body desperately needed a shower and a good night's sleep.

The first person I met when I entered the ready room was our squadron's senior LSO. His large, lanky frame seemed to comfortably fit his call sign of Horse. "Pretty dark night out there," he said, managing a smile. Horse was a natural pilot; there were a few of them around. The movement of the stick and throttles came instinctively to him, where I and many other pilots needed to consciously consider what we were doing in the air. His dad had been a navy pilot, so it was in his blood. He had grown up on the beaches of Pensacola, Florida, the cradle of naval aviation. He had watched the Blue Angels, the navy's elite flight demonstration team, regularly fly overhead, and so from an early age Horse was hooked. He knew all along that when he grew up he wanted to fly navy jets.

"It was black," I said. I finally thought I had a sympathetic audience and was hoping that Horse would give me a few words of encouragement or perhaps even a pat on the back.

"If you can't be smooth, be high. Welcome to the fleet," said Horse with a chuckle as he walked away. So much for sympathy. Our crew gathered in the back of the ready room to debrief the flight. Before we had finished talking about the departure from the ship we were interrupted by the grand entrance of the air wing LSOs. Generally speaking, the LSOs were selected from among the best pilots in the air wing, and I desperately wanted to be one. The senior air wing LSO was a feisty A-6 Intruder pilot whose call sign was Mad Dog. His title of CAG LSO meant that he was one of two lieutenant commanders who represented the commander of the air wing and who organized and trained the air wing's LSO teams. He walked briskly into the ready room and quickly picked out my face as the face of a nugget pilot after a scary night landing. "Hi, I'm Mad Dog, the senior CAG LSO." We shook hands, and I stood to face the judgment of this senior respected LSO and fellow aviator.

Mad Dog looked into the book filled with grades and comments for every single approach that had been flown that day. His finger moved down the columns of numbers and names until he found mine. "Settle on start, too much power on the come on in the middle, high in close, fly through down on lineup at the ramp, for a no grade taxi-one wire," barked Mad Dog. "If you had pulled off much more power correcting for that high in close, you might have hit the ramp. Remember, you must never recenter the high ball in close." This was a rule to live by, literally, and I had heard it thousands of times throughout my training. The comments and the grade for this approach were below average, and I was mad at myself for flying so poorly. A taxi-one wire was very bad. It meant that I had landed significantly short of the first wire and had in effect "taxied" the jet into the wire. I had been dangerously low.

Mad Dog continued his lecture. "If you didn't see a red meatball when you crossed the ramp, then you must have been spotting the deck." "Spotting the deck" was a cardinal sin and also extremely dangerous. It meant that the pilot tried to land by looking at the deck without looking at the meatball. It was a risky technique, since at night, almost all of one's visual cues are gone and one's senses can easily be fooled. I hoped that I was not already developing bad habits in my landings. "Just concentrate on scanning the meatball all the way to touchdown," said Mad Dog.

"Yes, sir, ahh . . . ahh . . . I did see a red meatball at the ramp," I said glumly, not pleased with my performance.

"Don't let the jet go low like that again. Just fly the ball and you'll do fine. Welcome to the fleet," said Mad Dog with a smile as he slugged me in the shoulder. He turned to leave, leading the traveling troupe of LSOs out of our ready room in search of the next pilot to debrief. I must have looked terrible. I had worked so hard and done so poorly. At least I was alive and in the fleet. I was in "the show" now.

This was the fleet, the major leagues of aviation, and night landings were the equivalent of a split-fingered fastball, a knuckler, a slider, and a spitball all rolled into one. I felt like the rookie centerfielder whose first major league at bat was against Nolan Ryan. After he struck out, his manager would tell him, "Just keep your eye on the ball and you'll do fine. Welcome to 'The Show.'" All I knew was that I would rather face Nolan Ryan's fastball than a pitching and rolling carrier deck at night. No matter how tough it was and how poorly I had done, I was still glad to be able to walk away from the landing. After over two years of training, I had finally made it to the navy's version of "The Show." Consoling myself, I recalled the words of Freddie Patek, a one-time five-foot-two-inch starting shortstop for the Kansas City Royals, who said, "I'd rather be the shortest player in the majors than the tallest one in the minors."

"Ahh, to hell with the LSOs," said Cave, who had a reputation for irreverence that was legendary. I had heard from the other junior officers, commonly referred to as JOs, that Cave was the only guy in the squadron who would, without thinking twice, challenge or argue with the commanding officer (CO) or executive officer (XO). He refused to be intimidated by anybody. "Cheer up," said Cave, "it was a safe approach, and you got onboard your first pass. You did all right."

"Thanks, Cave. I'm going to turn in. I'll see you in the morning." Our ready room was on the O2 level of the carrier, which meant it was one deck below the flight deck and two decks above the hangar deck. The stateroom that I was temporarily placed in was a two-man stateroom that I shared with one of the squadron's department heads, a lieutenant commander whose call sign was Kwyjibo. The call sign derived from a *Simpsons* television episode where Bart Simpson is playing his father, Homer, in a game of Scrabble. Bart declares victory after spelling the word *Kwyjibo*. Homer, doubting the existence of the word, demands a definition from Bart. Hesitating briefly, Bart is inspired by Homer's appearance and blurts out that a Kwyjibo is a "tall, middle-aged, balding, goofy-looking North American male." Bart's definition also happened to accurately describe my roommate, and so a call sign was born.

I found it awkward living with Kwyjibo for a number of reasons. I was commissioned as an ensign, the lowest rank in the navy's officer corps, and was promoted to lieutenant junior grade after having served for two years. Kwyjibo was a lieutenant commander with sixteen years of service. He was married and had two children, with a third one on the way. I was a bachelor and even though I was deeply in love with my girlfriend, Alice, children were quite a way off in my mind. The next promotion for me would be to lieutenant, and that would not occur for another two years. Then it would be another six years or so until I became a lieutenant commander. We simply did not have much in common.

Lieutenants, lieutenants junior grade, and ensigns were all considered to be junior officers. Rightly or wrongly, in our squadron there existed an invisible, but real barrier between the JOs and the lieutenant commanders. Every squadron has what is known as a Junior Officer Protection Association, or JOPA. Our squadron's JOPA was called UMPQUA which stood for Underprivileged Minions Perpetually Questioning Unlimited Authority. In reality, UMPQUA was the name of a dairy in a small midwestern town that was owned and operated by the family of one of our ECMOs whose call sign was Kamper. He had brought a number of patches from the dairy to the squadron and had proclaimed himself the founder of UMPQUA. Kamper was a large bear of an ECMO, and his family farm's Indian-head patch had become the symbol of our squadron's JOPA. I had not yet been given my patch, but I hoped that once I moved into one of the JO bunkrooms, I would be given one. I wanted to live with my peers as a member of UMPQUA, and learn from the shared experience of a first deployment. Kwyjibo was friendly, but I looked forward to the day when I could move into one of the JO bunkrooms.

As soon as I sat down in the stateroom I pulled out some paper and reached with my right hand up to the left shoulder pen pocket of my flight suit where I kept my trusted pen under a Velcro flap. It was a silver-plated Mark Cross pen that my grandparents had given to me as a high school graduation present. Now, after eight years of hard use, its silver-plated surface was scratched and rusting. But it still worked, and it was my good luck pen. It had never missed a flight with me since I had started flying in the navy over two years earlier.

Before I began to write to Alice, the woman I hoped someday to marry, I started to daydream. My mind drifted back to the first time Alice and I had met. Our fathers had been friends in college, but because her family lived in Texas and my family in Connecticut, we had never met. A job change for her father brought Alice's family to Connecticut in the mid 1980s, but it was not until December 23, 1989, that we actually met for the first time in her family's home at a Christmas party.

I will never forget that evening. She wore a black velvet jacket with black wool pants that fit well over her shapely long legs. Her eyes were hazel with a hint of brown to soften them. Her wavy dark-brown hair fell to her shoulders, and her jacket set off the string of pearls around her neck and made them glimmer. Large round earrings studded with a rainbow of colored stones covered her ears. In a word, she was stunning. I proceeded to follow her around for the duration of the party. We talked about her experience as a law-school student and about what she was hoping to do with her degree. I told her all about being a navy pilot and anything else I could think of that I hoped she might find interesting. She was helping her mother serve hors d'oeuvres, and I must have eaten several dozen crackers with smoked salmon, a bushel of vegetables with artichoke dip, and ten of anything else that Alice offered. I was smitten, and it showed. She was so beautiful, so elegant, so warm, and so intelligent. She was also probably accustomed to having men act this way in front of her. Yet, to her credit, she had the grace and charm to put up with me politely. Needless to say, I ensured that my family was the last to leave the party.

When my parents were finally able to drag me away from Alice, the conversation on the walk to the car was memorable.

"Sherm, I have never seen you act so uncool around a woman," said my younger brother, Alex, who was in college at the time and knew about cool. He was in a state of disbelief over my behavior.

"Alex, that's because I never have behaved like that. I couldn't help it, I was simply stunned. I can tell you right now that Alice is the woman I will marry." That comment promptly ended the conversation, because Alex took one look at me and realized that I was serious.

Soon after Christmas I flew back to Naval Air Station Whidbey Island, Washington, to complete my flight training, wondering how on earth I would convince Alice that we should spend the rest of our lives together. During the next eleven months, I wrote Alice brief, light, and newsy letters every ten days, just to let her know I was still alive as I continued through my training. It was not until November 1990 that I saw Alice again. When I had completed training and received my assignment to the *Midway*, I was told that I could go home for Thanksgiving before leaving for the Persian Gulf. My one thought was to see Alice again, and so I invited her to come spend Thanksgiving weekend with my family. Having not seen me for eleven months, she suggested that we first have lunch near her parents' home before we decided about spending the entire holiday weekend together.

The lunch was a great success and the weekend was nothing short of magical. I reaffirmed to myself my determination to marry Alice, and I believe she started to think that I had some potential, even though I could not possibly have been more geographically undesirable. After our weekend together, I promised myself that I would write her at least once a day during this deployment, and so far I had kept that promise.

With these thoughts in my mind, I put my lucky pen to paper.

12 Dec 90

Dear Alice,

I'm drenched with sweat and my brain is exhausted. Every now and then when I think about how dangerous it is flying around the ship it scares me. I just finished a flight with a poor landing and I'm angry. You can fly perfectly for an hour and a half and then be judged as a pilot solely on the last twenty seconds of the flight when you land aboard the ship.

My landings up until today have been excellent and I hope they will continue to be so. However, every once in a while that momentary loss of concentration can ruin your day.

Enough bitching; life is good, and I am really enjoying my new friends in the squadron. It looks like I may be able to call you on Christmas from some port in the Gulf. So hopefully this letter will keep you by the phone on Christmas day.

On days like today when I am a little angry and frustrated I want nothing more than to hold you in my arms.

All my love, Sherm

After I had sealed the envelope and written out the address, I heard a sound at the door. The next day's flight schedule appeared under the door. The squadron's emblem, a clenched metallic fist with lightning bolts emanating from all sides, was printed at the top of the page. It was this clenched metallic fist that gave our squadron its radio call sign of Ironclaw. Underneath the emblem, laid out in neat columns, was a slew of information. The flight schedule is every squadron's most important document. In one glance, an aviator learns his briefing time, launch time, recovery time, flight crew, mission type, required training, fuel load, ordnance load, operating area, coordination required with other units, questions of the day, meetings, notes, and a great deal more information, as well. Anything of importance that will occur in the squadron during a given day will be on the flight schedule.

My eyes moved slowly down the page looking for my name. A day flight would be nice, I thought, as my eyes studied the schedule. My name first turned up at the bottom of the first page in a daytime flight in formation with the XO flying the other jet. As I turned the sheet over, I hoped that I could rest tomorrow night; but no, there was my name. My mind flashed back to my struggle with the tanker and then it replayed my ugly approach from beginning to end. I felt so drained, so utterly exhausted. I could not imagine going through it all over again tomorrow night. But I needed to prove that I was ready to fly in combat, I needed to fly well during the day, so that I could approach the night with more confidence than I had now.

After learning tonight that one of the squadron's pilots, nick-named Pokey, had been grounded this evening after a poor landing, I felt even more pressure to perform. The squadron was now one pilot short. Pokey would not fly again until after a review board, which could take quite a while to set up. If combat was lurking in the near future, I needed to be ready.

CHAPTER THREE

Pretender or Contender

Later that night I awoke feeling uncomfortably alert, the way you feel when you have not been able to fall into a deep sleep because of feelings of anxiety racing through your head. The room was black. I could not see my hand as I brought it only a few inches from my face. It reminded me of the blackness of night when I am flying under an overcast sky and there is no moon. It is a lonely feeling in the jet. Even though there are three other men with me, it is still lonely, because I am the pilot. I am the one who must face the night, face my fear, and land the mass of steel and avionics onto the small deck floating in the vastness of the ocean. Why was I doing this? Why was I here? What was I thinking? Maybe I deserved those "The navy, are you crazy?" looks that I had gotten from many of my college friends. But somehow it felt right. Somehow I knew that this was where I belonged. There was a need deep within me to prove that I could hack it. To prove that I was not afraid of the night. Perhaps it came from early childhood nightmares lodged so deep in my memory that I could not even recall them. Whatever it was, I looked at the night as a challenge—a personal challenge.

The blackness in this stateroom was filled with the noises of the twenty-four-hour existence that is an accepted part of life on an aircraft carrier at sea. The mechanical sounds of the enormous elevators going up and down, carrying everything from aircraft to weapons and spare parts from the flight deck to the hangar deck, the loud clanking of metal on metal made by a sailor trying to fix something in the passageway and the pssssshhh sound of steam escaping from a pressure relief valve. There was always something going on and I had to get used to it soon, if I was going to be able to get any rest.

So much had happened so quickly in my life. During my senior year at Yale my interest in service had led me to seriously consider joining the Peace Corps. But, after many lengthy discussions with friends and family, I decided that the Peace Corps was not the organization for me. I wanted to serve the United States in a tangible way. My father had become an officer in the Marine Corps after he graduated from Yale during the Korean War. He urged me to explore my reasons thoroughly for entering the military. Following his advice, I laid out my thoughts. I wanted to do something exciting, something challenging, and something that served America; these goals led me to choose naval aviation.

I remember graduating from Yale and telling people that I planned to fly jets for the navy. The reactions that I got served to reinforce my decision. The look on their faces seemed to ask, "Why would you waste an Ivy League education on the military?" The military was still held in disdain by most of the students at Yale and many Americans of the Vietnam era. The message from my peers and many of my parents' friends was clear enough. They thought I was throwing it all away by joining the military. I wasn't sure what "it" was, but somehow I surmised that "it" was a golden future that would come easily if I followed the path of least resistance. My class graduated at the height of the leveraged buyout, hostile takeover, and junk-bond era on Wall Street, and the lure of the big money was sorely tempting. But for a young man who had grown up dreaming of playing centerfield for the New York Mets, a desk job had no appeal.

Sure, my friends might make more money, but I was convinced that many of them would give it all up in a heartbeat for the opportunity to fly a jet off a carrier. None of them knew how incredible it was to feel the acceleration of the catapult shot, the G forces from turning hard at low altitude, the tug of the arresting gear upon landing, the thrill of landing on a carrier during the day, and the terror of landing at night. It sounds like great fun during the day, and it is. At night, however, I earn my pay. Nobody I knew would want to trade places with me at night, and especially now that combat lies around the corner. It was with incredible foresight that my Yale classmates, aware of my unusual decision to join the navy, voted me "Most likely to die for a cause." Given my current situation, one had to concede that I had some clever classmates. But my stubborn nature fully intended to prove them all wrong.

The long road that had brought me to this black room in the depths of an aircraft carrier in the middle of the ocean started over three years earlier in Pensacola, Florida. Aviation Officer Candidate School (AOCS) was the home of men with really long names, such as Staff Sergeant Massey United States Marine Corps, and Master Gunnery Sergeant Bearup United States Marine Corps. The US Navy insisted that all naval aviators be trained by Marine Corps drill instructors, the toughest breed of military man. The United States Marine Corps was not a title or a suffix; it was part of their being. These drill instructors breathed the Marine Corps and had been selected to teach at AOCS because they were such model marines. I will never forget meeting my drill instructor, Staff Sergeant Massey, on the veranda of building 626 at Naval Air Station Pensacola on the afternoon of September 27, 1987. The sun was low in the sky, but its Florida heat made my Connecticut body sweat freely. It shone right onto the veranda, making small trickles of sweat run down my arms and neck as I stood there trying to decide whether to enter the door in front of me or whether to just wait until someone came out. Behind the door came loud shouts and screams, and my hesitation was justified. Staff Sergeant Massey made up my mind for me as he would do for the next few months. The door flew open and out he came. He was a live wire of a man who was in my face before I had resolved my moment of indecision. It was not your run-of-the-mill conversation. It went something like this:

"Don't eyeball me, boy," he shouted. My eyes could not help but try to look at the face that was attacking me verbally. "I said, don't eyeball me. Those eyes better be focused a thousand miles out in space." He circled me like a shark in shallow water, and all

I saw was the big Smokey-the-Bear hat going around and around me as I stood there sweating. The sweat started to roll into my eyes and when I raised my hand to wipe it off, he took another bite. "Did I tell you to wipe yourself, boy? From now on, you don't do shit unless I tell you to do it. Is that clear?"

"Yes," I said in a low intimidated tone of voice.

"I couldn't hear you. Do you like to whisper? Are you getting sweet on me?"

"No," I shouted as loud as I could.

"No, *what*, boy? Are you one of those disrespectful sweet things who wants to whisper in my ear, boy?"

"No, *sir*," I shouted again with conviction.

"Pick up your trash," he yelled. I looked down to my duffle bag and leaned over to grab it by the handle. "Stop! Stop! Stop! Hell no, get back to where you were." And I straightened up and tried to put on the thousand-mile stare. "When I tell you to do something, I want it done lightning quick. But, you will wait for the execute order. You will wait to hear the word *GO!* Is that clear."

"Yes, sir," I bellowed.

"You're whispering again," he whispered in my ear, the brim of his Smokey-the-Bear hat slicing into my temple.

"*No, sir!*" I screamed.

"Pick up your trash." I started to bend, but caught myself. It was just a game of Simon Says. "GO!" he yelled and I jolted downward to grab my bag and then returned to the standing position as quickly as I could.

"Take your trash over there against the bulkhead. Now, do it," he yelled. My feet moved toward the door—"No! No! No! Get back! Did I give the execute order?"

"*No, sir!*" I screamed.

"Then why the hell did you move your little feet, boy?"

This was a tough one. I took the honesty-is-the-best-policy approach. "Sir, I don't know."

"So you're a dumb ass, too. The navy is really stooping low these days. Now, we'll try it again," he paused and then shouted, "Take your trash over there against the bulkhead." I didn't flinch this time. "GO!" he shouted. I sprinted the ten yards with my duffle bag to what I figured was the bulkhead. I later learned that it was simply the navy term for a wall. I was realizing that there was an entire new vocabulary that I needed to master.

And so the interrogation continued through my name and my hometown and where I went to college. He got a lot of mileage out of the information he got.

"So, I bet you would rather be drinking those gin and tonics and playing tennis with your preppy buddies Muffy, Bunny, and Chip."

"No, sir," I shouted emphatically.

"What do you mean 'No, sir'? You really are stupid, boy. I don't know anyone in their right mind that would rather have me yelling at their stupid ass than playing tennis with some kids named Muffy, Bunny, and Chip."

"Sir, I want to be here. I want this training" was all I could think to say.

"That's bullshit. Why don't you just quit before it starts getting tough. Just go back to the pools and the tennis courts and leave the military to people who can handle it."

"Sir, I can handle it," I yelled, half believing it myself. I was determined not to quit, but I was in the minority. Staff Sergeant Massey was able to "persuade" over three quarters of my initial class to quit the program within the first twenty-four hours. The attrition rate due to the relentless combination of physical and mental abuse was sufficient to have the officer in charge of the school hold the remaining seven candidates in our class back one week so that we could go through it all again with the next class that came in. With only seven people left in our class, it would not have been economically worthwhile for the navy to send us through the entire four-month program as such a small group.

Even though at the beginning it seemed like random, senseless abuse, it was training in some ways. I did not understand it, but I was willing to accept it. I knew that I had to accept it, if I wanted to become a carrier pilot, and so I did. I played Simon Says, and I played it very well. For a while I followed orders from a hat. In fact, I do not think I even saw Staff Sergeant Massey's face for the first several weeks of the program. I did, however, get to know his boots quite well, because, as our class would be doing push-ups, he would walk back and forth along our line telling each of us, "Don't eyeball me, boy." As a result, I did not really get a good look at Staff Sergeant Massey United States Marine Corps until several weeks into the program.

Staff Sergeant Massey made an indelible impression on me in the four months that I ran, did push-ups, and studied everything from sea power to aerodynamics, in order to become an officer who might one day qualify to fly a jet off an aircraft carrier. I remember doing remedial drilling with Staff Sergeant Massey because, as a class, we were not that strong on our marching and parade rifle-handling skills. We were out on the "grinder," a huge parking lot on the base that was ideal for marching large formations of officer candidates. The expansive area was great because there were not many obstacles which we could run into. We were actually doing quite well when Staff Sergeant Massey said in typical unintelligible Marine Corps drill-instructor language, "Company, halt. Left face. Eyes up." Rapidly approaching from the distance was a tight formation of jets. The tightest formation I had ever seen. It was the Blue Angels returning from a rehearsal over the ocean to their training airfield less than two miles from where we were marching.

Once they had passed overhead, so as not to interrupt our gawking session, Staff Sergeant Massey said, "The slot man in that formation was marching on this grinder about six years ago. That can be you, if you want it bad enough." Without more than a minor pause for effect, he shouted the next series of commands: "Present arms. Right face. Forward march." And so we spent several more hours on the hot Florida pavement drilling with our rifles and imagining what it would be like to fly with the Blue Angels.

Every morning, we would wake to reveille at 5:00 A.M. Having slept in our running gear, we would be ready within minutes for our daily morning run. Marine Corps drill instructors love to run. The joy they feel leads them to sing while they run. The singing does tend to help take one's mind off the pain and stiffness that one feels at 5:00 A.M. These songs, called "jodies," also served to establish a cadence, enabling the entire battalion to run at the same pace. The cadence was steady and simple. Most of the "jodies"

referred to flying in one way or another. A few verses stick in my
mind. One in particular tried to capture the feeling of landing on
the small deck of the USS *Lexington*.

> *I want to be a Navy Pilot,*
> *I want to land on the Lady Lex,*
> *'Cause all my friends with the gold wings tell me,*
> *Carrier landings are better than sex.*

Another verse referred to a young pilot forced to interact with
nature in order to procure some new flight gear:

> *Running through the jungle in the middle of the day,*
> *A mean old alligator got in my way,*
> *I said, alligator, alligator, you'd better move,*
> *Before I make a pair of flight boots out of you.*
> *Smooth, shiny alligator hide,*
> *Gonna make a pair of flight boots just the right size.*

After four months of singing, running, push-ups, and other
more ingenious training techniques, I knew how to salute properly
with the fingers of my right hand aligned with my thumb and my
elbow raised to the proper angle with the right index finger coming up to the corner of my right eye. I could stand at attention and
have my hands placed just aft of the seam on my trousers, my heels
together, and my feet at a forty-five-degree angle. I could follow
orders and manipulate a rifle while marching. I could run an obstacle course with walls, ropes, tunnels, and sand. But I could not fly,
nor did I know whether I would have any aptitude for flying. It
wasn't clear to me at the time, but looking back, I had learned
some valuable lessons at AOCS. I now understood that an unfailing attention to detail and a relentless pursuit of perfection were
the cornerstones of an attitude that Staff Sergeant Massey United
States Marine Corps had successfully instilled deep inside of me. I
knew that in this way, he would be with me on every flight I ever
made.

On the bitter-cold January day that I graduated and was commissioned an ensign in the United States Navy, Master Gunnery Sergeant Bearup United States Marine Corps gave each member of my class a small card which I later had framed. Today, it is still sitting on my desk. The card reads:

> *You can divide naval officers into two classes: Pretenders and Contenders. The Pretenders are the ones who never sacrifice themselves. They will never know the meaning of "total dedication," therefore, they will never taste the glory. The Contenders are the ones who demand of themselves the absolute maximum limit and are willing to pay that price. They will be able to catch the glory.*
>
> *Life is that way. There are Pretenders and there are Contenders. The question is . . . which one are you?*

Since graduating from AOCS I had been seeking an answer to this nagging question. Which one was I? Did I have the spirit of total dedication to be a Contender? I believed I did, but realized that nothing would test that better than actually going into combat, or at least, so I thought. So as the presidential deadline approached for Iraq to withdraw from Kuwait, this is the question that kept ringing in my head: Was I a Pretender or a Contender? Since I was unable to answer this question with complete confidence, another question bubbled to the surface in my mind. It was a question of love.

Would Alice wait for me? Two weeks earlier, I had been busy falling in love. Now I was busy preparing for war. As I lay in my cramped, narrow, and lumpy bed in a room blacker than black, I thought back on what I had left behind. I smiled as I remembered the joyous Thanksgiving weekend in Roxbury, Connecticut, with my family and the woman who I was certain was the one for me. I remembered every moment of that weekend that we had spent together. One especially vivid memory rushed to the surface.

Alice and I walked hard for half an hour and then stood together on the top of what was called the Pinnacle, a large outcropping of rock on the top of a Connecticut hill overlooking Lake Waramaug.

The exposed summit gave us a magnificent 360-degree view of the countryside. The November wind was cold, and I gave Alice my jacket. The temperature dropped with the sun, and our faces became flushed from the cold air. Neither of us wanted to leave that spot. As darkness neared we grudgingly left the summit arm in arm. I was more certain than ever about my feelings for Alice, and I began to feel that she too was looking at me with a more serious eye.

I smiled in the darkness. Somehow, I needed to convince her that I was the one for her, that I was worth waiting for. In my typically well-planned manner, I had developed a strategy to court her from the Gulf. It was simple. Write at least one letter every day and she could not help but think of me. Then once I got home, I would be able to convince her in person that I was indeed the one for her.

With these happy optimistic thoughts, I drifted back to sleep and did not let the chains being dragged on the flight deck above my rack bother me. I had a lot to live for back home, and that made me quite scared about what lay ahead on this cruise. I just prayed that I would safely return home to Alice, so that I could convince her that we should spend the rest of our lives together.

Blown Away

"I've got him, he's four o'clock low," said Gucci, my rightseater, the strain of the 5-G turn affecting his voice.

"Is he in guns yet?" I asked, pulling the stick into my lap and feeling the G forces crush my chest.

"Not yet, but he's trying to saddle in behind us," said Gucci. I kept the pull on. My left hand was pushing on the throttles so forcefully that I was certain I was bending the metal. I was on the defensive, and I was simply trying to survive like a wrestler squirming on the mat, trying desperately to avoid being pinned. I could not see the bandit, because he was attacking from the right side, my blind spot, given the Prowler's side-by-side seating. I was trusting Gucci to be my eyes.

"He's almost in gun parameters," said Gucci. "Prepare to jink. Ready, *now*!" said Gucci. I snapped the stick to the left and then rammed it full forward. The G meter sprang to -2 Gs and everyone in the jet was thrown toward the canopy. All the dust and dirt that covered the floorboards of the jet was now floating in front of my face. The ocean filled the windscreen of the Prowler as we dove toward it, attempting to evade our attacker.

"Knock it off, Tank," said the XO to me over the radio. "Great move, you've got the lead, take me back to mother, I'm at 6.5 on gas," the XO snapped impatiently. The practice engagement was complete, and it looked like "Tank" was going to stick as my call sign if the XO was using it. It was derived from my first name, Sherman, as in Sherman Tank. It wasn't a bad call sign at all. I actually was lucky. Some guys got stuck with awful nicknames that they were never able to shake.

"Roger, knock it off. I've got the lead, and I'm 6.2 on gas," I said as I started to pull out of the steep dive. We had just completed several engagements of defensive tactics training. It was Prowler-versus-Prowler training within the squadron that enabled me to practice maneuvers I would need to use if I ever got jumped by an enemy fighter. I had learned the negative G maneuver that I had just used against the XO from a female flight instructor in Meridian, Mississippi. She had always said with a sarcastic smirk, "If you screw up this maneuver in the fleet, just tell them a girl taught you." She was one of the best pilots I had met going through flight training, and I considered myself lucky to have flown with her. Since the maneuver had worked, I didn't need to tell the XO that a "girl" had taught it to me, but I smiled as I imagined his reaction if I were ever to tell him. I needed to know such evasive maneuvers because the only way for a Prowler to survive an attack from an enemy fighter was to evade him. It was extremely frustrating to feel like a flying target, what fighter pilots called a "grape." But that was exactly what I was. Even though in our brief we had planned for the XO to lead the flight home, this was no time to bring it up. From talking with other people in the squadron, I knew that the XO might ask me to lead the flight home without having briefed it that way. It was not a big deal, but I knew that he was watching me closely.

Flying lead in a formation requires more administrative skill than stick and throttle skill. The most difficult part is remembering that you have a wingman reacting to your every control input, so being incredibly smooth takes on a new importance. Everything we were doing around the ship was now gearing up for a combat environment. Daytime recoveries were conducted "zip lip," meaning no communications. Everything was accomplished by prebriefed maneuvers, with each aircraft maintaining visual separation from all other aircraft. The procedures were actually quite easy; it was maintaining good situational awareness that sometimes got tricky. I led

the XO down to three thousand feet, which is where the Prowlers
and Intruders would circle overhead the *Midway* waiting to "break
the deck."

"Breaking the deck" meant that you were the pilot who landed
first, immediately after the last launching aircraft had taxied clear
of the landing area. If done properly, there would be only a few
seconds separating the instant when the final launching aircraft had
cleared the landing area to the impact of the wheels of the first
landing aircraft. It was something we all looked forward to doing.
To be the pilot who consistently broke the deck required a combination of timing, skill, and luck. It was yet another way for pilots
to be competitive and to measure ourselves against one another.

"Hey, we've got company," said Gucci. It was tough for me to
see the two Intruders that had joined on us because they were well
back to the right in my blind spot. I caught a glimpse of my two
new wingmen in my rearview mirror. Now I was leading a four-jet
formation and technically, I wasn't even formally qualified to be
leading a two-jet formation. I could feel the XO's eyes burning a
hole in the back of my head. *Don't screw it up* was all I could tell
myself as we circled the carrier, waiting for the right moment to
descend and enter the landing pattern.

Breaking the deck has an importance beyond just being a game.
Although it brings out the competitive nature of the air wing pilots,
breaking the deck critically reduces the recovery time during which
any carrier is forced to sail into the wind. To recover aircraft, the
captain is forced to turn into the wind and sail on a predictable
course until the recovery is complete. In so doing, the carrier becomes vulnerable and an easy target for the enemy. So it is critical
for the carrier's air wing to be as expeditious as possible in recov-
ering onboard. To break the deck a pilot needed "the gouge,"
which was navy slang for advice or wisdom that is passed from
senior aviators to junior aviators. "Getting the gouge" was the time-
honored way that junior aviators lived to become senior aviators.
The gouge for "breaking the deck" on the *Midway* was to start your
descent when there were five jets remaining to be launched in the
landing area. The lazy counterclockwise circle that we were flying

overhead the *Midway* was getting boring. On the first lap, the launch had just started and the deck was crammed full of jets. This time as we passed overhead I saw eight jets remaining to be launched. At least one more lap I thought.

Looking down at the flight deck from the holding pattern above still gave me the nervous tingling feeling all over my body that I had felt during my very first trap in a navy jet two years before. On that warm sunny day I was flying a Rockwell T-2 Buckeye training jet in a formation of four aircraft over the Gulf of Mexico; we were just southwest of Key West, Florida. The flight lead was an instructor from one of the Texas training squadrons whose call sign was Badger. He led three terrified students flying solo out to the USS *Lexington* for our initial carrier qualification. We had all been practicing our landings at the airfield for the past few weeks and now the navy expected us to land on that little boat in the water. *This is insane!* I remember saying to myself as I circled above the small World War II vintage carrier. Our LSOs had told us that as long as you concentrate on flying the meatball, there was no difference between landing on a runway or a ship. I had taken their word for it until I actually saw it. They were dead wrong. From where I was sitting, there appeared to be a goddamned huge difference between landing on a runway and landing on the bobbing flight deck of the Lady Lex.

It was the first real carrier landing for all of us. I felt like the guy who is stranded in a high place, when the people who are trying to rescue him keep saying, "Just don't look down!" The problem is, of course, that you do look down. When you realize that you shouldn't have looked down, it's already too late. That sunny day, two years earlier, Badger had led the three of us into the break, and then everything had happened so quickly that my memory is a complete blur. I executed the break turn, threw down my landing gear, flaps, and tailhook. The next thing I knew, I was kissing the T-2's dashboard and pulling the stick out of my chest because in all the excitement, I had forgotten to lock my seat-belt harness. Somehow, I had survived my first four traps and catapult shots. In fact, I had actually done well. But, now, even though I was in "the show," with about thirty day carrier landings under my belt, the *Midway* still looked small, and I still wondered if I was really going to be able to do it.

By the time we had completed another lap there were five jets left in the landing area and the timing was right. "We'll start down now," I said to Gucci. When we had reached the back side of the holding circle, I gently reduced power and lowered the nose. I wanted desperately to be the leader of the formation that broke the deck today, but I also needed to be smooth for the benefit of my three wingmen. The XO was tucked in tightly on my right wing and the Intruders were keeping the formation together. I was leading the flight in a descending left-hand turn sweeping down from three thousand feet to a point three miles astern the carrier at eight hundred feet.

"Your belly's clear," said Gucci's experienced voice. I had gotten so focused on the carrier that I had forgotten to look for potential traffic under our belly and to our right side as we descended into the initial point three miles aft of the carrier. Normally, I asked my rightseater to check the Prowler's belly to make sure there was no threat of a midair collision. I was definitely distracted by having these three jets on my wing. I had forgotten something that should have been ingrained in my brain. As the formation rolled wings level, precisely mirroring my control inputs, the altimeter in my cockpit was pegged at eight hundred feet. This was the altitude, according to the navy's procedures, where pilots initiated their entrance into the carrier's landing pattern, known as "the break." The break was a dramatic way to enter the landing pattern in which a pilot would roll sharply to a 90-degree angle of bank and perform a decelerating 180-degree turn in order to reduce his airspeed so that he could safely lower his landing gear and flaps. The final 180 degrees of turn were performed in this "dirty" configuration to an eventual arrested landing on the flight deck.

The worst part of leading three jets into the break was that I would be forced to break at the bow of the carrier. Breaking at the bow would allow my wingmen more room upwind and therefore more time, but it would force me to be rushed with my landing procedures. The landing pattern is like an intricate array of dominoes. If one pilot screws up, there will be a tremendous ripple effect that will disrupt the tempo and precision of this synchronized aerial event. I needed to perform the break turn at the bow so that all of my wingmen could break with seventeen seconds separating them. The interval of seventeen seconds at higher speeds would then translate into an interval of forty-five seconds at landing speeds in between the actual landings, which is what the air boss wanted to see.

As I rolled wings level at eight hundred feet and three miles behind the ship, I could see my wingmen tightening the formation to look good in front of the LSOs who would be grading our landings. I aligned our formation on the frothy whitish wake of the carrier and gently pushed the throttles forward to give the LSOs a good show. The jet was well trimmed and was riding steadily. The airspeed indicator climbed to 415 knots, much faster than I was accustomed to. I normally entered the break at 350 knots about one mile upwind of the ship, giving myself more time, but today I could not afford to do that. "Kiss 'em off," I said to Gucci just before I slammed the stick to the left. Gucci quickly signaled our break to our wingmen before the G forces took hold and we both groaned under the new weight of our bodies. The jet completed 180 degrees of the turn and I saw 300 knots on the indicator. "Shit, we are fast and wide," I said.

"Yeah," said Gucci, calm but alert.

I knew the two ECMOs in the backseat were ready for anything because they knew I was overloaded and they knew that it was not good for a pilot to be overloaded in the landing pattern. We were low and in a descending turn. The maximum landing gear extension speed was 250 knots so I watched the airspeed indicator carefully and as soon as it hit 250, I slammed down the gear handle. The approach was still salvageable at this point.

"Gear one two three down and locked, flaps thirty, stab shifted, slats out, hook's down, harness set, boards out, pressure's off, on speed will be 125 with 5000 pounds of gas," I sputtered out the landing checks as I shifted my scan outside the cockpit. I felt high and tight on the ship, but that was normal and I was just now realizing that it was the normal sight picture. The carrier was steaming away from me and the wind was blowing into me. These forces combined to make the correct approach path seem unrealistic. The feeling of "I can't get there from here" meant that I was probably on track.

My main problem was the solid red chevron on my Angle of Attack indicator. I was twenty knots faster than I should have been and one hundred feet higher. High and fast, it was an ugly place to be. I pulled back on the throttles as far as I dared and began to trim nose up to adjust my airspeed. As we rolled into the groove I scanned the lens on the left edge of the deck looking for something familiar that would help me fly the right glide path to the wires. Nothing, no ball, I was high. The Prowler was above the top lens of light on the Fresnel system. How embarrassing. It was a beautiful calm day and I couldn't even fly an approach well enough to get a ball on the lens. I was angry at myself and started to make the necessary aggressive corrections that were required.

I bunted the stick forward to start a rate of descent. Within a few seconds I saw the familiar yellow glow of the meatball appear on the lens, and I added power to slow my rate of descent. As I approached the deck the meatball started to sag below the green datum lights, telling me that I was going low and I responded with a forward thrust of my left hand, adding just enough power to clear the ramp and fly me into the wires. The last shot of power made the Prowler's glide path flatten out, and as a result I caught the third and final wire. The rollout brought our jet very close to the edge of the deck.

As soon as the deceleration stopped, allowing me to remove the stick from my stomach, I saw the yellowshirt out in front to the right of the jet, signaling me frantically to lift up my hook and taxi forward. In the midst of my self-congratulations for having landed safely I forgot that I couldn't relax yet. The XO's jet was right behind me, rolling into the groove, and I needed to clear the deck so that he could land. If I lingered in the landing area too long, the LSOs would be forced to wave off the XO, and then I would never hear the end of it.

I nudged the throttles forward and followed the directions of the yellowshirt, who was directing me forward to the *Midway*'s bow area. I was passed off to another yellowshirt standing up at the bow and I knew that I had made it safely out of the landing area, for over my left shoulder I heard the roar of the XO's engines as he landed in the wires just behind me. By the time I had taxied to the bow, both of the Intruders from our original formation had landed and I could already see the next formation behind them in the landing pattern. It was an amazing evolution; twelve aircraft would be landing at intervals of forty-five seconds on a ship at sea without a word being spoken. I felt proud to be a part of it.

Following the directions of the yellowshirts I turned at the bow and started taxiing aft on the port side of the bow area, where our Prowler would eventually be parked and chained to the deck. As soon as the yellowshirt gave me the signal that the jet was secured, I said over the ICS, "OK, guys, we're chocked and chained—let's safe our seats." Each crew member reached above his head and between his legs to lock the ejection seat handles into their safe positions so that nobody would accidentally set off a seat while getting out of the jet. Once everyone had confirmed his seat was safe, I shut down the Prowler's engines and raised the canopy.

The warm Gulf air blew into the cockpit and quickly dried the sweat from my face. As I started the treacherous process of climbing out of the Prowler's front cockpit, I noticed that the yellowshirts were taxiing an E-2C Hawkeye to the number-one catapult. This was unusual, because normally, no aircraft were launched after a recovery was completed. After I disconnected my G-suit, a nylon suit that fit snugly over my abdomen and legs designed with internal inflatable bladders to help me fight the effects of G forces, I unfastened my four-point harness and leg restraints. As I climbed out of the cockpit I waved to one of the A-6 bombardier-navigators, known as BNs, who had followed me into the break. He waved back and walked briskly past our Prowler on the way to his ready room. The most direct path to his ready room led him behind the number-one catapult where the catapult team was hooking up the Hawkeye to the shuttle.

From the Prowler's boarding platform I yelled because I could see what was about to happen, but it was no use. With thirty knots of wind over the deck for the Hawkeye's launch, nobody could hear my voice. The A-6 BN had his head down and was walking quickly toward the island on the other side of the flight deck. The catapult officer looked behind the catapult and didn't see the errant A-6 BN, because he was still hidden from view by a parked F/A-18 Hornet. The yellowshirt flung his arms into the "in tension" signal, and the E-2C Hawkeye pilot moved his throttles to their maximum thrust position just as the A-6 BN walked out from behind the parked Hornet. The BN was caught in the Hawkeye's prop wash before he knew what had happened.

The two huge propellers of an E-2C Hawkeye generate an air blast of hurricane proportions, turning the flight deck behind them into a wind tunnel. Instantly, the BN was blown down to the steel flight deck and his navigation bag opened and spewed out all his charts and code-word papers. When he tried to regain his feet, he looked like a tumbleweed cartwheeling on the desert prairie. He desperately grabbed for the small indentations in the flight deck surface known as "padeyes" which were the spots that chain hooks could grab and hold the aircraft securely to the deck. But his fingers could not find one. The BN's hands flailed hopelessly, trying to grab on to anything that would stop his progress down the length of the flight deck. From the right side of the deck I then saw a lone man sprint to the BN's aid. It was a textbook demonstration of open field tackling. This guardian angel dove at the BN, knocking him to the deck while at the same time grabbing on to a padeye. He pinned the BN to the deck, hoping that the catapult officer would now make the correct decision because he knew that he couldn't hold on to the padeye for very long.

The crucial decision now fell to the catapult officer who, seeing what had happened, had to choose between launching the Hawkeye or suspending the launch. If he gave the signal to launch the Hawkeye, it would be off the deck within three to five seconds. If he gave the signal to suspend the launch, it might take seven to ten seconds before the pilot actually retarded his throttles to idle, thus freeing the BN and his rescuer from their windy prison. But in seven to ten seconds the BN's rescuer might lose his grip on the padeye and both men would start tumbling farther aft along the deck. In less than a second the catapult officer made the right decision as he

touched the deck signaling to launch the aircraft. Within three seconds the Hawkeye was shot off the *Midway*'s bow, and the flight
deck personnel rushed up to the BN and his rescuer as they started
to relax their grips on the padeye and stood up together, both feeling the worse for wear.

By the time I got to the group I could tell by his flight deck float
coat that the heroic man had been a chief petty officer from our
squadron. "Helluva tackle, Chief Ross," I said with a smile.

"Thanks, sir, but I'm getting too old to do this shit. Tackling
stupid aircrew is for these younger guys."

"Well, I know Kooz is glad you were there," I said after taking
one look at the ghostly white face of the BN—which made me
realize just how thankful he was.

"Yeah, I guess," said the chief with a smile, knowing that he
would do exactly the same thing on the next recovery if he saw an
emergency. He simply reacted, based on years of flight deck experience. Without stopping to catch his breath, Chief Ross started
barking out instructions to the young flight deck crew attending to
one of our squadron's Prowlers. It was back to business for the chief
who had just saved a man from serious injury or possibly death. As
I walked down to the ready room I realized that what I had just
seen was business as usual and that I needed to get used to it. The
flight deck was a place to pay attention and keep your eyes open.

Our debrief was long and painful because it was done by the XO
who commented on every aspect of the formation flight from the
join-up to the point where we parked the aircraft back on the *Midway*'s deck. The XO was going to become our skipper within the
next week. I wanted desperately to understand this man who would
be leading our squadron into war. Even though he was now a pilot,
he had started his career in the Prowler as an ECMO. Very few
ECMOs were offered the opportunity to make the transition to
pilot. For those who made the transition, it was said they underwent
a surgical procedure called an "anchorectomy." It entailed the removal not only of an anchor from their gold wings (a naval flight
officer's wings had two anchors and a naval aviator's wings had only
one), but also the removal of any loyalty to the ECMO community.
As a result, the XO was regarded by many as an inveterate ECMO-

basher who took advantage of any opportunity to smash the already somewhat frail egos of junior officer ECMOs. As a pilot I rarely, if ever, felt the burning heat of the XO's wrath, but I felt it for my ECMO friends who often bore the brunt of his rage in the debriefs. The debrief's excruciating detail was necessary, but it was a long and painful process to undergo after a difficult flight.

When we finally broke up I saw Horse dressed in his LSO float coat. Things came easily to him in the cockpit. I envied him. Things that I would have to study and think about seemed second nature to Horse. I heard that it was the same way for him in his LSO duty. I wanted some of his naturalness to rub off on me. Perhaps it was just experience. Whatever it was, I wanted some of it. It was his team's day, and I asked him if I could join him for the next recovery.

"Sure, Tank, maybe we'll even get the pickle in your hand to-day," said Horse with a smile, referring to actually letting me control the recovery and grade the landings.

I didn't think I was up to that level yet, but I didn't hesitate to say that would be great. Excited about this possibility of action, I left the ready room and made my way forward to the "dirty-shirt" wardroom for a quick lunch. It was called the dirty-shirt wardroom because it was the only place where officers could eat in their flight suits. As a result, it was where the air wing ate. The skipper had approved my request to be an LSO, but the CAG LSOs had not yet placed me on a regular team. As a result, I would just go out to the LSO platform whenever I got the chance to develop the sight picture for the proper glide path and landing performance of the air wing's different aircraft. There were five teams of LSOs, and Horse was the team leader of one of the teams; Ren, our squadron's other nugget pilot, was a member of another. It was fun for me to be a freelancer not assigned to a team because I got to meet all of the LSOs and was picking up "the gouge" from lots of different people.

After finishing a grilled cheese sandwich and some french fries I started the long trek to the aft end of the carrier where the LSO platform was located. The walk along the port side of the carrier to the LSO platform was a treacherous one. The passageway started to twist and turn toward the aft end of the ship. High-stepping over the knee knockers (the apt navy term for the two-and-a-half-foot-high bases to the watertight hatches that were cut through every transverse frame of the carrier) made the walk a good workout and a real stretch of the legs. The walk took only a few minutes, but if you were in a rush you could run the obstacle course in less than a minute, depending on traffic in the passageway. The passageway was not wide enough to allow two men to pass each other so what would happen was when two men approached each other, the junior man would stop and put his back to the bulkhead and allow the more senior man to pass unimpeded. The traffic was light, and since the aft end of the ship right underneath the landing area was one of the primary enlisted berthing areas, I was senior to most of the men I passed on my way.

When I rounded the final corner I came upon Mad Dog and Horse studying "the book." There was an odd daybook and an even daybook, and at the end of each day the team leader was responsible for making sure that all the landing grades for that day got entered into the CAG LSO's computer for tracking the performance of the pilots. Every evening, the computer would spit out a squadron report with the landing grades of all the pilots who had flown that day. Then the squadron's LSO would transfer those grades to the squadron "greenie board." It was called a "greenie board" because the best landings were graded *OK* and were colored in green on the board. Yellow was used for an average landing (called a fair) and white for a below-average landing (called a no grade). At this point my grades had been all yellows and whites and I was dying for my first green.

"Hiya, fellas," I said cheerfully. "I missed you after the second recovery. I was flying 605."

"Hi, Tank. Sure let's see what you did out there," said Horse flipping back the page of the book. He mumbled *605* as he scanned the list of sidenumbers in the recovery from this morning. "Here you are. 605, high start underlined to in the middle, little not enough power on the come down in the middle, little low flat in close to at the ramp, fair, three wire. Nice job correcting off the really high start."

"Thanks, but I've got to fly a better pattern."

"Good corrections after the start, but remember, a good pattern leads to a good start which leads to a good pass," offered Mad Dog. Mad Dog was a tough LSO, but he could sense I needed encouragement. He needed to be tough on this ship. It was the most challenging ship in the fleet to land on, and if he didn't keep the standards high, then the chances for a mishap would increase. "Have you waved yet, Tank?"

"No. I've just been coming up and trying to get the sight picture."

"Well, you've gotta start sometime. Why don't you take this recovery and I'll back you up," said Mad Dog. "It's a small recovery and a steady deck, perfect for your first time."

"Sure, that would be great," I said, trying not to show my nervousness and excitement. I hadn't expected to get this opportunity for a while, and so I was thrilled.

The rest of the team began to gather as the jets continued to launch off the bow catapults. There was a representative from each of the different aircraft types in the air wing standing by as a subject matter expert, in case one of their aircraft should have any problems or emergencies. If an aircraft had an emergency, then they could provide information on the flight characteristics of the aircraft to the CAG LSO. Depending on the severity of the emergency, Mad Dog would decide whether or not he needed to control the recovery.

The beginning of a recovery was always hectic. I followed Mad Dog and Horse through the hatch that led to the flight deck. The rest of the LSOs followed in single file up onto the deck. Like the Seven Dwarfs, we were all dressed similarly with minor variations. We all were wearing white float coats made of canvas that had inflatable bladders to keep us from drowning in case we got blown off the deck. Getting blown over the side was extremely rare, but I had just seen it almost happen and so I thought the float coats were a good idea. The white coats had stenciling on their backs. Mad Dog's back said CAG LSO; the A-6s', EAGLE PADDLES, Horse's and mine, IRONCLAW LSO. "Paddles" was a nickname for LSO because LSOs used to use colored paddles to wave signals to the incoming aircraft. As a result, the terms *paddles* and *waving* continued to be used, even though technology had greatly changed the tools of the trade.

The other two important pieces of equipment that the LSOs all wore were small yellow foam earplugs and sunglasses. The "foamies," as we called them, could be squished tightly into one's ear to reduce the horrible effects of the howl of jet engines on your eardrums. And then there were the sunglasses. There was no standard, although the new wraparound Oakleys were quite popular. It was part safety and part image, but all of us had on our shades to protect our eyes from the sandblast effects of little bits of the deck's nonskid surface that would go flying down the deck each time a jet would land. A good LSO would watch the jet all the way into the wires, just like a good hitter in baseball would watch a pitch he was taking all the way into the catcher's glove. When doing this your face routinely got sprayed by little granules of coarse surface, which was a threat to an LSO's twenty-twenty vision.

The jets were all now well clear of the LSO platform which was right next to the landing area on the port side of the ship. Horse as the team leader ran the show and Mad Dog was there to supervise. Horse told me to raise the windscreen while he took care of the LSO PLAT display. I powered up the hydraulic system with the push of a button and then activated the motor, which raised a large windscreen at the back of the platform so that we would be protected not only from the jet exhaust of the aircraft in the landing area, but also from the nearly thirty knots of wind over the deck that we routinely had in order to land the air wing's jets.

"Intruders in the break," shouted Mad Dog. An aggressive flight of four A-6s were trying to break the deck. The lead A-6 had just entered the break overhead the *Midway*'s bow. I knew we had about forty-five seconds to get everything on the platform organized, and once again, I was feeling overloaded in a trial-by-fire environment.

"Tank, got your radio checks yet?" asked Horse.

"No, uhhh . . ." *How did it go? Oh yeah.* "Tower, paddles radio check," I said in a voice that surprised myself with its calmness.

"Loud and clear paddles, how me?"

"Loud and clear," I responded. I grabbed the pickle switch which controlled the wave-off lights and turned around to look at the lens behind me to test it. When my finger pressed the button, the bright red lights flashed rapidly and when I released the button, they were turned off. "Wave off lights check good," I screamed to Mad Dog.

"Roger that, mine too, and I've got a good back-up radio. All right, Tank, you just call the pass as you see it and don't worry if I change it."

"OK," I said.

"Don't use the word *OK* unless you are giving it as a grade."

"OK, uhhh . . . sorry, I mean *right*, got it." Horse stood just behind me poised with a pencil and the book ready to copy down my comments on each approach. The first A-6 was just turning the corner to begin the start of his final approach. In front of me was the LSO PLAT display which gave the LSO all the pertinent data he needed to control the recovery. In the center of the display was a miniature TV screen which presented the same picture to the LSO as it did to the rest of the ship from the flight deck's flush-mounted camera. Around the edge of the screen were various read-outs, such as wind velocity and direction over the deck, aircraft type, speed, deck motion (pitch and roll) of the carrier, hook-to-ramp clearance, and a slew of other information that I was too overwhelmed to even look at.

"Where is he, Tank?" asked Mad Dog.

"He's a little low," I said without much confidence.

"No, he's long in the groove. Time him," shouted Mad Dog. The pilot had turned too late from the downwind leg of the pattern and the combination of the *Midway* steaming away from him, the wind over the deck and his poor timing of his turn meant that his final groove length was far too long. Few things made Mad Dog madder than pilots who flew long in the groove.

My left hand held a telephone-style radio up to my left ear and my right hand held the pickle switch for the waveoff lights. As the jet rolled into the groove, the deck of the ship was still foul so I held the pickle switch above my head to remind myself that I couldn't let the jet land on a foul deck. Mad Dog also held his pickle switch above his head for the same reason. It was like tying a string around your finger to help you remember something.

The deck status light turned from red to green and we both

dropped our pickle switches down to our sides. It was a nice calm day and we expected the pilots to be able to fly under these conditions with little or no help from the LSOs. The recovery was expected to be "zip-lip," which meant in radio silence.

"Where is he now?" asked Mad Dog, checking to see how my eyes were calibrated.

"Little low."

"He's right on there, and his lineup is good," said Mad Dog, meaning that the A-6 was on the proper glide slope and lineup for his position on the approach. The A-6's engines seemed to smoothly respond to the steady inputs of the pilot. I became transfixed as I watched the jet getting bigger and bigger. It was flying right at me and only a small drift to the left would cause the jet's port wingtip to cut off my head at the neck. Even though I had been on the platform several times before, I still could not believe how close I was standing to where the jet landed. The air was so humid that I could see the vapors visibly swirling around the front of the Intruder's intakes as it roared over the edge of the ramp. If I had been standing on the edge of the ramp, the Intruder's tailhook would probably have knocked an apple from the top of my head like an arrow from the quiver of William Tell. There was not much room for error on these landings and today was as easy as it gets, daytime with good visibility and a steady deck. I could barely see anything worth commenting on as the Intruder slammed onto the *Midway*'s deck.

Mad Dog's voice in my ear startled me. "Call the pass, Tank," he shouted above the roar of the Intruder's engines.

"What was his groove length?" I yelled back to Stem, a Hornet LSO, who was timing the approach.

"Twenty-three seconds."

"Right, fair pass long in the groove." Horse nodded and copied down the comments in LSO shorthand notation. I turned my head to look at the book and was trying to remember what the A-6 had done and where he had moved on the glide slope. I saw that the next jet was about to roll into the groove. My mouth opened and nothing came out except for "Ahhh . . . he was overpowered and fast which made him go high then—"

"No . . . no . . . scratch that," Mad Dog said to Horse. "Tank, watch the next guy, I'll call that pass." Annoyed at myself for not spitting out the call quickly, I turned back around to watch the next jet. I heard Mad Dog rattle off the comments, "Little too much power on start, little high in the middle, little not enough power on the come down in close, drift left and land left at the ramp." I hadn't seen any of that and the next few approaches made clear to me how much more I needed to calibrate my eye. Every time a jet would land, I would get tongue-tied and would be unable to describe the approach that I had just witnessed. Each time, Mad Dog would tell Horse to erase what I had said and he would then proceed to describe in minute detail what the pilot had just done and how he had deviated from the optimum glide slope, airspeed, and lineup on the approach.

A few minutes later, after several more tongue-tied attempts by me, the final aircraft was approaching the groove and I was determined to spit out the comments quickly as soon as the jet landed. The incoming aircraft was the A-6 recovery tanker which was almost always the last aircraft to land, and from what I could tell, he was flying a great approach. If there were any deviations, he fixed them very smoothly. I decided to give him an OK.

"OK, pass," I yelled to Horse. "Little high start to in the middle, little too much power on the come down in close, little high at the ramp."

"Good call," said Mad Dog. "You're getting the picture. The first time is always tough."

"Thanks. They sure come fast and furious. I felt behind most of the recovery."

"You'll get the hang of it, Tank. Good job," said Horse. The other LSOs watching the recovery left the flight deck patting me on the back as they went by mumbling words of encouragement to me in deference to Horse who was their team leader. As I followed the group off the flight deck and thought about grading other pilots' landings, I wondered what it took to be a good LSO. I had often wondered what it took to be a good pilot. It seemed that the traits required for both would be similar: experience, practice, and the elusive quality of judgment. But, there was something else required for both jobs. For lack of a better word, I might call it levelheadedness. I believed I had it, because I had passed through all the wickets in training where some of my friends had fallen by the wayside. But it seemed like every day presented new challenges to overcome, so that you were never really sure whether or not you had all the required traits in sufficient amounts. The intense training involved in earning my wings of gold proved one thing: Everyone had an Achilles' heel. What mattered most was how you dealt with it when it was exposed. Some people could not get themselves past the hurdle, and in the end they stayed behind. Those of us who succeeded were able to overcome our weaknesses and control our fears.

Some of the common stumbling blocks were early on in the training at AOCS. One of them was the helo dunker, where you were strapped into a huge metal barrel simulating a helicopter, then dumped into a swimming pool. Once underwater the barrel flipped upside down and you were expected to extricate yourself from the barrel. The only catch was that you had to do it blindfolded, wearing swim goggles covered with black paint, so as to simulate a nighttime underwater environment. There were always a few people who proved themselves to be less than levelheaded in this situation. Then there was the parachute drop, where you parachuted into the ocean wearing over forty pounds of flight gear and were expected to disentangle yourself from your parachute in the rough water. Even the academic curriculum in engineering, aerodynamics, and navigation knocked a few people out.

One friend of mine from flight training set the record for the highest flight training grades in recent history throughout primary, intermediate, and advanced jet training. He went to Naval Air Station Oceana to fly F-14 Tomcats and excelled there as well, until it came time to land on the carrier at night. After always being the best in his class, he stumbled at the final hurdle of training; after two and a half years, the navy had found his Achilles' heel. He disqualified twice during carrier qualifications. In the end he qualified, but he left the navy at the earliest opportunity. So even those pilots who seem to have the "right stuff" in training were prone to fail on any given night in any given jet. Perhaps there were no real indicators of what it took to be a good pilot.

My Achilles' heel was exposed after a year and a half of flight training when I received a "down," meaning an unsatisfactory grade on a flight, for landings in the A-4 Skyhawk, the advanced training jet. It was equivalent to failing a test in school. In the end it proved to be a minor setback, and I bounced back quickly to demonstrate solid landing grades during my carrier qualification in the A-4 and above-average landing grades in the Prowler. But that one failure lingered in the back of my mind and when my confidence was low, the memory of that flight seemed to grow. I would wonder if it might happen again, if I might have problems landing. So far, in the Prowler my landings had been solid, but each and every landing was graded and "nuggets" were always under the micro- scope. I believed training to be an LSO would help me overcome my weaknesses, control my fears, and keep the bad memories of past landings out of my mind.

Having climbed down into the catwalk on the deck edge, I carefully stepped through the hatch into the passageway. Once the entire group was congregated, Mad Dog started to review grades for each pass to make sure that our comments were accurate. I quickly learned that this was where air wing politics came into play. Horse handed the book over to Mad Dog, who started down the list. For each approach he would read out the side number of the jet and then read the grade and the comments. If any of the LSOs had a problem with the grade, then they could speak up.

Halfway down the list Mad Dog got to a Hornet pass and read, "307, fair pass, high start to in the middle, not enough power on the come down in close, fly through down at the ramp."

"Ahh, Mad Dog," said Stem, one of the Hornet LSOs, "do you think those were hard comments on that pass?"

"Absolutely, Stem. I know that was Simba, but he flew a fair approach." Stem was trying to get an upgrade to an OK for his skipper, but Mad Dog would not waiver. He hurried through the rest of the approaches and there were no other comments from the gallery. It was easy for Mad Dog to critique Simba's pass in private, but it was going to be me who had to publicly inform Simba of his average grade.

"Now comes the fun part, Tank. You waved 'em, so you debrief 'em. Horse and I will back you up," said Mad Dog. "We'll see the rest of you guys at the next recovery." The crowd split up and Horse, Mad Dog, and I started to make the rounds to the various ready rooms to find the pilots who had just landed so that we could give them immediate feedback on their performance. The first few debriefs went fine. I introduced myself to the pilots whom I hadn't met yet and then told them their comments and their grade.

Just before we entered the Chippy's ready room, Horse tugged on my shirt and said cryptically, "Stay alert."

"Sure, no problem," I said not knowing what he meant. I pushed open the ready-room door and Horse smiled, pointing Simba out to me in the front of the ready room. I walked up to him confidently and extended my hand. "Hello, sir, I'm Lieutenant J.G. Baldwin, I've got your pass from the last recovery."

"Great, just what I need, another new LSO who doesn't know who his parents are," said Simba. I laughed at what I thought was a joke, but quickly realized he wasn't laughing.

"Sir, you were in 307 right?" I asked awkwardly not liking the deepening frown forming on Simba's face.

"Yeah."

"High start to in the middle, not enough power on the come down in close, fly through down at the ramp for a fair one wire," I said trying to visualize the pass as I read the comments.

"What was the last part, Lieutenant?" scowled the Hornet squadron commander. There was a storm brewing, and I was directly in its path. The front of the ready room started to clear out. The Hornet JOs had seen this before and they were looking for cover.

"Sir, what part do you mean? The part about the fair one wire?"

"Yes, that goddamned part. I don't know what jet you were looking at but that sure as hell wasn't me," shouted Simba, his voice rising as he continued. "That is the biggest bunch of crap I have ever heard," yelled the commander, working his way into a frenzy. "Get the hell out of my ready room," he was now screaming. His face was red, his veins pulsating on the sides of his neck. He picked up his nav bag filled with a kneeboard, approach plates, and charts. He looked down at it as if weighing it in his hand. In a flash I understood Horse's cryptic comment. I started to back up and then Simba hurled the bag at my head. Fortunately, I was able to duck out of the way as I backed out of the ready room sheepishly, meeting Mad Dog and Horse outside. Simba hurled more insults as the door closed. Several of the Hornet JOs followed us out of the room wincing with displeasure. Everyone was smiling at me.

"What an asshole—is he like that for every debrief?" I asked.

"Only when we give him a fair," chuckled Mad Dog. "He used to be a CAG Paddles so he thinks we should always give him OK passes. Don't let it bother you. He does that all the time after a bad pass. He'll apologize the next time he sees you." I walked away thinking that was an unlikely scenario.

I just hoped that the next time I debriefed him, he would be kind enough to actually fly an OK pass.

CHAPTER FIVE

Limitations

The preparations for our 1830 launch time were to begin at 1700 with a brief in our squadron's ready room. It was now 1640 and I was preparing to walk up to the ready room for the preflight briefing. Like last night, my mission was ESM, so I didn't have to worry about flying in coordination with other aircraft in formation. I was still a bit intimidated by night formation, and I had more than enough on my mind without having to integrate into a larger formation of aircraft. The mission would allow me to concentrate on my own flying and to focus on my landing. Tonight, all I needed to do was focus on two things: staying on top of the navigation, and then landing safely without scaring the LSOs, my crew, and myself as I had the night before.

As I got dressed in my temporary stateroom, I mentally rehearsed all the procedures for the flight. Throughout the day I had been reviewing procedures and thinking through every aspect of the flight from starting the engines to shutting them down. Visualization and mental rehearsal were the keys to successful flights for me. If I had enough time to prepare for a flight, it usually went well. If I didn't have enough time, then I often felt like I was playing catch-up during the entire flight. Most of the aviators onboard were hitting a middle of the deployment point in their proficiency level and I, having just finished training ten days earlier, was at a far lower level. The training matrix that the navy used to determine pilot proficiency estimated that a new pilot who has just completed training is proficient in only approximately 50 percent of the squadron's primary mission areas. The training is not more complete, because the navy expects the vast majority of pilots to enter their squadrons onshore in between major deployments, allowing them to finish their training in the squadron onshore before they deploy to sea. After the previous night I realized that one of those areas in which I was not proficient enough was night landings.

Even though the room I was occupying was better than what I could expect in the future, it was still extremely cramped. The room was approximately fifteen feet by eight feet and most of that space was taken up by beds, lockers, and desks. Everything was jammed into the small space right up to the ceiling in an attempt to use every conceivable bit of space for storage. All the furniture was metal and had a classic industrial look. Even though I was expecting to be moved any day, I quickly set up some semblance of a home in the small room. I placed a few family pictures on my desk and was still eagerly awaiting a picture that Alice had promised to send me. I was determined to keep her interested in me even though I could not possibly have been more geographically undesirable. I was determined to keep her interested and I prayed that my daily letters would keep me in the picture.

All morning I had been reviewing my procedures for shipboard operations. There were so many things to remember and so many ways to screw up. I just wanted to minimize my mistakes so that my name didn't quickly get celebrity status as a "colorful new guy." Color might be good in some businesses, but in naval aviation as a "nugget pilot," you did not want to have a colorful reputation. No captain of an aircraft carrier wants to have an inexperienced and struggling pilot landing on his ship at night or even during the day for that matter. If I wanted to have a chance to fly in combat, I at least needed to prove that I could perform the daily standard peace-time procedures correctly before they would consider sending me out on any strikes.

I made one last check to ensure that I had everything that I needed for my brief in the ready room and then I left the small stateroom and turned to climb the ladder well to the next deck. But there was a problem. The ladder well was covered by a piece of slick sheet metal, making it impossible to exit. The purpose of the sheet metal escaped me until I heard a young sailor shout, "Look out, sir!" A loud thud followed by a swishing sound made me look up to see a crate of lettuce come sliding down the improvised chute followed by a crate of cabbage, canned fruit, frozen meat, bread, and a host of other foodstuffs which kept coming down the chute one after another.

"We just completed the UNREP, sir. This chute will be tied up for a while," said the young sailor. *UNREP* stood for Underway Replenishment, which is how ships are resupplied at sea, and it had just ruined my plan to get to the ready room a few minutes early. My standard route was now blocked off by food delivery to the enlisted galley. I had to find another way to the ready room. Already my habit patterns had been disrupted; this did not bode well. One wouldn't think that this was a difficult problem, but the *Midway* was a ship built in the middle of World War II and it was slapped together with little or no thought to internal organization. It was built to fight, but it was not easy to get around the maze of passageways and dead ends. The small stateroom that I was living in was in a cul-de-sac of several staterooms and until now, I had assumed that what now was being used as a food chute was the only exit from the confined area. I now hoped that my initial assumption was wrong and there was another way out.

After a few minutes of walking around I found what appeared to be the only other exit point to the deck above. It was a vertical ladder leading to a small circular watertight hatch. I climbed the ladder and started to turn the watertight lever, loosening the clamps on the sides of the hatch. When I had loosened them sufficiently, I pushed up against the hatch, but I met with resistance. After a few seconds I pushed again and this time the hatch sprung open. When I poked my head through the small hole, four faces turned to gaze down at me with quizzical looks. I pulled myself up through the hatch into the middle of the kitchen for one of the enlisted galleys. Each one of the cooks had an expression on his face that seemed to say, "Those damned pilots sure are crazy. Who does he think he is popping up in the middle of my kitchen?" I didn't bother explaining myself because I could tell it would be pointless.

I just smiled and pulled myself up through the hole in their kitchen floor. As I walked through their kitchen I tried to seem nonchalant as though I took this route to the ready room every day.

After ducking under stacks of electrical cables, stepping over kneeknockers, twisting and turning down the labyrinth of passageways of the WWII vintage ship, I finally found my squadron's ready room. The door was painted maroon and the Ironclaw emblem was emblazoned boldly on the top half of the door. As logos went, it was a good one and I felt confident in knowing that our squadron had a strong reputation in the air wing. I entered the ready room eager to brief my upcoming flight.

The narrow entryway that led into the ready room was lined on the left with the officers' mailboxes. Inevitably, someone was standing in front of the mailboxes either putting paperwork into someone's box or checking his own box to see if anyone had put paperwork there since he had last checked. It was also the focal point of emotions, for it was at these mailboxes that we all received word from our families and loved ones. I was hoping that my mailbox would soon be filled with letters from Alice, but that had not yet happened. I slid sideways past my squadronmates who were intently rummaging through their boxes.

Next to the mailboxes was the coffeepot, another congregating area. Coffee was the lifeblood of most pilots. Industrial strength was how everyone seemed to like it. The closer to pure coffee grounds moistened with a hint of hot water, the better.

In the front right corner of the ready room there were two large, white boards. The one on the right wall was for the flight schedule; the one on the left, for briefing missions and illustrating tactics. Behind the board on the left was another one on a sliding track that allowed a briefer to double his available posting area. Behind the second white board were three corkboards also on sliding tracks that held charts of the Gulf region and various bits of daily-use information. It was an efficient use of the limited space available. To the left of the boards was the Squadron Duty Officer's (SDO) desk, above which were two televisions mounted in a cabinet suspended from the ceiling. One of them was always on the PLAT channel and the other could be used for anything from briefings on the ship's closed circuit system to watching videos from a VCR.

The SDO was the man in charge of this small kingdom. It was a job that rotated daily among the junior officers in the squadron. Today, Zwickster was the SDO and he was scurrying around the white boards at the front of the ready room, making last-minute changes to the flight schedule. Zwickster was an ECMO who also happened to be a lieutenant junior grade. We had met during training at Whidbey Island and he seemed like someone with whom I could form a strong friendship. He was a muscular, heavyset man who had the appearance of being a gentle giant—but a giant that you did not want to anger.

"Hi, Tank, how are you doing?" said Zwickster, eager to have another junior officer to talk to during his torturous day as the SDO.

"I'm fine. How's the duty going?"

"Surviving. Good news is that Horse just went to the LSO platform to catch the COD," said Zwickster describing the C-2 Greyhound aircraft that delivered our mail.

"That's great, it's been three days without mail. I'm really hoping that I might get some today," I said, thinking of Alice.

"You and me both," said Zwickster.

We both watched the PLAT TV intently as the C-2 cargo plane entered the picture from the right and rolled out on centerline. The lumbering propeller-powered COD, an acronym for Carrier Onboard Delivery, seemed to float in the air compared with the faster jet aircraft of the air wing. It appeared to stay centered on the crosshairs of the TV screen all the way down to the deck. *Nice pass*, I said to myself. The soft thud of the C-2 landing was peaceful compared with the violent crash performed by a Prowler landing on the flight deck. The welcome crackle of the ship's intercom, known as the 1MC, was heard in the back corner of the ready room. "Greenbush 207, safe on deck with five thousand pounds of mail!" announced a happy voice. Those in the ready room whooped and filled the small space with a chorus of cheers as everyone thought about the letters they hoped to be reading in a few hours' time once the mail was sorted.

Zwickster grabbed a marker and wrote in large block letters on the white board: 5,000 POUNDS OF MAIL AND NONE FOR KAMPER. The jab was a little mean-spirited, but Kamper, a senior lieutenant in the squadron and the founder of UMPQUA, took the joke well. And, it was true. Apparently, he didn't get much mail.

"So, Zwickster, are there any changes to the schedule?" I asked.

"If we have an up jet, you're taking it flying—the Skipper said you're the priority hop."

"Great, I better start getting ready for the brief. I'll talk to you later."

"Sure," he said in his friendly and relaxed tone. I looked at the board that kept the flight schedule current and saw that one of the jets was down for a maintenance problem, but the CO still wanted me to fly. I knew that I needed to fly again tonight. Flying again after a bad flight is similar to mounting the horse that just threw you. You need to shake off the bad memories and renew your confidence.

In theory, the SDO was the direct representative of the CO and was to keep him informed of all events that pertained to the squadron's operations throughout the day. In practice, he was responsible for keeping the ready room neat, the coffeepot filled, and doing whatever needed to be done to ensure the CO and XO were kept happy. It was an unenviable job, and a job that was hated by all junior officers. To keep the CO and XO happy today, Zwickster had been decorating the ready room for Christmas throughout the day. Many of the wives had sent decorations, and whoever was SDO was responsible for hanging new decorations as well as maintaining the old ones. Over the past few days the SDOs had covered the walls with ornaments and tinsel in order to get us in the holiday spirit. There even was a small fire-retardant Christmas tree in the briefing corner of the room with a few decorative boxes wrapped in festive paper sitting at its base.

There wasn't much room for a tree because almost all of the ready room's floor space was taken up by the large, industrially designed chairs made of sturdy metal frames and covered with comfortable, cushioned leather seats. Each chair had a broad flat metal surface on a swivel arm that could rotate up and create a desktop, just like chairs in large collegiate lecture halls. The chairs became each officer's desk at sea. Each one was labeled with the officer's job title; mine said PAO in large letters because the skipper had appointed me to collateral duty as the squadron's public affairs officer. There was a drawer for papers underneath the seat, so everyone kept his most current paperwork right there in the chair.

The reclining feature also made these chairs ideal for late-night, ready-room movie viewing. But unfortunately, unlike the other squadrons in the air wing that watched movies every night after flight operations, our ready room was usually quiet and intense late into the night because our XO would do his paperwork in his ready-room chair. As a result, our ready room had a much more businesslike atmosphere than any of the other ready rooms in the air wing. If the JOs wanted to watch a movie and relax, we were forced to escape to our bunkrooms.

Today the briefing card was blue. It was produced by the Carrier's Intelligence Center (CVIC) and included all of the day's code words and mission specifics for all events. It was a vast amount of information that was critical for aircrews to have in the air and was color-coded daily for ease of recognition. The rest of the crew for tonight's mission were now rolling into the ready room just as the brief was starting on the ship's closed circuit TV. Zwickster turned up the volume on the TV so that our crew could hear the brief.

"Hi, Cave, how are you doing?" I asked.

"Oh, not bad. Just rolled out of the rack, so I'm well rested," said the man whose job it was to fly with me on all my night traps, making sure that I didn't do anything really stupid. "It sounds like I'll get some more sleep on this mission."

"I wouldn't count on that," I said, knowing that Cave would be wide awake when we entered the night landing pattern.

"Well, you've got a point there . . . but it can't be worse than last night. You'll do fine," said Cave, cheering me up by teasing me. The problem was that we both knew it might be worse. I was lucky to be flying with someone so experienced and yet so relaxed. He was not nearly as uptight as some of the other navigators that I could have been teamed up with. Skippy and Wolfey, the two back-seaters for our mission, entered the ready room and quietly sat down next to Cave and me as we looked to the television for the beginning of the intelligence briefing.

"Hiya, fellas," I said to Skippy and Wolfey as they got out a kneeboard card on which to take notes.

"Hi, Tank," they said in unison.

The young intelligence officer's face filled the screen. The bright filming light used in the foreground made him look like a deer caught in the mesmerizing glare of headlights. "Good evening from CVIC. I am Ensign Lueb [pronounced *Lube*, explaining his nickname of *Jiffy*] and I will be presenting the Event Five cyclic ops brief," said the young intelligence officer from our squadron. The fifth event, our 1830 launch, had ten aircraft in it all doing different things. The fourth event had just launched a few minutes earlier and would be flying for the next hour and a half. Just after the ten aircraft in the fifth event launched, which was our event, then the event-four aircraft would land. This type of constant operations is called cyclic ops because it is based on a common cycle that can vary from an hour to several hours, depending on the amount of in-air refueling support available.

Using a pointer and a large chart, Jiffy highlighted all of the places where we shouldn't fly. The Gulf of Oman is crisscrossed by dozens of commercial airways, so it was extremely difficult to avoid all of these air routes. Since technically these were still peacetime operations, we did not want to receive any flight violations. If we flew out of a training area, off a corridor, or didn't communicate properly, we might get in trouble. One of my goals was to maintain a low profile. I certainly did not need any flight violations as a new guy. My credibility as a competent aviator would be sunk quickly. As a result, I was extremely nervous about tonight's flight. We were briefed to fly right up to the edge of the northern boundary in the Gulf of Oman and attempt to pick up any Iranian radar transmissions that might give us intelligence as we planned for our transit through the Strait of Hormuz into the Persian Gulf the following week.

My nervousness and inexperience showed in the crew brief that occurred after the television overview brief for the event. Everyone else in my crew was at mid-cruise proficiency and I was still feeling the steep slope of the initial learning curve. I had so much to learn and so little time that I just thought the best way was to ask a lot of questions and review the procedures as carefully as I could. As a result, I quickly developed a reputation as a briefer who delved into every aspect of the flight in excruciating detail.

Once the crew brief was finished, I sat down in my ready-room chair, organizing the various charts and kneeboard cards that I needed for the flight. The XO sat down next to me. "Hi, Tank, ready for your flight?" he asked.

"Yes, sir," I said, with as much confidence as I could muster.

"Do you have any questions about the procedures?"

"No, sir. I think I'm all set."

"I'm sure you're feeling lots of pressure to perform and impress people in the squadron. Nobody is expecting you to be a seasoned veteran, because you're not. Just do the job and do it safely. I can guarantee you will make mistakes. The trick is to avoid the ones that will kill you. The best way to do that is to fly within your own limitations," he said. *Easy for him to say*, I thought as I continued to prepare. The XO then got up and walked out. I had heard him say he was an education major in college. He had an interesting approach to psychology. He seemed to want to intimidate all the JOs, and it appeared that he had succeeded with only one exception. Cave was the only officer in the ready room who would stand up to the XO without hesitation. All the rest of us had a healthy sense of fear of him.

As I shuffled through the various cards and charts I would take with me on the flight I realized that I was still searching for a comfortable habit pattern here on the *Midway*. I had always developed a preflight ritual in places where I had flown before and I was looking for the same type of routine here, but I had yet to find it. I shuffled out of the ready room sideways because there was the usual group of people standing by the mailboxes shifting paperwork from box to box, trying to look as if they were getting things done. The paperwork in the squadron seemed to travel from box to box but never really went anywhere in particular.

The crew's first stop was in the squadron's paraloft. The more appropriate term would have been paracloset. All twenty-six aircrew had their flight gear in a narrow space across the passageway from the ready room. It was a tight squeeze for one person to put his gear on in this room let alone four people. So what usually happened was that one guy got changed in the room at a time while the other guys read the Aircraft Discrepancy Book (ADB) in maintenance control. The maintenance control office was filled with all sorts of ornery old salts: senior chiefs, chiefs, and the only officer in the squadron who could intimidate our CO and XO. We called him Beast. He, like Cave, was not easily intimidated. Kwyjibo was the nominal leader of the maintenance department, but in reality, it was run by Beast. This meant Beast was in control of the squadron's performance and could have a real impact on the CO's or XO's career. For this reason, they were intimidated by him and his power over his men.

I learned more positive things about leadership in the navy from hanging around maintenance control than from anything else I did. The sign above their door proclaimed the office "Mustang" country. Beast was the man in charge. He had been enlisted for many years and then had decided to become an officer; such men are called Mustangs. His manner was gruff, tough, and yet he had a deep sense of compassion hiding just below this hard surface. He had a heart of gold and a soft spot for his men. He had assembled around himself an outstanding group of chief petty officers. Of course I had very little to compare them to, but all of the senior pilots in the squadron said that we were truly blessed with an outstanding maintenance control team, which is the heart and soul of every squadron.

Being nervous and excited, I got dressed quickly before the rest of the crew came out of the ready room. My G-suit, leg restraints, torso harness, survival vest, and helmet were all brand-new and I felt self-conscious. I wished my gear looked as weathered and worn as some of the more senior guys in the squadron. *In good time*, I told myself. I felt a real need to be accepted as "a player" by the maintenance control crowd. Beast and his chiefs were a tough group to please, since they had seen lots of pilots come and go over the years. I wanted to impress them. The toughest and most ornery chief, in a friendly sort of way, was Chief Rat. He always seemed to be either smoking or acting as if he wanted to be smoking. Like most navy chiefs, he had grown up in the service when smoking was a way of life onboard ship. His lean, wiry frame was unusual among most chiefs who after years of service had often developed a significant protective layer around the waist. Chief Rat was lean and mean. If he didn't like you, he let you know. The dirty-blond hair on his head was retreating, a fact that added to his ornery nature. His troops loved him though, and they would work to their personal limits for him because they knew that he would be there to make sure the job was done right. Beast and Chief Rat had seen just about everything, and I knew that they considered me just another "nugget" pilot.

"Hi, Beast, how's it going?" I asked.

"It's been going fine. We haven't missed a sortie all day, and it will keep going fine, unless you break my jet."

"I'll try not to break anything," I said with a grin. "If I do though, remember that it's my ass in the jet and not yours."

"Yeah, but I'll pay the price once you bring it back." I flipped through the ADB focusing on the "pink slips," which were outstanding gripes—things wrong with the jet that had yet to be fixed. Below them were the yellow sheets, past gripes that had been fixed during the past ten flights. Reading through the ADB gave the pilot an excellent idea of what difficulties, if any, the jet might have during the next flight. "She's been flying great today," said Beast. "Three flights in a row." I hoped that the fourth would be as lucky. I signed the acceptance sheet as pilot in command, legally stating that I had read all the discrepancies and that in my best judgment, this aircraft was ready to go flying.

"I'll see you soon," I said as I put on my helmet and headed out the door to the flight deck. When I got outside, I was relieved to see that there were a few more minutes of daylight left before the tricky period of twilight began. This would be what was known as a "pinky launch." The preflight, man up, and engine start all went smoothly, if not quickly. Cave, Skippy, and Wolfey were all a step ahead of me throughout the start-up procedure. I was working hard to speed up the pace of my start-up procedures, but it would take some time for me to develop the level of proficiency and comfort that these three guys were at now. Fortunately, they all realized that and were patient with me. As I taxied the Prowler toward the catapult the sun touched the horizon.

The setting sun silhouetted the yellowshirt as he threw his arms upward in the familiar quarterback pose that told me the catapult was in tension and ready to fire. My left hand pushed the throttles forward to the stops while my fingers reached for the catapult grip. The palm of my left hand pressed firmly against the throttles and my fingers clutched the metal catapult grip that insured the acceleration of the catapult would not allow the throttles to retard to idle. My right hand began to move the stick in a deliberate counterclockwise circle, testing for the full deflection of all the flight controls. My eyes scanned the instruments in the cockpit and I searched for anything unusual. Each instrument had specific limits, each gauge needed to indicate the proper reading. When I was satisfied with the jet, my right hand came off the stick and I snapped a salute to the catapult officer. Seconds later, my head was slammed into the headrest of the ejection seat and once again, the 57,000-pound Prowler accelerated from a standstill to 150 knots within two seconds. We were airborne.

We flew directly north tonight toward the Strait of Hormuz. It was unfamiliar territory for the *Midway* and all other American aircraft carriers. The conventional wisdom had been that the Persian Gulf was too small for carriers to maneuver and hide from all of the potential threats. Needless to say, the area was unfamiliar to me, and I was quite nervous. This was not a part of the world where one wanted to lose track of the navigation solution.

Cave worked the radios easily and with great confidence. Within minutes, we had completed the standard series of radio calls and were on our E-2C Hawkeye's control frequency where we expected to be for the remainder of the mission. As we flew farther north the weather began to deteriorate. Cloud banks appeared ahead of us, so to maintain good visibility I decided to climb. The Prowler responded sluggishly above 25,000 feet and we were now climbing through 28,000 feet just to keep out of the clouds. Even though we were on the Hawkeye's radar we didn't want to rely on it to keep us clear of other traffic in the area. Lots of missions were being monitored tonight, so we wanted to be able to see where we were going.

There was only a small sliver of a moon but it was enough to illuminate the tops of the storm clouds to the east toward Iran.

"Those look pretty ugly over there," I said on the intercom to anyone who wanted to talk.

"Yeah, they sure do," said Cave.

"Ironclaw 606, Liberty 621 request."

"Go ahead, Liberty," said Cave.

"Ironclaw 606, we show you to be closest aircraft to Liberty 620. They have had a navigational failure and are out of comm range with us. It appears that they are currently heading toward Mustard airspace. Request you join on them and bring them back to Mother," said the air controller onboard the Hawkeye stationed to the south. "Mustard" airspace we quickly learned from our code-word card of the day described Iranian airspace.

"Roger, Liberty, give us a good vector and range estimate," said Cave, referring to the lost Hawkeye.

"Liberty 620 bears 073 for 50." On hearing the vector, I pushed the throttles forward and rolled the Prowler to the right until I picked up a heading of 073. When I rolled out on the heading, I was looking directly at the ugly weather that I had pointed out to Cave only a few minutes before.

"It figures, they would have to go and get lost in the worst weather in the area," I said.

"Yeah, it always seems to work this way," said Cave.

At an altitude of 28,000 feet we were traveling at over 400 knots true airspeed and we would close fairly rapidly with the Hawkeye, which was probably at best flying about 250 knots. I was excited; this was a great opportunity to prove my airmanship skills and at the same time really make a difference by helping these fellow aviators in distress. Our main concern was turning them around before they penetrated Iranian airspace which, given the current sensitivities, could well bring about an international incident. The Prowler was not the ideal aircraft for this mission because it does not have a fighter's air-to-air radar designed to pick out aircraft. The Prowler's radar is a ground-mapping radar used for navigation, so at this point, Cave and I were straining our eyes looking for the familiar anticollision light of a Hawkeye and hoping that their navigational malfunction was not caused by a broader electrical failure that could have knocked out their external lights as well.

"Liberty 621, Ironclaw, request updated vector," said Cave. Static was the only response. "We must be out of range for them now. I'll try to raise the E-2C that we're looking for. Liberty 620, Ironclaw, radio check." Once again, static came into our headphones. The minutes seemed to become longer and longer. I began to get concerned that we too would be straying into unfriendly airspace if we kept flying east much longer. I kept checking my ground-mapping radar to confirm that Iran was definitely at least twenty miles ahead of us. "Visual," said Cave, "two o'clock low, I think that's them." I banked to the right and pushed the stick forward and Cave talked my eyes onto the red anticollision light in the distance. The Hawkeye was flying at a lower altitude and the wispy clouds were obscuring the line of sight between us.

"I got him," I said finally. "Cave, I've got the radio for a minute," I said, since it was easier in formation flying to have pilot-to-pilot comms, thus eliminating the middleman whom the navigators become in such situations.

"Liberty 620, Ironclaw 606, radio check."

"Ironclaw 606, Liberty 620, loud and clear. Say your position," said a somewhat startled but relieved Hawkeye pilot.

"I'm two or three miles at your six o'clock. Need you to give me a right turn. You are almost Mustard." Immediately, I saw the right wingtip light dip lower and the pilot started to head south away from Iran. I smiled to myself thinking this wasn't going to be so hard after all. "Liberty, say your state."

"Ironclaw, Liberty state is 2.1," said the Hawkeye pilot with a distinct tone of anxiety in his voice. We still had bad weather and a night landing to go through and I could tell that this pilot was not thrilled with his predicament. I needed to try to give him confidence by leading him back to the ship quickly and safely. As the Hawkeye continued its right turn to the south we closed rapidly to effect an expeditious rendezvous. I set up the picture the way I had learned in training and started to close on the Hawkeye. The standard rendezvous speed was 250 knots, so I slowed to 300 and as the Hawkeye got closer I began to reduce the closure rate. At night it is extremely difficult to sense closure, so you need to operate using known airspeeds where the aircraft effecting the rendezvous controls the rate of closure and the target aircraft maintains a constant airspeed. I had slowed to 280 knots, but because he was low on fuel and uncertain of his navigation system, the Hawkeye pilot had reduced his airspeed to 180 knots to conserve fuel. So instead of 30 knots of closure, I had closer to 100. The next thing I knew the Hawkeye filled our windscreen and I pushed the stick forward and went just under the lumbering propeller aircraft. "Underrunning," I called in an embarrassed tone of voice. "Liberty, say your airspeed."

"Liberty's at one eighty."

"Roger," I said. "Damn it, Cave, he should have told me he was at one eighty," I said, frustrated by the screw-up.

"Yeah, but these Hawkeye guys hardly ever fly formation during the day and even less at night. We should have asked him." Now I was in an awkward position. I was looking back over my right shoulder, trying to slow down to an airspeed that was much slower than the Prowler could comfortably fly. The differences in the aircraft were going to make this job much more challenging than I had anticipated. The Hawkeye was a large turboprop aircraft with a very large wingspan and a surveillance radar dome that gave it very different flight characteristics from the Prowler. In training, I flew formation with only similar types of aircraft so all of the flight characteristics were the same. Now that I was in "the show," I realized everything was not so easy.

"This is a good heading for Mother," said Cave.

"Liberty, roll out on this heading for Mother. Can you bump it up to two hundred knots?" I said, trying to compromise between the normal 230 knots I would fly in a fuel conservation mode and the 180 knots that the Hawkeye pilot had been flying.

"Roger, two hundred knots," said my new wingman.

"You're descending," said Cave.

"Roger," I said. I was struggling with the rendezvous because as the Hawkeye sped up to 200 knots, I was trying to slow down so that his aircraft would go ahead of mine and I could complete the rendezvous. Because I was straining my neck looking backward, I couldn't look at my instruments, which would have told me I had started a gradual descent. I quickly scanned my instruments and saw 200 knots on the airspeed indicator. The Prowler felt as if it was on the edge of stall speed so I dared not go any slower. I added power and climbed back up to the Hawkeye's altitude and realized that I was actually now in a reasonable position to take the lead.

"Liberty, Ironclaw has the lead," I said, trying to sound self-assured.

"Roger," responded the Hawkeye pilot, knowing that I was anything but self-assured after that ugly rendezvous. The cloud layer had gotten thicker as we flew south toward the ship, and now I faced the unpleasant task of leading my wingman through the thick clouds at night at an airspeed well below the recommended penetration airspeed for the Prowler, which was 250 knots. It had probably been quite a while since this Hawkeye pilot had flown night formation in the clouds, so I was sure he was not relishing the thought either, but with his fuel situation, he needed to get back to the ship quickly. Cave started the radio drill as I started our descent to the ship.

"Strike, Ironclaw 606 is holding hands with Liberty 620, states are 10.0 and 1.9."

"Ironclaw, Strike, roger. Radar contact, switch marshal frequency," said the controller. Cave worked the UHF1 radio while I maintained pilot-to-pilot comms with the Hawkeye pilot on the UHF2. The Prowler's large earth-seeking nose wanted desperately to go faster than 200 knots but I reined it in and maintained the agreed airspeed so that the Hawkeye could keep up. The storm clouds were terribly dark and the air was bumpy. I felt sorry for the Hawkeye pilot trying to hang on to my wing. Within seconds of entering the clouds I noticed ice crystals forming on the Prowler's refueling probe.

"I'm showing icing on the fuel probe."

"Roger, I already have the anti-ice on," said Cave.

"Good," I said, thankful again for having an experienced right-seater. I was scanning my instruments, trying to concentrate as the Prowler was getting bounced about. My airspeed indicator showed we were losing airspeed so I gradually lowered the Prowler's nose to maintain 200 knots. But the needle continued to lose airspeed. I kept pushing the stick forward to increase what I believed was a decrease in airspeed, but what I had on my hands was an instrument failure. I didn't realize the problem until I heard the Hawkeye pilot's voice in my headset.

"Liberty is lost sight," said the frustrated Hawkeye pilot over the static-filled radio.

"Shit," I said as I fixated on my airspeed indicator as it unwound toward zero and I saw the angle-of-attack gauge race up to thirty units—the indicator of a stall. The turbulence of the storm hit us hard at that moment and I was convinced that the buffeting was because I had stalled the aircraft. I rammed the throttles and the stick forward looking for airspeed but it still indicated zero. I also wanted to get separation from the Hawkeye that was still in this cloud somewhere, and I didn't want to run into it. At least my attitude gyro still appeared to be working and so even though I didn't know my airspeed or my altitude, I knew that I was in a thirty-degree dive for the ocean. Our radar altimeter was set at five thousand feet. The baro altimeter was swinging around the face of the gauge absolutely useless. "Looks like a pitot-static failure, Cave," I said. "I've got the radalt set at five thousand feet."

"Roger, I think we can throttle back a little and test the radalt," said Cave wisely. I pushed the small test button and the alarm sounded on the radar altimeter which used a repeating radar signal bounced off the ground and then read by the aircraft to determine precisely the altitude of the aircraft. Thankfully, the Prowler's radalt was extremely reliable. After a few more seconds, I heard the reassuring *beep, beep, beep* in my headset, and I started to level off. Now that we were below the freezing level in the storm clouds, the ice that had formed on the pitot tubes which supplied the information needed for the airspeed, altimeter, and angle-of-attack indicator must have melted because they all came back to life and appeared to be operating normally.

"Marshal, Ironclaw checking in as a single on Mother's 350 at 35, state is 9.5. Has Liberty 620 checked in with you yet?"

"Ironclaw, Marshal copy your position and state. Marshal radial is the 270. We have just established radar contact with Liberty. They are on radar vectors to final now." I felt terrible that I had not been able to successfully lead the Hawkeye pilot down to the ship, but I had had my hands full with my own aircraft and I was sure he would understand. I just hoped he would land safely. We decided to monitor the approach frequency to listen to the Hawkeye's fate. Fortunately, his approach to the ship was uneventful. The pilot was able to shrug off his earlier navigational problems and block out the pressure of his low fuel state in order to land on his first pass. It was all about compartmentalizing. Good pilots have this gift. They are able to focus on the task at hand and accomplish it at all costs. I was getting better at this, and even though I was frustrated about my failure to successfully lead the Hawkeye all the way back to the ship, I was able to put it out of my mind, and I landed safely on my first pass that night.

The flight had been a big learning experience, because I realized that there were going to be a lot of things on this cruise that I had not yet seen in training, and as the XO had suggested, I needed to try to fly within my limitations. What I had attempted would have been difficult for a seasoned veteran at the ship, let alone a nugget like myself with just over a week of experience in the fleet.

When I walked into the ready room, Zwickster spotted me and shouted, "Hey, Tank, who is ART?"

"What do you mean?"

"Look in your box. We had mail call while you were flying and you got five letters from someone named ART," said Zwickster. My eyes and heart jumped into the mailbox along with my hand. *Five letters from Alice!* I was ecstatic. My pulse quickened as I walked to my chair, ripping open the letter with the oldest postmark. My eyes swallowed the first letter and the second letter within seconds. She "missed me . . . wanted to be with me now . . . wished I wasn't so far away." I devoured the third letter in which she "hoped we could spend time alone together." And then I tore open the fourth.

There was a photograph inside. My heart jumped. I pulled it out quickly, its back facing me and I turned it over to see a picture of a New York City brownstone building. Zwickster had snuck up behind me and in my excitement I had not noticed his presence until he started laughing.

"ART must be a real looker if she sends you a picture of her apartment instead of herself," he chuckled.

"Pound sand, Zwickster," I said, not doing a very good job of masking my disappointment. But, as I read through the fourth letter, Alice wrote that she intended to mail a picture of herself the next day. I immediately flipped open the fifth envelope postmarked the next day and enclosed was a beautiful picture of Alice. Zwickster gave me the satisfaction of smiling and saying nothing. I could tell he was favorably impressed.

Twenty minutes later, after we had finished our crew debrief, Cave stood up and called out to the ready room, "Anyone up for some sliders?"

"Sure, I'll join you," said Gucci, who was doing some paperwork in his ready-room chair. I could tell that the thought of a greasy cheeseburger sounded very appealing to Gucci. So our crew of four plus Gucci left the ready room and headed for the dirty-shirt wardroom.

There were two wardrooms for the *Midway*'s officers: the "clean shirt" and the "dirty shirt." The division between the two was clear. The "black-shoed" surface warfare officers ate in the "clean-shirt" wardroom where the dress code was khaki uniform, and the "brown-shoed" naval aviators ate in the "dirty-shirt" wardroom while wearing their flight suits. The dirty-shirt wardroom was the one place onboard the carrier where it was easy for the aviators from different squadrons to interact in a relaxed setting. When we met one another in our ready rooms, it was usually for a brief before a flight or a debrief after a flight, and then the focus was business. In the wardroom, we talked about everything else.

Our air wing had a cohesiveness that no other air wing in the navy could match. The *Midway* was the only American aircraft carrier homeported overseas, so as a result our air wing lived and worked together not only while at sea, but also when the deployment was over. All of the squadrons in our air wing were assigned to the same base in Atsugi, Japan, so friendships were easily formed across squadron lines. There was no doubt that having such a tight air wing enhanced our combat readiness a great deal. In contrast, all of the other American aircraft carriers were homeported in various coastal cities while their squadrons were scattered about in five different bases around the U.S. Even though this was my first experience in a fleet squadron, and I couldn't objectively compare our squadron and air wing to any others, I somehow knew that the *Midway*'s air wing was truly special.

Cave, Skippy, Wolfey, Gucci, and I walked single file through the passageway toward the wardroom located under the *Midway*'s catapults. There was no line at the stainless-steel counter in front of the grill, and we each greeted the young sailor who was serving food there. Cave ordered a "slider," a cheeseburger so greasy that it slides to the bottom of your stomach, and we all followed his lead.

"I almost hope we go to war so that I could focus more on flying instead of the stupid paperwork I need to do for my job," said Skippy, who as the assistant operations officer had one of the most responsible jobs for a junior officer in the squadron.

"Yeah, I guess your priorities would definitely change during wartime," I said, not knowing enough about what would happen if we went to war.

"If the shooting starts, the battle group will minimize message traffic to only what is operationally important," said Gucci, confirming what Skippy hoped.

"That would be great," said Wolfey. We looked at one another and smiled; we would all love to get out of doing our desk jobs if it meant more flying. The reality of getting shot at in combat was still too far away to concern us.

Within minutes our "sliders" were ready, and we all sat down at the end of one of eight long tables covered with blue-and-white-linen tablecloths. The chairs had slipcovers with the *Midway*'s seal sewn on their backs. Around the walls of the wardroom were framed photographs from each of the squadrons. It was as close to a family dinner as I could hope to get in the middle of the Gulf of Oman.

My squadron was now my family for the next few years, so I was eager to get to know them. "Wolfey, I saw you got some mail, too," I said.

"Sure did. A couple of letters from Lisa," he said, in his naturally deep voice. He received good-natured ribbing about his voice because it was rumored that a few of the wives in the squadron liked his voice so much that while the squadron was on shore in Atsugi, they would call the squadron when he was the duty officer, just to hear his voice over the phone.

"You're married to a Lisa, too, aren't you Skippy?" I asked.

"Sure am."

"Did both Lisas come to visit you guys in Singapore, last month?" I asked, knowing that the *Midway* had stopped there for a port visit about a month before I arrived onboard.

"They did," said Wolfey. "It was great. But it was also tough."

"What do you mean?" I asked.

"I know what you mean, Wolfey," said Gucci. "Kathy came to Singapore and I think it was both the best port visit, and the worst port visit we have ever had together."

"Why was that?" I asked.

"She could sense that I was nervous about the real possibility of combat on this deployment, and so our time together became very intense."

"That's exactly right," said Skippy. Gucci, Skippy, and Wolfey nodded to one another while Cave and I, the bachelors of the group, nodded because they were all nodding. As husbands, Skippy and Wolfey were definitely more empathetic than I was, and if they were nodding at Gucci's description of the Singapore visit, then I figured I should be nodding, too.

While I was nodding, a hand touched my shoulder and I turned to look up. It was an unfamiliar face, belonging to a pilot whom I had not yet met. He wore the Hawkeye squadron patch, and he looked tired but happy.

"I wanted to thank you for chasing me down out there tonight and leading me back," said the Hawkeye pilot.

"I'm sorry I lost you in the clouds, but I lost my airspeed indicator to icing as we started our descent."

"Well, you got me pointed in the right direction, and I appreciate it. I was having a bad night," he said in a weary tone of voice. "Thanks again, I'll see you around."

"Sure. Thanks for stopping by," I said, swelling with pride for the good deed I had at least tried to do.

"What was that all about?" asked Gucci.

"Well, uhh . . ." I hesitated.

Cave spoke up. "Let's just say that the next time Tank tries to rendezvous on a lost Hawkeye, at night and in bad weather, I hope that your ass is in the front seat with him and not mine." We all laughed at Cave's misfortune and continued to appreciate the deliciously greasy sliders.

After taking some more good-natured ribbing about my Hawkeye rescue operation, I retreated to the bunkroom where I put Alice's picture in a frame next to my bed. Then I reread her five letters until I fell asleep, feeling more happy and more confident than I had felt in weeks.

CHAPTER SIX

Clear Deck

After a week of flying twice a day, I was not too upset to wake up in the morning and see that my name was not on the flight schedule. My body felt as if it could use a breather, and my mind needed a day to catch up and take in all the new information that I was now expected to know. Trying to absorb all the knowledge and advice from all the pilots in the squadron felt like drinking water from a fire hose. It would take time for me to absorb it all.

"Hey, Tank, the flight schedule shows Sushi coming back to the boat on the Event three COD today. Looks like Bhagwan needs to make up his mind," said ET with his mouth full of toothpaste. He leaned over the small sink built into the wall of the bunkroom and spit out the blue-green foam from his mouth. I had heard he was called ET because after downing a few beers at the officers' club, he began to look and act like the extraterrestrial in the Spielberg movie.

"Yeah, I noticed that," I said. "If Bhagwan hasn't moved in there by noon, I'm going to take the slot in the other bunkroom." ET nodded agreement as he walked out the bunkroom door. This morning had become the culmination of a two-week-long dilemma of where to put the new guy. After a week with Kwyjibo I was moved to BK#10, one of the JO bunkrooms, to sleep temporarily in the bed of a guy called Sushi who was in Riyadh, Saudi Arabia, doing strike-planning coordination with the air force. He was scheduled to return today, so I needed to find another place to sleep. The pilot I had replaced had left the squadron, leaving a rack open in BK#19, the more spacious JO bunkroom, but as the new guy, I did not have any claim on this spot. It needed to be offered up to a more senior JO in the squadron. As a result, Bhagwan and Pez, two of the most senior lieutenants in the squadron, had spent nearly two weeks since my arrival debating the relative merits of uprooting themselves and their possessions and moving to the other bunkroom. Now that Sushi was returning from Riyadh, their hands would be forced. I was not planning to sleep on the deck, because they could not make up their minds. Pez had announced the day before that he would stay put and so now it was up to Bhagwan.

I was hoping that Bhagwan would also decide to stay put so that I could move into the other bunkroom. The three other JO pilots, Horse, Ren, and Pokey, as well as some of the more senior JO ECMOs, were in the other bunkroom and I believed that living with them would really help me learn the tricks of the trade much more quickly than living with all of the most junior ECMOs.

I walked over to the bulkhead sink and turned the spring-loaded faucet. As soon as I let go of the faucet the spring snapped it back to the off position, thereby saving precious water from being wasted. I still hadn't gotten used to the spring faucets nor the faint smell of JP-5 jet fuel in the water. I knew that within another week it would not even be noticeable to me, but now I still grimaced whenever I leaned over the sink. After I lathered up my face I heard the door to the bunkroom open and I turned to see ET again.

"I just ran into Bhagwan in the ready room and he said he is going to stay put," he said.

"Oh, really," I said not wanting to seem too enthusiastic because ET did, after all, live in this bunkroom. "Well, it looks like we're not going to be roommates after all," I said.

"Yeah, it would have been good to have you here but I'm sure you'll like it in the other bunkroom," said ET.

"I hope so," I said as I finished shaving and started to think about packing up my things and making the move to Bunkroom #19, the

"BK of the Stars," as its inhabitants referred to it. The familiar crackle of the 1MC in the background interrupted our conversation.

"Mail call. Mail call," said the voice in a very bland way. ET and I looked at each other, both saying a quiet prayer to ourselves that there would be some letters for us today.

Having the day off from flying would give me an opportunity to move my belongings to what would be my final resting place for the remainder of the deployment. It would be my second move within the two weeks I had been onboard, and I was very eager to have a rack that I could call my own.

BK#19 was closer to the ready room than BK#10 and it also was more convenient to the wardroom where I would be eating. I soon realized that the only places I really needed to know how to find were the wardroom, to eat, the bunkroom, to sleep, and the ready room, to plan and brief my missions. Needless to say, my new bunkroom was in a great location especially for a new guy like myself who really didn't know his way around the carrier at all.

It took only a few minutes upon hearing the news of Bhagwan's decision for me to pack everything into my two big duffle bags and start the struggle down the passageway toward my new home. The door to BK#19 actually had BK OF THE STARS stenciled on it. I had thought they were all joking about this but it quickly became clear that my new roommates took it seriously. I dropped my bags in the passageway and opened the door. The room was dimly illuminated by red bulbs that offered just enough ambient light so that you could walk around without stumbling, but not so much that it made it difficult to sleep. Having the red lights on meant that someone in the room was asleep and that everyone should be courteous and quiet. I soon learned that the red lights were almost always on, and at any given time of day there was someone asleep.

The room was rectangular and had four sets of bunk beds lining one of the long walls with desk and closet space filling the opposite wall. Eight of us were to share this tiny space. From out of the shadows appeared Ren, a tall, lanky pilot from North Carolina who would quickly become one of my closest friends in the squadron. Ren had arrived only three months before I had, so we were both quite new to the squadron. But he was no longer the new guy—I was. As a result, he was ensuring that I got the "new guy's rack" in the bunkroom.

The "new guy's rack"—it was no surprise to find out—was awful. To start with, it was a top rack, so it took a considerable amount of agility to get into bed. That, however, was not the worst part. Right above the rack there was a steam pipe that leaked. It had obviously been worked on numerous times, but it still leaked, and apparently Ren had solved the problem by hanging a sheet of plastic under the pipe. The resulting dripping sound on the plastic was extremely annoying because it was not rhythmic.

"It takes a while, but you'll get used to it," said Ren with a smile as he moved his belongings from the shelf next to the rack and the drawers below it.

"It doesn't look like I'll have much choice," I responded with a chuckle.

"I'll see you later, I've got to wave this next recovery," said Ren.

"I'm hoping to get assigned to an LSO team soon," I said.

"That's great, I'll see you later," said Ren as he headed for the door.

After emptying my duffle bags into the vacant locker I took a closer look around the bunkroom. Judging by the rhythmic snoring, I could tell that someone was asleep, so I kept quiet. The deck of the bunkroom was covered with carpet remnants that at one time had probably been several different colors but were now various shades of charcoal gray. The textures were all different as well. One section had shag and another was sculpted. I decided that it would not be wise to ever walk on this carpeting in my bare feet. I did not even want to think about the last time this carpet had been cleaned.

The ceiling was typical of the rest of the *Midway*. Within this small space there were cables, wires, ducting, piping, and metal beams running crisscrossed all over the ceiling. Wires were always added, as opposed to being replaced. As a result, the ceilings around the ship were inundated with wires and nobody knew what they all did. But nobody cared as long as all the systems worked properly when they had to work.

At the end of the row of bunkbeds there was a small area which could accommodate four or five guys sitting and one or two standing. It was our version of a living room, if it could be called that. At one end of this living room was a refrigerator with a television on top of it. The fridge was covered with aviation and travel stickers from the past JOs who had lived in this room. The *Midway* got around and its list of ports was displayed on this fridge: Thailand, Singapore, Hong Kong, Korea, the Philippines, Australia, and Hawaii. There were also many colorful stickers about naval aviation and the mighty Prowler. Around the corner from the fridge was a head, which was considered one of the benefits of this room. Few rooms had their own heads, so we felt privileged even if it was rarely cleaned. I stood there in the near darkness wondering what I should do next.

"Hey, Tank," said a raspy voice that sounded like its owner had just woken up.

"Yes?" I responded as I turned around to see Kamper's face peering out from behind the curtain covering his rack.

"Welcome to the BK of the Stars. I've got something for you," he said as he extended his hand toward me in the dimly lit room. I took a few steps in his direction, and I saw the Indian-head patch in his hand. Kamper was welcoming me to more than the BK; he was welcoming me to UMPQUA. Now, I too, along with the rest of the squadron's JOs, was considered an Underprivileged Minion Perpetually Questioning Unlimited Authority.

"Thanks, Kamper. I was hoping I would get a patch when I got to the BK."

"No problem, I just didn't think it would be right to give it to you while you were still living with Kwyjibo."

"I understand. Well, I am glad I'm here now." I clutched the Indian-head patch in my hand and stuffed it in my pocket. I smiled, thinking that the patch would soon be on my flight jacket.

"Sure," he said expressing little emotion. "Right, now I'm going to try to get some more rack time in before my brief."

"OK, I'm on my way out—I'll see you later," I said, trying to downplay how excited I was to be included in UMPQUA.

"Yeah, see you later," said Kamper, sounding as if he were already half asleep.

I realized that if Ren was going to wave that meant there was a launch and recovery very soon. I had been thinking about finding my way to the tower and this seemed to be a good opportunity. If I couldn't fly today, at least I could watch. Watching a launch and recovery would be a form of study and preparation for me. I did not watch passively. I would mentally place myself in the cockpit of each jet as it taxied around the deck and think about all of the procedures that I would need to follow in order to get off the deck safely. Such mental rehearsal would be excellent for me, and I knew I would enjoy watching the way the deck worked.

From what little I had seen in training, I knew it was a dynamic environment in which each launch was specifically choreographed so as to ensure maximum efficiency for the given mission. We were not yet at war, but we were training for it, and every launch became a serious drill. The taped delay CNN broadcast that we watched on the ship made it clear in everyone's mind that Saddam Hussein was not likely to pull his forces out of Kuwait. Everyone from the eighteen-year-olds fresh out of high school to the Vietnam veteran aviators started to ask themselves, "Am I good enough? Will I get the job done?" From the way I had seen the *Midway* operate so far I felt confident in this ship's complex team. Each man had his own specific responsibility that when done properly, made the ship run like a precise machine.

As soon as I had put away some of my belongings, I threw the rest of my bags on my rack and left the bunkroom headed for the tower to watch the launch and recovery. The passageways wound around the O-2 level of the carrier and I ducked under bundles of wiring and jumped over kneeknockers in order to get to the island on the starboard side of the ship. The narrow metal staircase led me upward in a never-ending series of tight switchbacks for several levels until I could go no farther without going to the captain's bridge. I decided I did not need to bother the old man today, and so I retraced my steps and noticed a small stenciled sign on the level below that said PRIMARY FLIGHT, which was the ship's tower.

I pulled on the lever connected to the latches of the watertight hatch and pushed open the hatch that led to a catwalk and the fresh sea air. I paused outside on the catwalk on the outboard side of the island and watched the pilots and their jets circling above the *Midway* just as I had done the day before. They were waiting to break the deck, waiting for the right moment. It always felt great to get outside and feel the wind on your face and smell the salty air. Most of the time it was too busy and crowded to walk out on the flight deck. This section of the catwalk was shielded from the flight deck by the island's superstructure and offered a protected pocket of fresh air that was hard to find on the carrier. I would have to remember this catwalk as a place to come when I needed time to myself. I turned and went up a small ladder to my right to the next hatch that had PRIMARY FLIGHT stenciled in bold black letters on its gray exterior.

The tower, known on the carrier as Primary Flight, was the home of the air boss and was located just below the level of the captain's bridge. Typically, an air boss held the rank of commander and had recently commanded a squadron on another aircraft carrier. He was responsible for conducting safe and efficient launches and recoveries of the *Midway*'s aircraft. He owned the flight deck and all the men who worked on it, and he reported directly to the *Midway*'s captain.

Closing the hatch quickly behind me I entered the air boss's domain. Here in this fishbowl up above the flight deck this navy commander was king. He was responsible for the smooth and orderly conduct of flight operations on the *Midway*, a responsibility that made most of the men who had the job ornery and impatient. An air boss understands that on the flight deck mistakes often mean lives at risk, so his tolerance for mistakes was negligible. I walked behind his high chair, mounted to give the king full view of his realm, and took my place in the row of junior aviators who were actually up there standing watch. Each squadron was expected to have a qualified aviator in Primary Flight for every daytime launch and recovery. The purpose of his presence was to answer questions that the boss might have about their aircraft in the case of emergencies.

The squadrons all maintained a copy of their Naval Aviation Training and Operating Procedures Standardization manual and

pocket checklist in Primary Flight so that the boss could better help
and advise pilots who were struggling with an emergency. To the
junior officers forced to stand in Primary Flight throughout every
uneventful launch and recovery, it was a tremendous waste of time.
But to the pilot with an airborne emergency, it was very comforting
to know that you had a squadron mate with the checklist only a
radio call away if you were flying a jet that had its warning and
caution lights flashing in your face like a Christmas tree.

The boss had already called for pilots to start their engines for
the launch, and now the first jets were taxiing toward the catapults.
The first jet to position itself on catapult number one was a Hornet
from the VFA-195 Dambusters. The squadron had been named in
honor of the navy pilots who had blown up a seemingly invincible
dam during the Korean War.

"That's our skipper," said the young Hornet pilot next to me.
"It must be good to be the king," he said as he wistfully watched
his commanding officer taxi into position on the catapult track.

"Yeah, Simba thinks he's king all right," I said. "I recently debriefed him on a fair pass."

"Ha-ha," chuckled the Hornet pilot. "I heard he nearly got you
with his nav bag."

"It was pretty close," I said.

I stared at Simba's Hornet and his white helmet in its cockpit. I
wondered what he was thinking right now. Given his experience
level I wondered if he might be so confident that he could afford
not to really concentrate on the upcoming launch. No, I realized
that he would not have survived to become so experienced if he
didn't know how to concentrate and compartmentalize his
thoughts. We are taught it from the beginning of our training.
When you are flying, you need to be focused, to lock out other
thoughts, because if you made a mistake in flight, the other things
would probably not matter anymore.

The final checker was a young enlisted troubleshooter from the
Dambusters' squadron who raced around the jet checking for any
common prelaunch problems. The Hornet had established itself as
an extremely reliable aircraft, so nobody was surprised when the
final checker popped out from under the jet with his thumb raised,

telling everyone that as far as he could tell, the jet was ready to go flying. Unbeknownst to him, Simba, or anyone else on the flight deck, there was a small clamp on the main fuel line in the jet's main wheel well that was loose.

The *Midway* had just turned into the wind and the display panel that was right next to the boss's chair showed that there were twenty-one knots of wind down the deck. It was an ample amount of wind but not as much as we had grown accustomed to during the past week. The launch light on the railing just below the windows in the boss's fishbowl turned from yellow to green, signaling that the launch could begin. The yellowshirt gave Simba the "in tension" signal and Simba pushed his throttles forward to full military-rated thrust. As he held his engines at full power he moved his stick and rudders, checking out the control surfaces of his Hornet.

Simba had rogered a weight board of thirty-nine thousand pounds, a standard launch weight for the Hornet. The *Midway*'s steam-powered catapult system was not quite powerful enough to get the Hornets enough airspeed by the end of their deck run without the Hornet pilot selecting afterburner just prior to the catapult shot. So afterburner launches for the Hornets were standard procedure for the *Midway*'s Hornet pilots. On the flight deck the catapult officer saw the yellow light change to green and he initiated the launch sequence by pumping his arm up and down in the air with enthusiasm, signaling Simba to select afterburner, or "blower," as Hornet pilots affectionately referred to the Hornet's awesome engines. The tail feathers of the Hornet's tailpipe opened slightly, and the roar of the engines reached a higher pitch of intensity. Everything seemed fine. I saw Simba's head take one last look at his instruments and then he snapped a salute at the catapult officer. The catapult officer went down on one knee and checked forward and aft and then touched the deck. Seeing this signal a young enlisted man on the starboard catwalk just below the level of the deck looked forward and aft and then hit the catapult's launch button. Immediately after hitting the button the young man raised his arms above his head to ensure there was no confusion about when he actually had touched the firing button.

Simba already had his head back against the seat. The Hornet squatted with the acceleration as it hurtled down the catapult's track and into the air. Simba was now flying, but the tremendous force of the catapult shot further loosened the clamp on the main fuel line. With the engines operating in afterburner the pressure on the line was just too much; the clamp broke and the main fuel line separated. Off the catapult the resulting catastrophic fuel leak sprayed jet fuel into the air, which instantly ignited when it reached the afterburner's exhaust, creating a fireball just aft of Simba's Hornet. It was just like spraying an aerosol can over a burning flame—only magnified in intensity a thousandfold.

"Hornet airborne off Cat One, you're on fire. Deselect afterburner and check for secondaries," said the air boss with a sharp edge in his voice.

Simba immediately deselected afterburner and raised his landing gear and flaps as he scanned his cockpit, looking for secondary indications of an engine fire. Loud bangs or vibrations, dropping oil pressure, or controllability problems are typical secondary indications of a fire, yet Simba did not feel or see any such indications. As soon as the Hornet's engine came out of afterburner the flame disappeared but the fuel leak continued. The vaporizing fuel appeared to be white smoke pouring out of the rear of his jet.

"Chippy 407, your fire appears to be out, but you are still smoking. Do you have any secondaries?"

"Boss, 407, I don't have any secondaries for an engine fire—but it looks like I have a major fuel leak. I need someone to check me out. Climbing to angels two and turning downwind. Request clear deck."

"Chippy 407, estimate fuel remaining," queried the boss. There was a pause on the open circuit.

"Seven minutes," said Simba with a cool voice belying the severity of his situation. He knew that the flight deck was cluttered with jets and to clear them in less than seven minutes was going to be extremely difficult.

"Roger, you'll have a clear deck in six minutes," said the Boss.

"Copy, six minutes. I'll make a straight-in approach." *There is no way they can have a clear deck in six minutes*, I said to myself as I looked down on the flight deck. It was packed with aircraft from stern to bow.

"Roger," acknowledged the boss. His face was taut with the pressure of the moment, but I could tell he was confident in his men on the flight deck. The boss grabbed his microphone for the loudspeaker. "Attention on the flight deck, we need an emergency pull forward, this is not a drill. An emergency Hornet inbound needs a clear deck in six minutes. Let's make it happen." I looked at the flight deck, then looked at the boss's face and I knew that this was going to be close. The boss could only watch now as his men worked. There were still eleven jets in the landing area that needed to be launched to give Simba a clear deck to land. I still didn't think it was possible.

As Simba performed the climbing turn to two thousand feet his Hornet's main fuel pump kept pumping fuel through the line that was no longer connected to the engines. Once he had leveled off on downwind another Hornet flown by his squadron's XO closed on him, performing an aggressive rendezvous. The two Hornets flew two miles abeam the carrier on downwind as Simba started to set up for his emergency approach.

The atmosphere in the fishbowl grew tense as the activity on the flight deck continued to become more and more frantic. Every man out there understood that the flight deck they were standing on was the only place that the Hornet pilot had to land. It was now clobbered with eleven jets waiting to launch. If they could not clear the deck within the next six minutes Simba was going swimming or worse, and the *Midway* would lose one of her jets.

"How many more to launch?" asked the boss.

"Eleven," came the reply from the young enlisted man who was tracking the progress of the launch.

The math was not difficult. At best, utilizing the *Midway*'s two catapults, it would take the ship five and a half minutes to launch the remaining jets that were parked in the landing area. Not to mention the jets and equipment that would need to be towed out of the way once the launched aircraft had left the deck. Everyone knew that this was going to be close.

The boss reached for a telephone and hit speed dial for the

bridge. "Captain, we have a Hornet inbound with an uncontrollable loss of fuel, expecting his approach in about five minutes," said the boss over his private line to the *Midway*'s bridge. The captain must have acknowledged the boss's call because the latter quickly hung up the phone and got back to work monitoring the job that the flight-deck crew was doing. One minute had passed and two more jets had been launched.

"LSOs to the platform, Emergency Hornet inbound," said the Boss over the 1MC, a sound system that worked throughout the ship. I knew that Ren and his team were already waiting in the wings for the launch to be over. I watched as the flight-deck crew worked their magic. Yellowshirts, blueshirts, greenshirts, redshirts, purpleshirts, and brownshirts were running around the flight deck, their heads constantly turning to ensure that the sweeping exhaust from a turning jet would not blow them over the side. The color of each man's jersey defined his job on the flight deck, but now every man was pitching in on whatever job needed to be done. The tailpipes of the jet engines were all about four to five feet above the deck, so many of the deckhands would run behind the wheels and under the tailpipes in order to avoid the powerful thrust of the exhaust. As jets were turning, their tailpipes would sweep around, threatening to blow over anybody who was not watching out.

"Chippy 407, tower," said the boss in the most calming voice I had ever heard from a boss.

"Go ahead, Boss," said Simba with more than a trace of anxiety in his voice.

"Ready deck in three minutes, say your state."

"Estimating four minutes fuel remaining—I'll be normal configuration. I'm at five miles turning inbound," said Simba.

At 150 knots with a one-minute turn inbound and the separation that the *Midway* would make during the Hornet's turn, Simba could expect to arrive just after three minutes had elapsed. He couldn't afford to be early before the deck was clear because he would then have to waveoff, and he might not have enough fuel remaining for another approach. If he waited too long to make his approach, then he might also run out of fuel. I could feel my heart rate increasing gradually and my face began to feel flushed. Even though I was a junior pilot I knew what it felt like to operate an aircraft that wasn't working as advertised. Emergencies were never fun, but they were a part of the job, and we all had had them at one time or another. Today it was Simba's turn.

Five minutes had elapsed since Simba's first radio call. The deck had successfully launched nine jets and the final two were approaching the catapult now. One of the two jets was a Prowler with its wings folded; the other was a Hornet which now had its wings spread and was ready for the launch. The LSOs were setting up their platform and making sure that their radios worked. "Tower, paddles, radio check," said Mad Dog.

"Paddles, Tower, loud and clear," said the boss.

"Tower, Paddles, loud and clear," said Mad Dog.

"Chippy 407 is inbound with a fuel problem; he is only going to have enough for one pass, so we need to catch him," said the boss.

"Roger, Boss," said Mad Dog, knowing that what the boss really meant was that this pilot coming in is probably nervous so don't let him screw up his one opportunity at getting aboard.

"Chippy 407, Paddles."

"Go ahead, Paddles."

"407, just remember you are lighter than normal. Don't let yourself get overpowered."

"Roger" came the terse response from a pilot who had a lot on his mind.

The yellowshirt gave the spread-wings signal to the Prowler as it approached the catapult and the right wing began the slow downward motion into the locked position for flight. But to everyone's horror, the left wing did not budge. It rarely happened on these reliable Grumman aircraft, but every now and then, one of the wings would get stuck. We referred to it as the Grumman salute. Any other time and it would have drawn some chuckles in the tower, but now time was critical. The boss needed a clear deck within the next ninety seconds. As I watched the deck's reaction I saw one man run full tilt at the Prowler and vault like an Olympic gymnast onto one of the jamming pods, thereby hoisting himself onto the wing of the Prowler. It was Chief Rat. Once on top of the wing he solidly pushed the wingtip and unseated what was a blocked hydraulic line and the wing began to descend to the locked position. Within seconds he was off the wing and back on the deck, having completed his mission. The Prowler taxied to the cat, and Simba's Hornet continued to close the gap, getting closer to the ramp and to zero on his fuel gage.

Simba was now about a mile and a half behind the *Midway*. From the tower we could see a white cloud of fuel emanating from the Hornet's main wheel well. I looked down onto the flight deck at the frantic activity. Men were scurrying around the deck driving small yellow tow trucks and starter carts out of the landing area. Almost everyone was running away from the ramp and the potential for fire, but there was a small group positioned at the ramp and the roll-out point. The red light indicating foul deck was still on as Simba started his descent at three quarters of a mile.

"407, Hornet ball, 2.8, one pass," said Simba, indicating his fuel remaining—and that the fuel-loss rate would only allow him this one chance at landing.

"Roger ball, you're a little high," said Mad Dog in a honey-sweet tone of voice that always helped calm nervous pilots. Some LSOs called this phone sex. The last jet had launched just seconds before, but for some reason the deck was still foul. The LSOs held their hands above their heads to indicate visually to the boss that they were aware of the foul deck. Now it was a matter of seconds. The deck was clear, but the arresting gear was not yet set properly. Simba's Hornet kept coming, and everyone in the tower started mumbling out loud, "Come on, come on . . ." Miraculously, the deck light changed from red to green and the LSOs dropped their hands to their sides. Simba had a clear deck.

"You're overpowered," said Mad Dog. "Don't climb." On that last call Simba cleared the ramp and the Hornet crashed down into the wires. Fuel spewed all over the deck as Simba rammed his throttles forward in case his hook skipped the wires. Once safely aboard, Simba shut down the Hornet, and what little fuel was left reduced its rate of dumping significantly.

"Great job, flight deck. Now let's get that fuel cleaned up before the next recovery," said the boss. My heart was still pounding but I realized that this was business as usual. I was not yet accustomed to carrier life. I knew intellectually that things like this happened on occasion. I had heard stories from my flight instructors during training, but to see it in person was very different. Everyone on the flight deck started back to their normal work routine. I saw a few supervisors pat their guys on the back, as an acknowledgment for a job well done. It was the quiet gesture of one man saying to another, "Good work." It was just another day at sea for the flight deck crew, but I realized and appreciated the fact that a few seconds either way and at best, Simba might have been forced to eject into the harsh and unforgiving sea, and at worst, might not have made it back at all.

Amazed that the flight deck crew had cleared the entire deck in six minutes, I left the tower and climbed down the narrow switch-back ladders to our ready room. Once inside the door I took two steps to the mailboxes and looked inside. There were a few folders pertaining to articles that I had written and on top of them stacked neatly were three letters from Alice and one from my parents.

Perhaps we might overcome being separated by the globe. Perhaps we might continue our courtship by mail for the next four or five months. I was beginning to understand how emotional the mail can be when one is at sea for long periods of time. The mail provides the lifeline to your loved ones. It provides you with the reasons for working so hard, and it builds the hopes that keep you yearning for home.

CHAPTER SEVEN

Total
Scrutiny

The feeling of my body compress-
ing against my ejection seat's padded surface made me smile, because it was a dark night and that compressed feeling reassured me
it was a good cat shot. The pitot-static airspeed indicator in the
Prowler was quite good, but had enough of a lag to be worrisome.
It didn't give a precise indication of airspeed until the jet was airborne. During the critical one and a half seconds the Prowler hurtled along the deck of the ship, the acceleration was too rapid for
the gauge to measure the pressure differential in the air accurately.
So in the end, I judged a good night cat shot more by how it felt
in the seat of my pants than by what I saw on my instruments.

Those initial seconds of a night flight were always unnerving.
We were held hostage by the power, or lack of power, of the *Midway*'s steam catapult system. We all hoped it would have enough
juice to get us up to a hundred thirty knots before we reached the
pointy end of this massive gray floating island. This time it did, and
on our first flight as a new crew, Gucci, Wolfey, Skippy, and I were
flying.

After two and a half weeks and twelve traps I was no longer flying
with Cave. I had cleared the first nugget hurdle. The crews had
been rearranged, and now if we went to war my primary crew would
be the one I was flying with this night. I often wished that their
call signs didn't all end with what sounded like a diminutive "i" or

"y," but it was a well-known fact that you never got to choose your own call sign. A nickname was much more likely to stick the less you liked it. In fact, more often than not, call signs were somehow connected to an embarrassing moment in the aviator's past. I had never met a guy nicknamed *Maverick*, and generally, if someone said his call sign was *Hollywood* or *Iceman*, you could bet that he was trying to give himself that name—but that rarely worked. Somehow the call signs of Gucci, Wolfey, and Skippy fit each member of my crew and I accepted that fact.

Gucci was a broad-shouldered, handsome Italian with jet-black hair. He appreciated the finer things in life such as a good bottle of wine and a nice pair of shoes. As a lieutenant commander he was the senior man in the crew, and was also our mission commander. The relationship between the command pilot and mission commander can be a difficult one for a nugget pilot. As mission commander, he was responsible for the successful conduct and completion of the mission. As the pilot in command, I was responsible for the aircraft and safety of the crew. On many occasions these two realms of responsibility overlap and cause conflict. It made for a powerful dynamic with regard to crew coordination. Gucci struck me as a strong-willed individual, and I hoped we would not be butting heads all the time over decisions in the cockpit.

Wolfey looked a lot older than he actually was because of the gentle curve around his middle, combined with his rapidly receding hairline. Enhancing his middle-aged appearance was a velvet voice that resonated from deep within his chest. The steel-rimmed glasses that he wore made him look nothing short of professorial. And yet, somewhere within the complex personality of this prematurely middle-aged man was a child who adored electric train sets. Perhaps it was his Germanic blood expressing its fondness for precision locomotives. I will never be sure. His was an unimaginative call sign which simply was a derivative of his last name. I suppose he could have been labeled *Wolfman* and to tell the truth, I tried to make that stick, but everyone in the squadron had already become accustomed to *Wolfey*, so *Wolfey* it remained. I still am not sure where the nickname Skippy came from and I don't believe it has anything to do with peanut butter, but it somehow was uniquely suited to the tall, smooth, and easygoing man from Montana.

Soon after clearing the deck my left hand released its tense grip on the throttles and moved a few inches forward to raise the landing-gear handle. My eyes, now recaged in their sockets, continued to scan the instruments, confirming that the Prowler was indeed climbing into the dark night and not sinking toward the dark sea. After waiting a few seconds I glanced down at the landing gear indicator and said, "Got three up and locked; passing one eighty-five; flaps are coming." My hand flipped a lever and within a few seconds three small windows on the flaps and slats indicator all said UP, so I flicked the hydraulic isolation valve and reported to the crew, "I'm up, clean, and isolated. Instruments look good. Climbing to nineteen thousand feet."

"Roger," said Gucci as he turned his attention to the navigation system, satisfied that we had no immediate problems with the jet. There were enough thin cloud layers to make visibility difficult and disorienting under the faint glow of the moon. As a result, I decided to remain on the assigned departure heading until I climbed through ten thousand feet where the cloud layers seemed to dissipate. I rolled the Prowler to the left as we continued our climb toward the rendezvous altitude in search of the two Intruders and one Prowler that we would be joining.

Tonight was my first mirror-image strike, and I was nervous. During the three months *Midway* had been at sea prior to my arrival, the air wing had developed intricate strike plans for many actual targets that would be attacked in the event that Iraq refused to pull out from Kuwait. Since *Midway* was still in the Gulf of Oman, we were flying practice missions that used the same planned headings and distances, but relocated about five hundred miles south of where we might be flying real strikes in the future.

These mirror-image strikes were the best training possible and I had hoped to get to fly one because I believed such a mission would help me understand how all the pieces fit together in a massive carrier air wing strike. I had not been told as much, but I felt as if this flight was a "combat check flight" for me. We were simulating an entire mission and I believed that the skipper had his doubts about my ability to handle the steep learning curve presented to me. After my first encounter with the Iron Maiden it was discovered that I had damaged the jet's refueling probe during disengagement from the basket. It was an easy repair, but the squadron couldn't afford to have me breaking refueling probes every time I tanked. Since tanking was going to be critical to the success of every combat mission, I needed to prove I could tank without damaging the jet. So tonight I felt that I was under the total scrutiny of everyone, not only in my new crew, but also in the formation. With Dawg, our squadron's operations officer, as the pilot in the other Prowler, and Gucci, our squadron's electronic warfare officer, in my right seat, I knew that they would both offer our skipper a crisp analysis of my performance tonight. After being onboard *Midway* for only two weeks, I would be tested, and I hoped more than anything to pass muster and be considered combat ready.

There were going to be twenty-two *Midway* jets rendezvousing tonight with three US Air Force KC-135 tankers, then pressing on to two different hypothetical primary targets located in the desert. Our division of four jets—two Intruders and two Prowlers—would rendezvous overhead *Midway* and then fly together in formation to meet tankers using the call signs, Mako 5, 6, and 7. At the tankers we would meet up with our High Value Unit Combat Air Patrol (HVUCAP). These two Hornets would escort the Prowlers throughout the mission in order to deter our imaginary adversary of the evening. The HVUCAP was necessary to protect the Prowler, a High Value Unit, from enemy fighters because the Prowler had no air-to-air weapons capability. The Prowler's mission, the suppression of the enemy's air defenses, was absolutely critical to the success of any strike. As a result, the air wing needed to protect its Prowlers with some of its fighters. The Prowler performed its mission like a blocker on a football field. By firing High-speed Anti-Radiation Missiles (HARM) at enemy radars and also by jamming their radar systems, we would blind the enemy and create a safe path for our bombers to get to target. Tonight, after a mock attack on designated targets, we would return to the carrier. The mission was scheduled to last nearly three hours. I was thankful that this was actually one of the shorter mirror-image strikes.

"One thousand feet to go," said Gucci, bringing my attention to the required level-off.

"Thanks," I said as I simultaneously reduced the power and lowered the nose to level off the Prowler two hundred feet below the agreed altitude. I didn't want to fly at the rendezvous altitude of nineteen thousand feet until I had my eyes on my playmates. I knew I was the last one airborne, so I was aggressively scanning the horizon looking for red anticollision lights. With twenty-one other jets meeting at five different altitudes the sky was filled with twinkling red anticollision lights. I found it challenging enough to rendezvous with one jet at night at one altitude; I couldn't believe I was about to join three other jets overhead the carrier in the same piece of sky that eighteen other jets were using to rendezvous.

We were flying in a left-hand turn through cloud layers of varying thickness when I began to feel the first twinge of vertigo, or as pilots call it, "the leans." Because there was no clearly discernible horizon it was difficult to tell which way was up and which way was down. I had heard stories of pilots with severe vertigo mistaking the white lights of small fishing boats on the black ocean at night for the stars in a black night sky. The potential danger of such a misperception for a pilot is obvious. My sense of balance and orientation was being fooled by deceptive messages that my body was sending to my brain. When I leveled the Prowler's wings according to my instruments, my body still believed it was in a left turn. I had only felt this once or twice in training, and now I knew that I was flying in the type of weather known to induce vertigo. They also told me in training that you should alert your crew if vertigo occurs and they can help talk you out of it with reassurances that the aircraft is actually flying straight and level. So far, I was confident that my vertigo was not that bad, and because of the total scrutiny I was under, I did not want to reveal it to my crew. Except for admitting the problem, I began to do what I had learned in flight training: I eased my angle of bank, focused on my instruments, and hoped that the feeling would go away soon.

"Tally, at two o'clock," said Gucci. His voice emanated a confidence I was not feeling at the moment so I leveled the Prowler's wings in order to see what he was pointing at. What I saw made me grimace. The crossing angle was terrible. And what was worse was that the three aircraft were already flying in tight formation. Once again I felt behind. I needed to rendezvous expeditiously so as not to slow up the mission. The three-plane formation crossed in front of our nose and I rolled hard to the left, added power, and pulled back on the stick to keep the nose of my aircraft ahead of the formation, thereby increasing closure rate and expediting the rendezvous. Given the vertigo I was feeling, I needed to crosscheck my instruments inside the cockpit even more frequently than I would have normally. I needed to convince myself that my instruments were telling me the truth.

I knew I was performing the best possible maneuver, but by banking so hard to the left, I lost sight of the three-aircraft formation as the right canopy rail rose to obstruct my view out of that side of the Prowler. The fact that I had momentarily lost sight was to be expected, but was still unsettling. We were hurtling through the air toward a three-jet formation and I couldn't see them. As I craned my neck in an effort to regain sight I unintentionally allowed the Prowler to start a gradual rate of descent. Not adhering to your assigned altitude is the cardinal sin of night rendezvous because only one thousand feet below are four other aircraft joining up in the same way. Many navy pilots have been lost at sea during night rendezvous because they descended into another group of aircraft and had a collision. *Many of them probably had vertigo,* I told myself as I battled the contradictory signals to my brain.

"Altitude," said Gucci, who did not have vertigo and was not about to let himself become the focus of a squadron safety lecture about the Prowler crew who busted their altitude and had a midair collision.

"Got it," I said, having caught the descent just as Gucci had mentioned it. My neck strained to get sight of the three jets I was joining over the Prowler's right canopy rail. At 325 knots I knew I was being aggressive but I wanted to impress the more senior Intruder pilots and Dawg. The lead Intruder, piloted by one of the Intruder squadron commanders whose call sign was Nitro, continued his left turn as I closed rapidly on the three jets turning to the left. I was focused on the lead Intruder, trying to maintain the proper rendezvous angle as I approached. I reduced power and started to slow the rate of closure to keep the rendezvous under control.

"We need to get onboard. There are some clouds coming up," said Gucci. I knew that if I was not close enough to the other jets by the time we entered the clouds, we would lose sight and it would take much longer to complete the rendezvous. I inched the throttles forward and increased my angle of bank, placing the nose of my aircraft well ahead of the formation. This maneuver made my line of bearing more acute and served to increase my closure rate. The bearing line that I was flying was quite acute now and the rate of closure felt very uncomfortable. Each aircraft in the formation started to get bigger quickly. At the last possible instant I reduced power, popped my speedbrakes, and wrapped up the Prowler in a tight left bank, barely keeping sight of the third jet in the formation. I struggled to position myself properly, flying just six feet away from Dawg's right wingtip. He was the third jet in the echelon formation as we penetrated the clouds. It had not been a pretty rendezvous, but it was expeditious, and under these conditions I was relatively pleased.

Flying formation at night in and out of clouds can be extremely disorienting for a pilot. I knew that my crew was probably more nervous than I was. I could just imagine Skippy and Wolfey's conversation over the backseat ICS: "He's gonna kill us all!" Wolfey would say. And Skippy would respond glumly, "Yeah, what a way to go." I was struggling to keep sight of Dawg's jet, which was struggling to keep sight of the second jet, which was struggling to keep sight of the lead. Flying formation means controlling relative motion, and for me, tonight it also meant controlling and eliminating my sense of vertigo. The goal of flying good formation is to zero out relative motion between multiple aircraft. The second plane reacts to the actions of the lead, and those reactions are compounded as you get farther from the lead aircraft. The third reacts to the second, and by the time the lead's small increase in power and stick deflection had reached me, as the fourth jet in the formation, it already had been magnified by two other pilots, so my correction was much larger.

Nitro, the lead Intruder pilot, soon rolled out on a good heading, taking the formation toward the tanker track. Now that I was flying off Dawg's wing I was no longer able to crosscheck my instruments, because I needed to stay focused on his aircraft due to low visibility. I just hoped my vertigo would disappear soon.

"The system seems to be good in the back," said Skippy in his smooth Montana voice that somehow made me think of the deep-blue western skies and many other places I would rather be. "We are going to run a few more checks, but everything we need for the mission looks good."

"Roger that," I said, trying to sound as calm as Skippy and knowing that I didn't.

"Ready for the combat checklist?" asked Gucci. We had briefed this and it was no surprise, but I was so focused on keeping sight of Dawg's Prowler that I was not in the mood for any checklist at this point. But I knew it was a good idea to get used to it, because we might actually be using it for real someday soon. Gucci began the challenge-response checklist that covered everything from lowering visors on our helmets to the switch position on the missile control panel for the High Speed Anti-Radiation missile we were carrying on Station Two on our port wing. All of my responses to Gucci's questions were somewhat slow and deliberate because I was so reluctant to lose sight of the formation.

According to the brief, it would take us about forty-five minutes to fly from overhead the carrier to the tanker track. As we flew west toward the Saudi Arabian peninsula the sky did not improve. We maintained our echelon formation and altitude at nineteen thousand as we had briefed. I grumbled to myself that if Nitro had been a considerate lead he would have climbed out of the cloudy weather and given his wingmen a chance to relax on the way to the tanker. However, he did not do that and we continued toward the tanker track with virtual silence in the cockpit because my crew could tell how hard I was concentrating just to keep the formation in sight.

"This is stupid," said Gucci. "We should at least try another altitude."

"I'm with you on that one," I said, glad to hear Gucci say what I had been thinking for the past fifteen minutes. Mako 5, the tanker that we were to rendezvous with, was supposed to be at our present altitude so I was sure that Nitro just believed it would be simpler to stay where we were, versus climbing and then having to descend later. It was a judgment call and he was the lead. As the wingman I was expected "to join up and shut up."

"We are running a little behind on time," said Gucci.

"Yeah, but we built in a fair amount of slop at the tanker, so we should be OK," said Wolfey from the backseat, interjecting his first remark of the flight.

I could never be as trusting as these backseaters. In the Prowler the ECMOs had absolutely no forward visibility, yet somehow they still loved to fly and they trusted me with their lives on a daily basis. It was a responsibility that I took very seriously, but at the same time I could not relate to the way they could just happily accept the fact that they had no control over this gray warhorse that plowed through the sky now in search of fuel. All three men in my crew were married, so the feeling of responsibility was automatically doubled in my mind.

"The nav is tight and we should be at the tanker track now," said Gucci. Just then Nitro started an easy left turn to start searching the skies for the tanker. Neither the Intruder nor the Prowler is equipped with air-to-air-style radar, so it was going to be tough to find tankers in this weather. The cloud layers had dissipated somewhat, so visibility was a bit better, but it was still going to be a difficult rendezvous without an effective radar. I chuckled at Gucci, who had his head stuck in the radar, fiddling with its controls, trying to set it up so that he might pick out the KC-135s in front of us. I had never heard of anyone using the Prowler's ground mapping radar to search for airborne targets, so I was certain that he was wasting his time. I scanned the horizon when I could but I was still primarily focused on flying good formation off Dawg's aircraft.

"Gucci, why are you wasting your time watching the radar?" I finally asked, beginning to feel that he really should get his head up and help me look for the tanker.

"I'm not wasting my time, because I see them about ten degrees left of the nose," responded Gucci with the pride of a navigator who knows his stuff.

"Yeah, sure," I said skeptically. "We'll see." A few seconds later our formation increased its angle of bank to the left and off the nose I saw the three bright white lights of Mako 5, 6, and 7. "Damn, you're good," I said. "How did you use the radar to do that?"

"I just raised the angle of elevation, reduced the azimuth angle, and increased the scan rate. Tactical aircraft are almost impossible to pick out, but these huge tankers aren't so tough," said Gucci, taking justifiable pride in his radar operating skill.

Fortunately, the weather had improved a little and my vertigo had disappeared, so when Nitro began to maneuver the formation for the rendezvous I was feeling fine. Large rapid turns with three aircraft flying off your wing is frowned upon, but when you're the CO of a squadron you don't tend to be concerned with what lieutenants think about your formation flying. It was clear that Nitro didn't care at all what we thought, because he maneuvered his Intruder without regard to the three pilots desperately trying to hang on and keep up with him. As the tail of the whip I got jerked around and I nearly lost sight of Dawg's aircraft just as the tanker entered a large cloud formation conveniently located on the tanker track.

The only positive thing was that it was definitely an aggressive and expeditious rendezvous and our four-plane formation was soon flying off the left wing of the massive tanker. Gucci automatically switched our front UHF radio to tanker frequency and I heard Nitro's bombardier/navigator say, "Mako 5, Maverick 17, port observation, nose cold, switches safe, looking for 8.0."

"Maverick 17, you're cleared in for 8.0," said the air force voice on the other end of the circuit. Nitro waited for the boom operator to do his thing. It took a few seconds for the boom to be lowered from the tanker and the basket extended before he slid his aircraft into position. Nitro may not have been much of a smooth formation lead, but he stuck his Intruder's refueling probe into the Iron Maiden's basket on his first attempt and had no problem staying in. *Experience is a good thing*, I said to myself, wishing that I somehow could get a dose of it intravenously. Nitro maneuvered a bend in the hard rubber hose to maintain a constant flow but still had enough leeway so that he did not unintentionally disengage. When he was done he slowly backed off and just as pretty as you please took his position on the tanker's starboard side ready to watch his wingmen engage the Iron Maiden.

The next Intruder pilot was a seasoned lieutenant called Rooster, who I assumed got the call sign because of his cocky attitude. However, I soon learned that he had something to be cocky about, because he approached the basket and placed his Intruder's probe in it on first attempt. A few minutes later he was complete. He then backed out, and slid to the right to be next to his skipper.

Now it was Dawg's turn and I watched closely as he slid to the right in what seemed to be an awkward fashion. After several small wing dips he was finally ready to make his approach to the basket. Just as he commenced his closure on the basket the massive tanker started its left turn which kicked the basket to the outside of the turn. As a result, Dawg's first approach was ugly. His refueling probe caught the edge of the basket and the Iron Maiden slapped at the nose of his Prowler in a most resentful way.

As Dawg began his second approach I started to prepare myself for my meeting with the Maiden. I lowered my seat and selected "in air refueling" on my control panel so that fuel would be efficiently distributed to the Prowler's tanks through the refueling probe. Then I tried to relax as I watched Dawg's next attempt. The tanker was still in a turn and as a result, the basket was out of alignment slightly and Dawg missed it again. I winced for him. He was an excellent pilot, and I knew that this must be killing him, knowing that the Intruder skipper, one of the air wing's most senior pilots, was on his right and I, the newest pilot in the air wing, was on his left as he stabbed again at the basket and missed.

After one more missed attempt I knew that something was wrong. "Tank, Dawg on squadron tactical, I have a touch of vertigo, I'm going to take a break." The voice was slightly weaker coming in over our backup VHF radio but I could hear it without any problem. I knew he must have a bad case of vertigo for him to admit it to me, or perhaps he was just displaying the maturity that I lacked. I watched him descend with small wing dips that signaled to me he was struggling with a really bad case of vertigo as he passed under my jet and positioned himself on my left wing.

It was my turn to wrestle with the Iron Maiden, and this time I felt ready for it. Since my first nerveracking introduction to the basket at night I had been able to take some daytime practice plugs, so I had built up my confidence. But I knew that night's shroud of darkness made all things more difficult in the air and I started to focus on the task at hand. If I broke the refueling probe this night the chiefs in maintenance control would make my life absolutely unbearable. I could just imagine Beast convincing everyone that my call sign should be changed from *Tank* to *Can't Tank*. I didn't like the thought of that and I, like all naval aviators, hated to look bad, so I was determined to tank without incident tonight.

I maneuvered the Prowler to a position about ten feet behind the basket and started to wiggle my toes. I could feel my hands relax their grip and I felt more confident. I never understood the connection between my toes and my hands—but it seemed to work, so I just kept wiggling. My left hand scootched the throttles forward slightly to develop a closure rate on the basket. Even though my eyes were focused on the basket, in the periphery I could see that the tanker had started to roll. Once again it was at the end of its straightaway, and I was in the wrong place at the wrong time. I pushed the throttles again and made a minor correction for the anticipated swing of the basket to the right. The refueling probe slammed into the center of the basket and I rolled to the left to match the turn rate of the tanker. The basket swiveled nervously around the fuel probe of the Prowler, and the hard rubber hose gyrated under the tension, but the probe remained seated and I heard the sweet words from Gucci, "We've got good flow." I felt confident that I could stay plugged, but it was *unplugging* that had caused me problems in the past. I had been breaking the probe tips on the disengagements, so that is what I now started to worry about.

A few minutes later Gucci's voice came through my headset saying, "A thousand pounds to go." I would soon need to disengage from the Iron Maiden. I could tell that he was as concerned as I was. He had been sitting in the front right seat a few nights before when my disengagement had resulted in the basket slamming down onto the Prowler's nose cone right in front of him. Tonight would be better, I hoped.

The light on the underbelly of the KC-135 went from green to yellow, indicating that I had taken on as much fuel as I was going to get. It totaled almost seven thousand pounds on our fuel gauge and I was pleased that I had stayed engaged the entire time. The trick to disengaging was to pull the probe straight out of the basket. If the aircraft disengaging had a slight upward, downward, left, or right vector then the probe tip could get dislodged by scraping the steel rim of the basket on the way out.

My right thumb was twitching on the electric trim switch on top of the stick, trying to perfectly stabilize the fully fueled Prowler before I attempted to withdraw the probe from the basket. My right hand relaxed its grip on the stick momentarily and the aircraft seemed about as stable as could be expected. I felt as if it was taking forever and I knew that the tanker was about to enter another turn, so I wanted to disengage before that happened. I gently pulled the throttles back, reducing power as I concentrated on the basket. Gradually the hard rubber hose extended, and the bend that I had worked so hard to create disappeared. Now the moment had come where the hose and basket were taut, and the final feeling of disengagement came as the probe tip broke its lock with the basket. I watched the tip cleanly exit the basket as I released a deep breath. Once clear of the basket I kept fading back until I could cross beneath and below Rooster and come back up on his right side.

Now it was Dawg's turn. I knew that he only had a few minutes to get his gas before we would be negatively impacting our timeline.

"Our HVU CAP is in loose cruise to our right," said Gucci. The Hornets had completed their tanking and were now waiting and watching as Dawg approached the basket. This time he looked steady and we all were relieved when he plugged on his first attempt. Within a few minutes he had topped off his Prowler's tanks and we were ready to depart the tanker track.

Compared with the rendezvous and tanking, the rest of the mission was uneventful. We were able to fly our timeline and simulate the launch of our HARM missile just prior to the Intruder attack on mock targets. The value of the mirror-image strikes lay in practicing the logistics involved in a joint navy/air force integrated air strike on a large scale. It had been a successful night and I think Gucci was as convinced as he could be that I would be able to handle myself in combat. In the end, he too had to worry about how he would handle it, because it would be a new experience for everyone.

CHAPTER EIGHT

The Calm Before the Storm

Through the fog of an alcohol-assisted sleep I awoke to hear the telephone ringing in the BK. The previous night was Christmas Eve and we had celebrated. It had been our second night in the Persian Gulf port of Abu Dhabi in the United Arab Emirates, and on both nights my squadron mates and I had partied well into the morning. Somehow, I had gotten myself back to the *Midway* and into my rack so that I would be onboard in time to stand watch as the squadron duty officer that day. *Brrriinng . . . Brrriinng . . .* the annoying telephone kept ringing.

I pulled myself out of my rack and stumbled across the room toward the incessant noise. "Hello," I said hoarsely, praying it was not anyone in a position of authority on the line.

"Tank, it's ET. We've got turnover now."

"Shit. Sorry, ET, I'll be down there in a minute. Is there anything going on?"

"Yeah, it's Christmas and I want to get off this boat, so hurry up and get your ass down to the ready room."

"OK, OK. Bah humbug to you, too. Calm down, I'll be there in a minute," I said groggily as I hung up the phone. I quickly shaved and put on my khaki uniform. Since I was the new guy, I was not at all surprised to be assigned duty this day. But that didn't mean I wasn't upset about it. I was far away from home, family, and friends. The only thing that cheered me up was the fact that I was with five thousand other Americans on the *Midway* who were in the same situation. *What a concept,* I thought to myself, *Christmas on an aircraft carrier, in a Muslim country, in the middle of the Persian Gulf.* It just felt strange. I was determined to have as happy a Christmas day as I could, given the circumstances. I knew that there were a lot of young sailors onboard the *Midway* who would be terribly homesick today, and I hoped to make some of them feel better.

As I walked to the ready room to turn over the watch I thought about what had happened the night before. I had been drinking at a squadron party most of the afternoon before I decided to call Alice from the hotel room where I was staying. It was wonderful to hear her voice again, and we spoke for quite a while. Intoxicated not only by love, but also by lager, I was feeling happy and talkative. I remember saying, "I love you" to her. She immediately dismissed it, saying it was simply the beer talking. But I adamantly insisted it was not. We ended up laughing about it, and I hoped that I had not overstepped my bounds. What was done was done, and there was no taking it back. I just hoped that perhaps someday the feeling would be mutual.

The ready room was empty when I got there, except for ET and a young petty officer who would also be standing watch during the next twenty-four hours.

"Hi, ET, sorry I'm a bit late."

"Yeah, yeah, I've already logged out. The skipper is in room five thirty-seven at the Sheraton if anything happens. Fortunately, last night was quiet."

"Really? None of our guys got into any trouble at all?"

"None that I've heard about."

"That's great. I hope it stays that way," I said. In port, the worst part of the SDO's job was dealing with situations when members of the squadron got into trouble with local authorities. Since this was a Muslim country, and especially given current tensions in the region, the captain of the *Midway* had made it clear that there would be very stiff penalties for any troublemakers. We had all wondered how effective his promise would be, but it appeared to be working. I knew that our sailors respected the captain, a former fighter pilot from the Vietnam era, so I, for one, was not surprised by their good behavior.

I picked up the logbook and a pen and made my first entry: "0745: Lieutenant Junior Grade Baldwin assumes the duties of Squadron Duty Officer." Now if anything happened to anyone in the squadron it would be my problem to deal with for the next twenty-four hours. ET smiled; he was free. "Have a good Christmas," I said.

"You too, Tank," said ET as he turned to leave.

I arranged with the duty petty officer a schedule that would allow us both some time to eat our meals and attend Christmas services. I planned to go to one of the services because I felt that singing some Christmas hymns was just what I needed to chase away my homesick and lovesick feelings. The first Protestant service was at 1000, so I killed a few hours by reading magazines in the ready room and watching parts of the movie that was playing on closed-circuit television. As agreed, the petty officer came back to the ready room at 0945 so that I could go to the chapel.

The ship's chapel was quite small, located off the hangar deck near the bow. I had actually not yet been to a service onboard the *Midway* even though I had been unofficially talking to the Lord regularly about my night landings during the past several weeks.

To get to the chapel I needed to traverse the hangar bay, which was always an adventure. It was a maze constructed from the wings, noses, tails, landing gear, and fuselages of aircraft. This was where jets were brought for more lengthy or serious repairs that could not be accomplished on the flight deck. The hangar bay was a work in progress. It was never neat and tidy; it was always in transition. I walked past a Hornet with only one engine, an Intruder lifted up into the air on jacks, and a Prowler with its fuselage fuel cell being replaced. It might be Christmas, but preparations for combat were still underway.

When I got to the chapel what few seats existed were already filled. I found a spot against the glistening white bulkhead and faced the altar where the chaplain stood speaking cheerfully with the captain. I was impressed to see the captain on the ship. He certainly could be in town at a fancy hotel relaxing, but instead, he was celebrating Christmas with his men. To me, that was leadership. *Not bad for an old fighter pilot*, I said to myself. He was tall and slender and his aquiline nose gave him an appropriately distinguished look. He clearly understood that for sailors, actions speak louder than words. His reputation was that of an intellectual Renaissance man. He struck me as a thoughtful, quiet man who would listen carefully, then speak decisively only after he had formulated something worthwhile to say. I had often seen him walking around the flight deck talking with the men when there was a lull in the flight operations schedule. You could tell that he enjoyed being captain of this massive warship. Command at sea remained the defining challenge for naval officers just as it had been for centuries.

He did command the *Midway* and her men, but another navy captain, the CAG, commanded the air wing. There were close to five thousand men on the *Midway*. The *Midway*'s captain was responsible for the ship's company, approximately half of that number, and the CAG was responsible for all the aircraft onboard as well as the men who flew them, fixed them, and enabled the squadrons to function. The air wing comprised the other half of the total number of men onboard. The relationship between these two men was generally excellent, but their responsibilities often seemed to overlap, creating tension between them. But we all knew that these two men handled tension better than most.

Late one night the previous week, during the final recovery, a Hornet pilot was struggling; he could not get his jet to land back onboard. The *Midway* had been steaming into the wind in the same direction for well over an hour. After going to the tanker once, the Hornet pilot continued to bolter and the carrier was getting dangerously close to Iranian waters. The captain needed to turn the *Midway* south in order to avoid an international incident, but the CAG argued that the Hornet pilot did not have any friendly divert fields, and that if the carrier turned out of the wind it would be impossible for the pilot to land. The captain delayed his turn to the last possible moment, giving the pilot one more approach. Fortunately, the LSOs were able to talk the frazzled pilot into the wires on his last approach. It was an example of teamwork and coordination between the *Midway*'s two most senior officers that we pilots would not soon forget. We all had confidence in their leadership.

The CAG was a Vietnam veteran A-6 Intruder bombardier navigator who had more traps in the A-6 than any other person in the navy. He had been one of the first BNs to fly the Intruder, and he had done little else for the past twenty-plus years. He knew the A-6, and he knew carrier aviation better than anyone. The *Midway*'s captain was also a Vietnam veteran who had flown F-4 Phantoms, but he had taken a different career path after commanding a fighter squadron. He had been selected for sequential command in the prestigious aircraft carrier pipeline, and had spent the past few years commanding other large navy ships in preparation for the *Midway*. The two men were equivalents in rank, but history had shown that the aircraft carrier captains were on a faster track, which virtually guaranteed them flag rank. The CAG was an aviator's aviator and enjoyed flying too much to give it up and drive a boat.

I wondered where the CAG was celebrating this Christmas Day. Wherever he was, there probably was not a five-piece orchestra preparing to play Christmas music. Four enlisted men and their instruments sat patiently next to the altar waiting for their cue from the chaplain. But one of their number was missing. I wondered who it was. The mystery was soon solved as the captain himself returned to his seat with the band and picked up his trumpet. Following his lead, the band started to play processional music as the chapel continued to fill with sailors from all areas of the ship. There were young men whom I recognized from the flight deck, from the wardroom, and from our squadron. But there were many more faces that I had never seen before. Crowded into the small chapel were black faces, white faces, and many faces of color that completed the spectrum in between.

All of them knew their captain, and they all watched him as he played his trumpet. I could tell that they appreciated his presence. They knew that he didn't have to be there, but wanted to be. The chaplain had wisely selected some of the most well-known Christmas hymns, so the fact that there were not nearly enough hymnals to go around didn't matter in the least. The ones that were available were being shared by three or four men. As I sang the familiar words I smiled. I felt my heart lifted up by the many voices joined together with a common purpose. It seemed that we all hoped our families back home could hear our music. Each man looked as if he was projecting himself elsewhere as he sang. We each, for a moment, had the pleasure of singing these songs with our families in our minds and hearts.

The service was short and to the point, following the fine tradition of military chaplains. Grape juice, instead of wine, was served at communion, in accordance with navy regulations. I watched as the men took their communion. There was a seriousness of purpose about these young men. They all knew that war might be around the corner, and we all were asking ourselves the same question: *How will I measure up?* All of us there that day were seeking the strength we needed to carry on. I believe it was the determined nature of the faces around me in the chapel that morning that made me realize war was at hand.

CHAPTER NINE

Rugers in the Ready Room

"Attention on deck!" shouted the new XO. Everyone in the ready room snapped to the unfamiliar position of attention. The squadron's change of command had just occurred the day before we pulled into the port of Abu Dhabi for Christmas, and it was clear that life in the squadron was going to be different. In the traditional manner, after eighteen months of being second in command, our XO relieved our CO and took over command of the squadron. His job as XO was filled by a new navy commander, who in turn would serve as XO for eighteen months and would then take over as CO. It was an ongoing process designed to groom squadron commanders, ensuring that they knew the squadron well before they commanded it.

During his eighteen months as XO, our newly appointed CO had earned himself the behind-the-back nickname of "Alpha Charlie." To the uninitiated this seemed a harmless enough nickname, but to those in the know, the words *Alpha Charlie* stood for the letters AC which were the encoded initials for the "Anti-Christ." The junior officers in our squadron believed that the squadron was given its sense of unity by a shared hatred of this man. With regard to the leadership question of "Where do your loyalties lie—to the mission or to your people?" Alpha Charlie was definitely a "My loyalty is to the mission" leader. He would not hesitate to flatten, squash, and slam dunk the career of any JO who he felt interfered with the successful accomplishment of the squadron's mission. Now he was in charge, and it was clear that Christmas was over.

Our new XO had come from the fleet replacement squadron at Whidbey Island, where he had a reputation as a tough man with a short temper, which was why he was known as *Nitro*. It was tough to read his mood, a fact that he not only knew but in which he also seemed to take pleasure. He was capable of creating an immutable facade concealing his emotions. The facade seemed to magnify his natural intensity. He struck me as a man who was willing to endure much pain in order to prevail.

Our new skipper walked down the center aisle of the ready room with a seriousness of purpose in his stride and a sobering presence that made me realize that wearing the mantle of command really had changed the man. His disarming smile and rolling gait had disappeared. It was impossible to put my finger on it, but I could tell that this man had undergone some subtle transformation. Only the day before he was our XO, but today he was our skipper, our squadron's leader. "Take your seats," he said, his voice steeped with newfound authority. His lean, wiry frame and gaunt face marked him as the distance runner and fitness fanatic that he was. He did not look pleased as he looked out over his audience.

The skipper was now trying to act relaxed by leaning against the white board at the front of the ready room. It was not working. He looked uncomfortable, and the invisible yet heavy weight of command seemed to be too much for his shoulders. But, giving him the benefit of the doubt, I figured that it would take him a little while to get accustomed to his new position. I sat down in my ready-room chair as did the other twenty-five pilots and ECMOs in the room.

Once the shuffling and settling into chairs had stopped, he started to speak. "I am very excited about taking command and have been thinking about this day for a long time. It is indeed good to be king." A few random chuckles followed this comment. "This afternoon we will start flight ops again after a five-day layoff in port. As always, everyone will be a little rusty, so I want all of you to be extra careful out there. Back each other up in the cockpit and follow your procedures." I looked around the ready room and saw that the guys were losing interest. It was shaping up to be a boring "be safe" speech which the air wing considered mandatory immediately following a port call. But, sensing this reaction, the skipper changed his tack to recapture the interest of an audience he realized he was losing.

"We also need to focus on the fact that in a little over two weeks we may be at war. I am not convinced that it will happen, but I am convinced that you guys are not ready. We are at mid-cruise, and you are not where you should be in terms of your proficiency. Right now, there are a number of you whom I would not allow to fly in combat, because I don't think you can handle it. So if you want to keep your wings and fly in combat, then you need to get with the program. ECMOs in particular—you need to think more like pilots. You've got to stay ahead of the aircraft. You've got to keep situational awareness and understand the geography of the area in case you get shot down. You've got to have an evasion plan of action. You need to convince me that you are ready. I have seen lots of international crises that have been defused at the last minute because the carrier deployed off the coast of the hot spot, but this situation is different. The Iraqis are digging in and hunkering down. They are preparing for a fight. And if you are not prepared, you will get nailed.

"We need to take ourselves to a higher plane of professionalism and performance, and we need to do it now. First, we will improve our professionalism by abolishing UMPQUA. From this day forward nobody in this squadron is to be seen wearing an UMPQUA patch on his flight suit or flight jacket. This group has acted unprofessionally and I will not accept it. Second, we will improve our performance by focusing on the potential for combat in everything we do. I want each of you to start flying with the Rugers that we ordered for this deployment. Arnie, break out the weapons."

Arnie, a junior officer ECMO, and our armaments officer, walked to the front of the ready room amid a stunned silence in response to the skipper's announcements. This was not an uplifting speech. I could tell immediately by looking at the somber faces of the JOs around me that the ban on UMPQUA was a serious blow to morale.

Demonstrating the spirit of UMPQUA, Kamper, not intimidated by the new skipper, asked, "What is unprofessional about UMPQUA?"

"It has developed in a negative way and that is all I intend to say about it. No more UMPQUA, and no more questions," said the skipper. "Now, let's turn to the Rugers." Kamper, although not intimidated, was not stupid. He realized this issue had been decided, and on the basis of rank he had no argument to make.

Before I had arrived, the squadron had ordered 9mm Ruger pistols for everyone instead of the standard navy issue .38-caliber service revolver that aviators were issued if flying in combat. The Rugers were newer and more powerful and we all were willing to spend the money to carry them with us instead of the old .38s. I had not been able to order one but Wolfey said that he would sell me his. The pistols were expensive and Wolfey was not convinced that he would really need anything more powerful than the navy issue .38. I suppose Wolfey had simply resigned himself to the fact that if we were shot down, he was as good as dead in the hands of Iraqis.

Arnie had established a system for keeping track of the weapons and the ammunition clips. Each Ruger was sold with two clips, so I got the box marked WOLFE and promptly scratched his name off and wrote BALDWIN in big block letters so that there would be no mistake whose weapon was inside. I had never owned a pistol before and I felt a rush of power and excitement. The only time I had ever shot a pistol was at AOCS with Staff Sergeant Massey United States Marine Corps looking over my shoulder. The Ruger was black and heavy. Once the clip was shoved up the pistol's handle it felt very solid.

Some of the guys in the ready room knew what was what with a pistol and some of us did not. My hands struggled with the unfamiliar motions involved with disassembling and reassembling the weapon. As I looked around the ready room there seemed to be "shooters" and "nonshooters." Even though I was a "nonshooter" in terms of my lack of experience, I felt confident in my resolve to use this weapon if required. Ren and Gucci shared this resolve. I sat down with them and watched as they broke down the weapon into more manageable pieces for cleaning. The cardboard box that the Ruger was packed in contained some small cleaning instruments which I needed to learn how to use. I could tell that Ren knew what he was doing.

"Have you ever shot a Ruger, Ren?" I asked.

"No, but I've shot some other nine mils, and they were pretty similar." His powerful hands worked the slide of the weapon, pulling the pin allowing the slide to be removed. Even though UMPQUA had just been officially disbanded, this gun-cleaning session was a strong bonding experience for the squadron. The twenty-six of us were sitting in close quarters cleaning weapons that one day might be used against an enemy. I was where I wanted to be. After all the training I had been through this was what I had hoped for as a military professional, being in a ready room on an aircraft carrier with a dedicated group of men preparing for war. Or at least I thought that was what I wanted. Combat was still far enough in the future that the reality had not yet set in. I still viewed the entire concept of war as a remote and glorious boyhood possibility— something which all true heroes always survived.

"If I'm surrounded by a group of angry Iraqis I would first remove one shell from the first clip, then fire my two clips at the bastards and then chamber the final round in order to put myself out of my misery before they captured me," said Ren, in his easy North Carolina accent. I nodded in agreement. I could not even imagine the kind of torture that they would impose on an American pilot. The real torture would be far uglier than what we had faced at the United States Navy's Survival Evasion Resistance Escape school, where in training we had simulated the experience of a pilot shot down behind enemy lines. Even if the Iraqis didn't capture us we knew that the desert itself could be just as evil.

"Did you guys hear about Lepp's quote in *Newsweek*?" asked Gucci. We all shook our heads collectively, wondering how a crazy Marine Corps F/A-18 pilot on loan to one of the *Midway*'s Hornet squadrons would get quoted in *Newsweek*. "When he was asked whether he thought the US should go to war against Iraq, Lepp said, 'Can't save a dime, can't keep a girl, might as well go to war.' "

"No, did he *really* say that?" I asked incredulously.

"*Newsweek* says he did," said Gucci.

"He's crazy," I said.

"What would *you* have said?" Gucci asked me, looking for something a bit more profound than Lepp's caveman attitude.

"All I know is that if we fight, I hope we have the support of the American people. I don't want to hang my ass out on the line for something that nobody back home cares about," I said. Gucci and Ren nodded in agreement. We were haunted by the thought of Vietnam veterans coming home to confusion and facing resentment for what they believed was a war fought in support of freedom and democracy. Such a scene was more than my stomach could handle. And so, becoming involved in what might turn out to be an unpopular war was my greatest fear.

Across the ready room I saw Stealth attempting to disassemble his weapon. He was definitely not a "shooter" and he was also a loner. He was a mumbler and one of those people who is very difficult to talk with because you can barely understand what he's saying. This is not a good trait to have in a tactical aircraft where cockpit communication can either keep you alive or kill you. It was easy to see that nobody really understood Stealth, myself included. He was a lean, wiry guy, which had more to do with his vegetarian diet than any specific athletic workout schedule. He was considered an intelligent ECMO, but he did not relate well to the other aviators. I sensed that he felt he was in the wrong business, and he seemed woefully depressed because now a war loomed over us and he had nowhere to go.

After a while an imperceptible layer of oil made the blackness of the weapons shine brightly under the flicker of the ready room's fluorescent lights. We each had now thoroughly cleaned the Rugers and were ready to pack them away. The senior parachute rigger in the squadron had developed a gerry-rigged holster that would allow us to pack the Ruger into our survival vest without making it too uncomfortable in the cockpit. For now the Rugers would remain locked in a metal box, and after the brief for a mission, we would sign our weapons out from the SDO along with our ammunition. Drawing my weapon from the armory would now become a regular part of my habit pattern. We were one step closer to the war that now seemed imminent.

"Let's head back to the BK," said Ren.

"OK," I said. We dropped off our Rugers with Arnie, who checked them for all their parts and to see that all rounds were in the clips. Once we were outside the ready room Kamper and Horse came up behind us.

"I can't believe that prick is banning UMPQUA," said Kamper in a low but angry tone of voice. "He probably found out that we call him Alpha Charlie behind his back."

"He just feels insecure about having command," I piped in.

"Well, he should," Kamper said. "Without UMPQUA we definitely need a war to take our minds off of having such a jerk for a skipper. UMPQUA will simply have to go underground for a while. And even without the patches, the spirit will live on in the BKs."

"He certainly knows how to eliminate morale in one bold stroke," said Ren. Gucci took a left out of the ready room while the rest of us returned to the BK with thoughts of war in our heads. When I got back to the BK I wrote Alice the following letter:

29 Dec 90

Dear Alice,

I have no idea how long it is taking for my letters to reach you in New York. I hope that you have received a few of them by now and that there will be a fairly steady arrival rate until the next time I see you. Writing letters has always come easily to me more out of a sense of discipline than a sense of pleasure. However, writing to you is a great pleasure, and I find myself taking breaks every day to walk to the privacy of my room to write you a letter. To know that receiving a letter from me will make you smile is more than enough to make me write every day.

The squadron has started to involve me in the planning for possible strikes that our air wing may fly. I am working hard to learn lots of new things and do not seem to have time to sit back and think that we really may be going to war. The air wing is ready and so am I, but we all hope that it can be avoided. Your picture is so beautiful, and I miss you more with each passing day.

All my love, Sherm

CHAPTER TEN

Into the
Valley of
Death . . .

The veterans in the air wing who had been saying that they had seen it all before and that they expected Saddam Hussein to succumb to international pressure were now realizing that perhaps this time was indeed going to be different. The presidential deadline was less than twelve hours away and it looked like we were going to strike. This was one of the rare times when all eight of us were in the bunkroom at the same time.

"What do you think, Ren?" I asked. "Do you think we're going to make Iraq the biggest parking lot in the world?" The bunkroom was crowded. Everyone there was thinking about the upcoming challenges.

"Whatever we do, I just want to get on with it and get home," said Ren, who had just gotten engaged before the deployment and was scheduled to be married in July. The idea of a protracted conflict scared him more because such a war might interfere with his wedding plans than because of any danger he might be in from flying over enemy territory. The waiting and anticipation was tough, although I was sure it was not nearly as bad for us as it was for the guys on the ground in the desert. The infantry guys knew that Saddam Hussein had been fortifying his defenses since August, and now it was January and we were planning to attack. I did not envy them at all. They knew that Iraq had chemical and biological weapons and that it was not afraid to use them since it had used them regularly in its war against Iran. Those guys on the ground were the real heroes in my mind; the thought of this war from my perspective was downright civilized compared to what they would go through. I would fly my missions and if I did return, it would be to a hot meal, hot shower, and dry bed. I thought of the poor army and marine grunts whenever I got in the mood to complain about our situation. I knew that there were a lot of young Americans who had it much worse.

All the planning for the first few waves of strikes had been completed weeks earlier; now it was a matter of executing against real targets what we had practiced in the mirror-image missions. A question I needed to face now was whether or not I should write Alice a letter to be sent to her in case I got shot down. It was a tough decision to make. I knew that she would appreciate such a letter, but if I put my feelings on paper it would make it harder for her to let her memory of me fade. I decided that such an impassioned letter would only be selfish, and that I wanted her to wait for me only until the end of this deployment. It was too much to ask her to go through the long wait that might ensue if I were shot down and called missing in action.

So while Skippy, the only married guy in the BK, was writing to his wife, I lay in my rack and wondered on which strike my name would first appear. I knew that the first air wing strike called for three Prowlers—two go-birds and one spare—so I was sure that my name would not be on that mission list. But I also expected that the second strike would not be far behind this first predawn strike. So with only five pilots in our squadron, my name by necessity would come up quite quickly.

The skipper called a squadron meeting at 2200 in the ready room. We all rolled out of our racks a few minutes before and slipped on our flight suits and boots and rubbed our eyes to wake up as we stumbled single file down the passageway from the BK to the ready room. Kamper, Horse, Pokey, Ren, Lawboy, Arnie, Skippy, and I made up the "BK of the Stars." All of these guys were senior to me since I was still a lieutenant junior grade, and I felt happy to be a part of their group. We were all nervous with anticipation. None of us knew what lay ahead and yet we all felt the kind of excited apprehension that you feel on an athletic team before a big game. Not to belittle in any way the historical significance of an attack against Iraq, but from the junior officer perspective, from the young Americans in the cockpits on these aircraft carriers in the Persian Gulf and the air force and marine pilots on the ground in Saudi Arabia, it was game day. The adrenaline was flowing through our veins and we were ready to do what we had trained so hard to do; strike and win.

The ready room was abuzz by the time we got there. Gucci was one of the first people I saw. He grabbed me and said, "Tank, it's a go. CAG received the execute order and I'm going to fly in the first strike with Dawg, then do a quick brief so I can fly in the second strike with you, Skippy, and Wolfey just after dawn."

"Roger that," I said, not knowing what I should say upon hearing that I would soon be getting shot at by people who would like nothing more than to torture me for a few years if they got their hands on me. At the front of the ready room was "the lineup." Damn, it even sounded like a baseball game. The starters were no surprise: our three most senior pilots, the Skipper, Dawg, and Horse were assigned to the first strike which would launch at 0100 with a time on the two targets of 0330, and back on deck at 0530. Most of our senior ECMOs, including Gucci, would go with them. The second major strike would launch as soon as possible after the first strike package returned. There was the grim realization that we might need to make changes, depending on the attrition rate for the first strike. Wolfey, Skippy, and I would plan to start briefing our mission at 0400 for a 0630 launch. We would need to fill in Gucci upon his return from his first mission with Dawg. Ren would fly in the same event with us but he would be going to a different target with a different strike package. The third mission would include the same crews as the first. These were the preplanned missions, the results of which would need to be evaluated before choosing the next targets.

"Attention on deck," shouted our new XO. Once again the skipper walked in the door and a sea of JOs parted in front of him as he advanced down the center aisle of the ready room. I had been caught up at the front of the room and needed to sidle out of his way as he approached the front. Like the rest of the JOs, I quickly scrambled for my chair.

"Take your seats," said the skipper as he strode toward the front of the ready room. Pointing behind himself he said, "As you can see, I have selected crews that will fly the first missions. At this point there are no indications that the strikes will continue beyond these first two initial events. But I have a strong feeling that they will. Good luck. Now I want to turn it over to Jiffy, who will explain a recommended evasion plan and hand out your blood chits."

The tall ensign intelligence officer from Colorado stood up and walked to the front of the ready room. But before he could say a word about the stack of papers in his hand, the 1MC in the corner of the ready room began to crackle. The small box came alive. "This is the captain speaking, attention on deck for the admiral." The 1MC was piped into every space on the ship. For the first time, many of the enlisted men onboard would now hear that we were actually going to enter a shooting war. "Within the last hour we have received the execute order to strike targets in southeastern Iraq as part of what will be called Operation Desert Storm. At this point I do not know how long this conflict will last, but I do know that the men on the *Midway* will do their utmost to defeat this enemy with dispatch. In a few short hours we will launch our first strike at the enemy. To the sailors and crew, keep alert and let's run the tightest of ships; and to the aviators, let's make each bomb count. I turn to the chaplain now for a benediction." There was a shuffling sound over the microphone and then the softer voice of a chaplain came on the airwaves.

"Lord, give these brave aviators the courage to carry out their difficult mission and the strength to return safely to their home here on the *Midway*. May you in your infinite wisdom bring peace with justice again soon to this troubled region of the world. Amen." It was a hopeful prayer and I believe echoed accurately the feeling of everyone on the ship that night.

The ensign cleared his throat at the front of the room, drawing our eyes back to him even though our minds were still focused on the admiral and the chaplain. Regardless of where our minds were he began his presentation. "What I have here is a 'blood chit.' During World War II, Korea, and Vietnam, American pilots used them as a negotiating tool. The blood chit itself was made from an indestructible fibrous paper. Each piece of paper has written in Arabic a statement that says if you guide this man safely alive to US troops or US allies, then the US government will pay you a cash reward of fifteen hundred dollars. So your average goatherder if he can read will probably help you out, unless the strike you were on killed his entire family," said the ensign with a nervous chuckle that was not returned by the rest of the ready room.

After handing out the serial-numbered "blood chits," the intelligence officer reached into a second file folder and pulled out another set of papers. "I also have brought your personal security folders for review and update. As you know, the information on this card will be used by special forces to authenticate your identity before effecting a rescue. The number that you choose and sentences that you write should be personal in nature and should identify you clearly to rescuers." He passed the stack of folders out and I looked at mine closely. All the official name, rank, and serial-number data were correct, then my eyes moved down the page to the personal section. I had my own personal number which I would never forget even after a few days in captivity. I just hoped that I would be able to add and subtract correctly after a few days in the desert. The identifying sentences I used were strictly personal: "My first dog was named Honey. My first at-bat in Little League I hit a home run. My first car was a Red Toyota Supra." These were the kind of personal memories that I would not forget even in a stressful situation and that nobody else would know about.

Within a few minutes everyone had verified their cards and the skipper stood up once again. "The XO and I have carefully selected the crews that are flying these missions because we believe that you can handle it. We have decided to set up a rotating SDO watch with Pokey and Stealth sharing the duty on a twelve-on, twelve-off, rotation. This will allow the rest of you to focus on your flying

In-flight refueling, also known as tanking, is one of the trickiest parts of flying lengthy missions from an aircraft carrier. Here an EA-6B Prowler approaches the extended basket of an Air Force KC-10 tanker. A majority of the tanking during the Persian Gulf War was conducted by the KC-135, which has a much shorter hose than the KC-10. The different design characteristics of the KC-135 tanking system made it more difficult for Navy jets to tank, a fact that gave rise to the KC-135 being nicknamed the "Iron Maiden." *Courtesy U.S. Navy*

The pilot of the Prowler has successfully "plugged" the basket, enabling him to refuel. *Courtesy U.S. Navy*

` The Fresnel lens, known as the "meatball," is the visual-landing-aid system that provides the carrier pilot with glide-scope information on final approach. *Courtesy U.S. Navy*

Two EA-6B Prowlers flying in section cruise formation. A much tighter formation is used when breaking the deck. *Courtesy U.S. Navy*

The mission of the EA-6B Prowler is to Suppress Enemy Air Defenses (SEAD). The Prowler accomplishes this mission by using jamming as a "soft kill" technique and by firing High-speed Anti-Radiation Missiles (HARM) as a "hard kill" technique. By degrading or destroying enemy radar systems, the Prowler creates a safer path to the target for the bomber aircraft. *Courtesy U.S. Navy*

An F/A-18 Hornet poised for launch from one of the USS *Midway*'s two bow catapults. *Courtesy U.S. Navy*

This photo, taken in the Pacific Ocean in 1984, shows the different types of aircraft, grouped together on the flight deck of the USS *Midway*. Aircraft shown are F-4 Phantom II, EA-6B Prowler, A-6 Intruder, E-2 Hawkeye, and SH-3 Sea King helicopter. *Courtesy U.S. Navy*

The USS *Midway* back in 1947 before it was rebuilt with a modern angled flight deck. *Courtesy U.S. Navy*

An aerial shot of the USS *Midway* taken in the Indian Ocean in 1979 clearly shows the angled flight deck. *Courtesy U.S. Navy*

The crew of the USS *Midway* posed for a photograph on the ship's bow while sailing in the Arabian Gulf in 1987. By 1987 the USS *Midway's* air wing had added the new F/A-18 Hornet and retired the F-4 Phantoms and A-7 Corsairs. This air wing composition was what the USS *Midway* had during Operation Desert Storm. *Courtesy U.S. Navy*

An aerial shot of the USS *Midway* and the USS *Independence* docked in Pearl Harbor, Hawaii. It is easy to see how much smaller the USS *Midway* is than the USS *Independence*. *Courtesy U.S. Navy*

Navy ordnanceman loading an AGM-88 HARM missile onto an EA-6B Prowler. *Courtesy U.S. Navy*

ADC Doug "Rat" Rathbun, aka "Chief Rat" (*left*), and LTJG Rob "Beast" Smith (*right*) were key players in ensuring the aircraft for VAQ-136 kept flying during the heavy demands of combat flight operations. *Courtesy U.S. Navy*

BELOW LEFT: Here I am in the cockpit of an EA-6B Prowler getting ready for a mission shortly after Operation Desert Storm. *Courtesy U.S. Navy*

BELOW RIGHT: The photograph of Alice that she sent to me while I was on board the USS *Midway*. *Norine R. Toole*

and mission planning. And remember, if we do our mission effectively, then we should bring everyone on this ship home with us
once the shooting has stopped. The first group of crews brief in
half an hour. Good luck and fly safe."

The meeting broke up quickly after the skipper left the ready
room. Ren and I walked back to the BK together. I understood
Pokey but not Stealth. "What's the deal with Stealth? Why is he
standing watch?" I asked Ren.

"I heard that he quit."

"But he's still wearing his wings," I observed.

"You've got a point there. Maybe he's med down," said Ren,
giving Stealth the benefit of the doubt that the flight surgeon might
have actually grounded him for medical reasons.

"Well, if he did quit, it would be for the best. From what I've
heard, he's a liability in the air. He could get somebody killed," I
said.

"Yeah, you're right about that."

I wondered if one of the grunts on the ground could just decide
to quit. I wondered what would happen if one day a soldier just
woke up and said he had had enough, that he would like to stop
now. I bet his commander in the field would court martial him for
cowardice. Apparently, it was different in naval aviation. I suppose
the navy assumed we were all crazy to begin with. After all, one
could make a strong case that anyone who volunteered to fly jets
off a ship at sea was already crazy. So when someone said he had
had enough of naval aviation, he proved himself sane and could
keep his wings. I guess things had changed, because it did not work
that way for Yossarian in *Catch-22*.

Once we were back in the BK I looked at my watch. I had several
hours to sleep before my brief at 0400. Yet I was not confident that
I would be able to get any rest. My mind was filled with images of
not only my upcoming mission, but also of the men who were
preparing to hit the hornet's nest. The thought of being in the
second strike did not appeal to me. It was like following the daring
kid who ran up and smacked a hornet's nest with a stick and then
handed you the stick and dared *you* to do it. Now, of course, the

hornets were all pissed off and ready to sting anything that came near their nest. This second strike in the daytime was the same type of situation. The first strike would go in under cover of night and spank the Iraqis, and they would just be getting their heads up again and their sights recalibrated when we would fly overhead a few hours later.

"Hey, Ren, this second strike in the daytime plan really sucks," I said.

"Yeah, I know what you mean. Those Iraqis are going to be really pissed off by the time we get there."

"Exactly what I was thinking," I responded. The questions kept popping into my mind to ask my fellow Prowler guys. *What was the AAA like? Did you see any SAMs launched? What radars were radiating? Were there any radars up that you were surprised by?* The A-6 guys were going in low on this first night in a traditional A-6 Intruder attack. This initial low attack was where heroes would be made. What would be the attrition rate? How many would not make it home?

It was frustrating to me that our jamming and missile system on the Prowler was only capable of defeating and destroying surface-to-air-missile sites. It had no real effectiveness in protecting the strikers from antiaircraft artillery and small-arms fire, which was really the greatest threat on the type of low-level attack they had planned. I had mixed feelings about my role as a Prowler pilot. A big part of me wanted to be piloting a bomber that would fly through the worst of the flak and AAA and drop my bombs on target, whatever it might be. It would be the A-6 guys who would win the Distinguished Flying Crosses, if there were any to be won. But another part of me was glad that my mission, called SEAD—Suppression of Enemy Air Defenses—was a directed mission against definite military targets. We would jam radars that were illuminating strikers and then shoot antiradiation missiles at those radars. I liked the fact that the weapons I would fire would be directed against someone who was definitely and actively trying to shoot at me and my comrades. However, compared to the grunt on the ground, any pilot's version of war is a clean and sterile one at best. I didn't know how I would react if I had to look at a man's eyeballs as I stabbed him with my KBar knife or my bayonet. Once again, even though flying off a floating hunk of steel was crazy in and of itself, I was glad to be resting on the *Midway* before my first look at combat, rather than being curled up in a foxhole.

The time disappeared as I sat there in a small web beach chair watching the PLAT—Pilot Landing-Aid Television—and thinking about the morality of warfare. The TV sat atop our bunkroom refrigerator. No one knew when the refrigerator had been placed in the room, but the earliest dated sticker was one from the 1988 Olympics in Seoul, South Korea. It had probably not been cleaned in the intervening years. How many other JOs had sat and stared at this same TV, wondering if the jet just launched would ever come back? I didn't know the answer but I felt as if I were sharing feelings with a lot of fellow aviators from the past.

I could hear the level of activity picking up on flight deck. It was the first strike beginning to man-up their aircraft. I looked at my watch; half an hour before launch. Soon the air boss would start the same old litany that each aviator on the flight deck had heard before: "Let's man your aircraft for the 0100 launch. Stand clear of jet intakes and watch out for jet exhaust. . . ." Only this time the launch would definitely be different. The atmosphere would be more serious, and what smiles were made would be fleeting and nervous. In some ways I felt it was worse to be in my rack imagining all of this rather than being on the deck experiencing it. It would only be another few hours before my turn would come.

I sat there listening to the sounds of the flight deck and watching television as jets laden with bombs taxied in a serpentine pattern across the deck. The clackety-clack-clack-hiss of the catapult being tested, the whirring noise of the jet blast deflector being raised and lowered, tie-down chains rattling across the steel deck, and the high-pitched screech of huffer carts used to start the jets were all familiar sounds, yet tonight they sounded more purposeful and deliberate. Within a few minutes the first two A-6 Intruders were on the bow catapults. The standard flurry of activity was taking place around the jets as the pace of the yellowshirt's "taxi forward" signal became slower and slower. The hold-back fitting was now taut on the first A-6 and the yellowshirt gave the tension signal as the A-6 went to full power. My stomach tightened as I watched and realized that I would be testing out my controls on the catapult in a few hours. Once the controls had been checked the pilot switched on his lights, the yellowshirt touched the deck, and the catapult fired. The glow of the A-6 tailpipes disappeared into the blackness and fuzz of the TV screen.

One after another their engines roared to life, then came the clackety-clack-clack-hiss of the catapult stroke followed by the roar of another engine and the clackety-clack-clack-hiss of the next catapult shot. The noise was repeated every thirty seconds until more than twenty *Midway* aircraft had been launched. Then there was a pause and quiet as if the *Midway* were breathing a mother's deep, tearful sigh having sent her children off to war and praying for their safe return.

It was awful not being part of the first strike, but I knew my turn would come soon enough, and I also knew that I needed to get some sleep. So I switched off the TV and jumped into my rack. In between flight deck sounds I intermittently heard the splash of a single drop of water on the plastic sheet above my bed. Whenever I was close to dozing off, the drop of water would splash again. It was a form of Chinese water torture that I had not yet gotten accustomed to, so my mind kept racing.

The first four days and nights of strikes were already scheduled. There was little planning to do for the next few days; it was pure execution. After the first few days we would then begin the constant process of battle damage assessment in order to determine which targets to hit next. As an air wing we had practiced and practiced our plans, so we were confident in what we were doing. We only hoped that Iraqi air defense would be less effective than we anticipated. They had been fortifying their positions since August and the presidential deadline left little to guesswork. They knew we were coming and knew where we were coming from. Perhaps they doubted our resolve? Perhaps they never thought we would really attack? Our squadron's job was to ensure that every *Midway* aircraft that launched came back safely. If we did our job of suppressing Iraqi air defenses, their surface-to-air missiles would be ineffective, their fighters would not have the support of ground-based search radars, and our guys would get in and out unharmed.

Our strike plans were good because they were simple and straightforward. One of the targets this night was an airfield in southeastern Iraq that had some Iraqi fighters on the ramp. It was going to be a traditional low-altitude A-6 attack. I felt nervous just thinking about it; the guys airborne now must be really wired. The attitude in the air wing over the past month had been low key and matter of fact. During that time it had been interesting to watch people and see how they reacted to increasing pressure and the realization that war lay ahead. Most of the guys in the air wing were ready and willing to fight, but there were some who did not share our enthusiasm.

Stealth was the guy in our squadron who decided that combat was not for him. Rather than turning in his wings, he developed a mysterious inner-ear medical problem. We all thought him a coward, but we were perhaps harder on him than was fair. In reality, it was probably a good thing that he would not fly with us because he would have endangered any mission that he was on. It took a lot of courage for him to admit that he was not able to fly under combat conditions.

I had no right to judge him, but I did anyway. I had certainly not yet proven myself in combat. Perhaps Stealth knew himself better than I knew myself. Maybe I would panic and lose control when I came under fire. I would not know until I was there. Stealth made all of us nervous even though we didn't talk about it. We were all trained and ready to face the pressures of combat, yet the question lingered in the back of each aviator's mind: *Can I handle it?* I hoped that Stealth would be removed from the ship, but we soon realized that he would continue to wear his wings and stay onboard throughout the remainder of the deployment.

Half a world away, Alice was studying hard in law school and watching CNN. I knew she too was wondering if I could handle combat. After seeing footage of the first strike on Iraq, she wrote me the following letter:

17 Jan 91

Dear Sherm,

Well, it's war. What an unbelievable scene! I've seen it all today. They even showed the night attack on Bhagdad. You all are very BRAVE people. Now Saddam has attacked Israel. He is a true barbarian. I imagine you will have unbelievable stories to tell.

I received your New Year's Eve letter today. Wow—HAPPY NEW YEAR from the Gulf! Hopefully sometime in the next few years you'll be spending a New Year's Eve somewhere with Alice instead of on some boat waiting for war.

Well, Sherman, the next time I see you I'll bring the champagne and I imagine it will be the best ever!

People are behind the forces over there and everyone is constantly glued to the TV. This is an unbelievable experience for everyone here, but for you all out there it must be something else. Who knows when you'll get this and who knows what the state of affairs will be. I just hope that you will be OK. I really am only certain of one thing right now and that's that I love you, and I want to tell you that in person.

Love, Alice

CHAPTER ELEVEN
What You Don't See Will Kill You

Slam-screech-roar-whirr! woke me up from a deep sleep. It was the sound of a jet landing. *Slam* was the wheels and tailhook hitting the *Midway*'s steel deck; *screech* was the violent squeal of the hydraulically powered arresting gear as the jet's tailhook dragged the steel cable down the deck; *roar* was the jet's engines spooling up to full power; and the eventual *whirr* was the cable retracting to its original position in preparation for the next jet. I looked at my watch; it was only 0345—something was wrong. The first strike package should just be egressing from the target; not landing. *Slam-screech-roar-whirr!* Another jet had landed.

"Ren, what the hell is going on," I asked. I jumped out of my rack and turned on the PLAT screen in our room as the two A-6s taxied around the deck with some hung ordnance. "They must have had a system failure. I think that's CAG's jet," I said, referring to the commander of the air group.

"I don't know, but let's go up to the ready room and find out," said Ren, who was getting dressed.

"Yeah, we're briefing soon anyway," I said as I slipped on my flight suit and laced up my boots. By the time we got to the ready room there were some other interested faces glued to the television screen watching the A-6s shutting down their engines. It was a disheartening sight to see these warhorses return to the ship with their bombs still hanging on the wing. But CAG had flown throughout Vietnam, so we were confident that something major had happened to make him turn away from the target. It demonstrated a level of maturity and patience that was a valuable lesson to all of the more junior aviators. There is a fine line between being brave and being foolhardy. We learned later that both CAG's aircraft and the spare aircraft had been unable to get their bombing systems or ECM suite to work, and that after struggling with the systems for the first two hours of the flight, CAG decided it would be best to try it again later. Without being able to bomb accurately or to detect SAM launches, CAG knew that the mission would be unsuccessful at best and suicidal at worst. Knowing that the air wing would view it as a great disappointment, he had made a truly brave decision, for he saved the lives not only of his crew but also that of the spare jet's crew, who probably would not have had the guts to turn around if CAG had not done so himself. CAG's wingmen, Bucket and Kooz, pressed the attack on an airfield in Kuwait all by themselves.

Our gaggle brief started at 0400 in the Chippy's ready room because their skipper, Simba—my old friend—was going to lead the strike. It was difficult to focus on the specifics of the brief because everyone was thinking about our squadron mates who had just dropped their bombs and shot their missiles and were now desperately trying to fly away from their targets in Iraq and Kuwait without getting shot down. Maybe some of them had been hit. We wouldn't know for sure for another half hour or so.

I had helped plan the mission we were about to fly, so I was familiar with the target and knew the tactics. The Air Tasking Order had been sent out to the *Midway* late the night before from the air campaign's headquarters in Riyadh. The staffers in Riyadh picked the targets and it was our job to figure out how to best take them out. On this strike, the Prowlers were to conduct a Suppression of Enemy Air Defenses (SEAD) mission along with a section of Hornets acting as HARM shooters and the main strike package would use laser-guided bombs to destroy a major Iraqi communications node in southeastern Iraq near Basra. Once Simba had briefed the big picture and the logistics of the combined air wing action, the group split into smaller element groups. We went back to our ready room to brief the SEAD element.

Ren was not very happy about the combat crew assignments, because he had been put in the new XO's crew. He would be under close scrutiny, but it also meant that he would certainly get to go on some good missions. The XO gave the overall SEAD brief detailing the expected locations of the variety of surface-to-air missiles (SA-2s, SA-3s, and SA-6s) in the area of the strike. The Hornets and Prowlers would have several preplanned HARM missile shots that would attempt to hard kill radar sites associated with the surface-to-air missiles. The preplanned shots would be fired on a detailed timeline in order to offer maximum protection to ingressing bombers. A steady rain of missiles would shower down on any Iraqi radar that chose to come up during the three and a half minutes strikers were in the heart of the SAM envelope. Or at least that was the theory.

Slam-screech-thud-whirr! The recovery of the first strike had begun. The XO finished up his brief and answered questions that some of the Hornet pilots had about their preemptive HARM shots. Our ready room slowly emptied as the aircrew from other squadrons headed back to their own ready rooms in order to brief the final small details of the mission, such as emergency procedures, and to clear up any last-minute rendezvous or tanking questions.

One after another the jets returned, and within a few minutes both of our Prowlers were safely on deck. Before long we heard an announcement over the 1MC: "Recovery complete, recovery complete. All Event-One aircraft launched have landed." A small cheer went up in the ready room as we all hoped that the same thing would happen on our launch. This was a streak nobody wanted to break. I finished briefing with my crew and we all split up to follow our individual rituals. My ritual was becoming second nature. I was about to leave the ready room to make a head call when a roar erupted from the A-6 ready room next door.

My curiosity got the better of me as I opened the door that separated the two ready rooms and poked my head around the corner. There watching the TV screen were about twelve of the A-6 JOs. "Hey, Tank, come here. This is some great footage of our strike," said Regbo, one of the A-6 pilots who had taken the low, and extremely dangerous, route to the airfield target. I couldn't believe it. I was about to fly my mission and could watch the previous strike on videotape. It was a homemade video because Regbo had convinced his parachute riggers to design a custom-fitted holder that would enable him to place his camcorder in the cockpit to film his mission.

I was drawn to the television, which had mostly a black screen with a faint glow of red on the lower part from the cockpit's instrumentation. The comm between the pilot and the BN was slow and measured, but soon the tempo began to pick up as did the brightness of the screen because the Iraqis started shooting. The sky lit up with tracers and flares, and the tone of Regbo's voice and Viktor, his BN, also began to raise the level of tension. The view from the camcorder was straight out over the nose, and the arcing lines of AAA tracers and SAM launches were alarming to watch. The camera angle twisted quickly and irregularly as Regbo flew his jet in a jinking maneuver so as to make it a difficult target for the Iraqis shooting at them from the ground.

As they approached the target both Regbo and Viktor switched to hot mike so that they didn't need to press a switch to talk on the intercom. As a result, their breathing as well as their words conveyed the fear they were feeling. "Small-arms fire coming up on the left," said Regbo, "and, on the right."

"Roger, keep moving. Steering is now to the target eight miles to go," said Viktor.

"Barrage fire ahead," gasped Regbo. "Breaking left."

"No! No! Break right, break right, SAM at three o'clock!" shouted Viktor. "Keep the pull on, not tracking, it's not tracking us. Press to the target. Five miles to go."

"Waiting for the hammer," said Regbo as he anxiously anticipated dropping their bombs.

"I'm in attack mode now," said Viktor, having switched his

display to better provide the necessary information for the attack.

"Roger," said Regbo. "Shit, jinking," said Regbo, responding to heavy AAA tracers off the nose of the jet. Regbo rolled the jet almost ninety degrees to slice through the hail of bullets. *Beep-beep-beep!* went the radar altimeter, followed by, "Shit, I got it!" as Regbo pulled up, nearly hitting the rising terrain.

"Three miles to target. Keep it moving, lots of shit coming up at us," said Viktor, who felt that with all the bullets in their area the A-6 loaded with bombs was not moving fast enough for his liking.

"I've got the throttles to the stops," said Regbo. Then the light show really began—on the screen it was like thousands of fireflies over a field at night. They were closing on their target airfield and it was obviously well defended. AAA and small-arms fire intensified and the TV's screen started to flash and glow. "We're getting close, and they're pissed!"

"I'm completely inside now," said Viktor as he lowered his head to the radar screen, hoping to acquire the target. He began preparing weapons to be linked to the A-6's bombing system for a release calculated by the computer to ensure the best trajectory and the most damage.

"Roger, I'm committed. Now we're on government time, Viktor," said Regbo, realizing that this was what he got paid for. He handed control of the weapons' release to the computer and continued to jink violently, avoiding outbursts of fire whenever he could see them. Another few seconds and they were over the airfield and the A-6 delivered its bombs on target on time. Regbo pulled up and away as aggressively as he could, probably overstressing the airframe, but it didn't matter, because they had survived. I looked at my watch and swore under my breath. It was my turn.

"Way to go, Regbo, great job, Viktor—gotta go flying," I said with as much of an upbeat sound in my voice as I could muster, having just witnessed the hornet's nest our strike would be entering. The communications node we were striking was not all that far from the airfield that Regbo and Viktor had just nailed, so I was sure that the Iraqis would not be pleased to see us.

"Take it to 'em, Tank," shouted Viktor as I left the Eagles' ready room.

I was scared. Skippy and Wolfey were almost finished getting into their flight gear when I entered the room. "I just watched a video of the A-6 strike. Looking on the bright side, I think we either have God on our side, or these Iraqis have really poor aim, because with all the crap they shot up in the air it's a miracle they didn't shoot our guys down."

"Great," said Skippy. "Let's pray that they won't get better with practice."

I had now flown with my Ruger in my survival vest for the past two weeks, but it still felt heavy and uncomfortable. The only place for the holster was in a front pocket of the vest. I didn't quite have the same full stick deflection aft that I wanted, because pulling straight back on the stick made my hand hit the protruding bulge of the holstered weapon. The other pilots had the same complaint, but it looked like one of those things we were simply going to have to work around and compensate for. I was confident that once the adrenaline was coursing through my veins I would have no problem achieving full stick deflection.

The skipper's crew and Dawg's crew had just entered maintenance control and were discussing problems they had experienced with their jets. Now dressed for the flight, I walked up to them and listened to what they had to say. The only thing that concerned me was that Dawg's jet, the one I would be flying, had trouble with the initial alignment of its Inertial Navigation System (INS). They were forced to input the ship's course, speed, and position manually instead of taking it electronically from a cable linked to the ship's own INS. It wasn't that much of a problem, but at least I knew we would have to watch our navigation closely. I flipped through the ADB and with my good-luck pen signed the acceptance sheet, taking responsibility for the aircraft and my crew. It was the first time going flying that I let the thought enter my mind that I might not come back.

"Tank, we've got to keep our eyes out of the cockpit, and watch out for the oil platforms near Bubiyan Island. They were shooting at us the entire time we were in our jamming orbit. Remember, what you don't see will kill you," said Gucci, who now, after just returning, had to climb right back in the jet with us. We had agreed that Skippy would brief Gucci while I preflighted our jet, so I turned for the hatch to the flight deck.

"Tank, we had to evade an SA-2 that started tracking us," said Arnie. "Just watch for the flash on the ground, and soon you'll be able to tell whether or not it's coming after you."

All I could do was nod and say, "I'll keep my eyes open." I felt completely intimidated as I tried to disengage from the group so I could focus on what lay ahead.

As I walked toward the hatch leading to the flight deck I felt a tug on my arm. It was Beast. He had been watching the entire sequence of events and could tell that I needed encouragement. He looked me in the eye and said, "Don't break my jet," followed by a wink and a pat on the back that made me laugh. I was thankful that I could still recognize sarcasm in my heightened state of nerves. Beast had known just the right thing to say to break the tension for me.

"Don't worry, I'll bring it back up and up," I said, referring to both the front- and backseat systems of the Prowler as I opened the hatch and felt the rush of warm salty air enter the passageway. The flight deck was busy as always, but combat exposed an added dimension now. The ordies were loading real bombs and missiles onto the *Midway*'s aircraft. There was no more practice; this was for real, and the ordies stepped smartly around the deck, realizing that their job was now an indispensable part of the *Midway*'s mission.

Chief Rat and Clement stepped up to greet me at the front of the Prowler. "Sir, we think the alignment problem for the last crew was a cable problem. We're in a different spot for this launch so a different cable should give you a good alignment."

"Sounds good—everything else look OK?" I asked.

"Looks great, sir. She's ready to kick some Iraqi butt," said Clement with an enthusiastic grin. Airman Moren, the plane captain for this Prowler, followed me around the jet during my preflight inspection to make sure that if I spotted anything wrong he would quickly find the best person on the maintenance team to come and inspect the problem. The jet looked sharp. It was clear that the plane captain had worked hard to prepare this Prowler for its mission. My preflight was another ritual that I had developed in which I started at the left engine intake and worked my way around the jet clockwise until I ended back where I had started. This time the yellowshirts had parked this jet TOW, which meant "tail over the water," so I couldn't check all the things that I normally checked when I inspected the aircraft tail.

As I ducked under the tail I noticed the glow of the sun to the east on the horizon. I stopped what I was doing and took a deep breath. The sun was coming up again even though there was a war going on. Even though I was in the middle of war, the sun was still rising in the morning and setting in the evening. I believed in what I was about to do; I believed we were doing the right thing by trying to unseat Saddam Hussein from Kuwait; and I believed that it was important for the world community to condemn this kind of unbridled aggression. For the first time in my life I was being confronted by evil in the world. But the sun would keep rising and setting whether or not we risked our lives flying in between Iraqi bullets.

"Hey, Lieutenant, anything wrong?" asked Airman Moren still following me around.

"No, just enjoying the sunrise," I said. I am a pragmatist at heart, and I knew that the only way to get Saddam Hussein out of Kuwait was to kick him out, and that is exactly what we intended to do. I completed my preflight inspection of the jet and everything looked good.

I cinched tight the chest strap of my torso harness and tucked the loose end of the strap under itself. I had become accustomed to the forty-plus pounds of survival gear a long time ago, but now it was definitely heavier than it ever had been before. A large part of it was the Ruger pistol and two clips of ammunition that I had stuffed in the front of my survival vest. But a great deal of the new weight was extra survival gear that I had added out of fear of getting shot down. The other things I carried were personal items such as additional water bottles, an extra pair of socks, sun block, a hat and gloves to protect me from sunburn, sunglasses, a Swiss Army knife, a Bic lighter, a Snickers bar, some fishing leader and a hook, and some sponges to help with water collection. This personal gear was in addition to the standard-issue US Navy gear which was quite extensive, including a variety of flares and other signaling devices. The survival vest added to the weight of the G-suit, leg restraints, torso harness, helmet, and oxygen mask which were standard carrier-pilots' gear.

With my torso harness tight I then zipped up my survival vest, buckled the waist straps, and climbed up the Prowler's ladder to the boarding platform. After going through a quick twelve-point visual check to the ejection seat, I carefully removed the eight pins that mechanically safed the seat's explosive rocket motors, and stowed them in a storage bin alongside an extra bottle of water. I then contorted my body to fit under the canopy and into the seat. The habit pattern continued, and as I had done hundreds of times before in different navy aircraft, I started to preflight my cockpit. Starting at the back left, I touched every switch, making sure that it was in the right position for start-up. In primary flight training we had done a blindfold cockpit check in which we would need to run through our emergency procedures without seeing the switches. We had been told it was to simulate a situation where you might have smoke in the cockpit and couldn't see anything. So now in the Prowler my fingers could tell just by feeling the switch which one it was and whether it was in the right position. This took me about two minutes to complete. Gucci had just climbed into the cockpit, so I needed to give him a minute to get settled. He scanned the space quickly and checked the switches that were critical, then leaned toward me and said, "Ready for power." I leaned over the edge of the canopy rail and gave the power signal to the plane captain.

Within ten minutes we had started our engines, gotten a good alignment on the INS, and were ready to taxi to the catapult. The *Midway*'s deck was running incredibly smoothly. Of course, I had nothing to compare it with because this was the first fleet carrier I had ever been on. But all the chiefs and more experienced aviators were saying that the *Midway*'s deck crew was the best they had ever seen. I felt fortunate to be in their hands as the yellowshirts passed me up the deck toward the bow catapult.

Once again the familiar kick of the catapult slammed my head back, and we were flying. By Persian Gulf standards it was a cool, clear dawn, so the rendezvous and tanking were relatively easy. By now I had become proficient enough at dealing with the Iron Maiden so that I didn't break the jet's refueling probe when I disengaged. After completing our tanking we joined up with our HVU CAP, a section of Hornets that were primarily focused on two preemptive HARM launches to help keep the Iraqis' heads down when our bombers flew over the target. We also carried a HARM for a preemptive launch against an SA-3 that was in the area of the target.

Our jamming orbit would be right off the coast of Bubiyan Island in southeastern Iraq. We would be directly overhead several oil platforms that had reportedly been sending up a significant amount of AAA. Our intelligence was that the Iraqis had placed lots of radar-guided 76mm and 57mm cannons on these platforms and some shoulder-fired SAMs since the Iraqi invasion of Kuwait in August. Now these oil-platform gunners were getting their chance to take potshots at us. But that was not my worst fear. We would be flying at an altitude of nineteen thousand feet which would be above most of the AAA. My worst fear was from fighters. The Iraqis had a small, but technologically advanced, air force, thanks to the former Soviet Union. The thought of a MIG-29 Fulcrum or an Su-27 Flanker on my tail was terrifying because I did not have any way to defend myself other than diving for the deck in the hopes that I could scrape them off my tail at low altitude.

We all knew that the first aircraft they would want to shoot down was the Prowler because we would be jamming their air defense radars. If they could eliminate us then their SAMs would have an easier time targeting our bombers. This is why the US Navy called their Prowlers High Value Units (HVUs) and kept a fighter CAP with them constantly. Our strike was going to attack an important node in the Iraqi command and control system, and if we could destroy it, we would significantly disrupt their communications along the main ingress corridor for many of our future strikes.

The hollowness in my stomach was now dissipating as we flew

into the morning sky. The act of flying always made me feel better, no matter how poor I felt on the catapult. It was the reassuring feeling of my hands on the stick and throttle, knowing that I now controlled not only my own destiny, but also that of three other men as well. I thrived on the feeling of responsibility and independence. The Prowler was a very solid aircraft and its bulk made me feel confident in the air as its wingtips sliced through another thin wisp of a cloud. My right thumb continually flicked the electronic trim button on the top of the stick in an effort to balance the jet perfectly in the air. At just the right moment I rolled aggressively to the left and intercepted the next heading en route to our HARM launch point. Even though I was scared, I knew this was where I belonged.

"Let's go through the combat checklist," said Gucci.

"Roger," I said. We had been using this checklist for the past few weeks, but it had seemed unreal until now. This day we all realized that any one of the items on this list could save our lives, so we focused and paid attention.

"Stow all loose gear," challenged Gucci.

"All set here," I said.

"Good in back," said Skippy.

"O2 on and visor down," said Gucci.

"All set," I said, followed by, "Good in back," from Skippy. The checklist went through the essential items in the cockpit and it took only a few minutes to complete.

"The nav is tight. Just did a radar update off of the tip of Failaka Island and we are right on. Follow steering," said Gucci, satisfied that things were starting off well on our first mission. The steering needle superimposed on my compass rotated freely and gave me drift-corrected headings to fly based on the information calculated by the onboard computer. ECMOs loved to tell pilots to just follow steering. Some pilots just listened; I usually asked a few questions.

"What are the winds?" I asked.

"260 at thirty-five knots according to the INS," responded Gucci. That corresponded closely with the forecast winds at this altitude and I felt satisfied that the steering was good.

"Great," I said. "Is the chaff and flare program set up?"

"Yeah, the system is set up as briefed," said Gucci. Our squadron had decided to use a preprogrammed system that would deploy both chaff and flares to protect us from the widest array of possible threats.

"Picking up a lot of activity on the system," said Skippy nonchalantly from the back. That meant that the Iraqi search and acquisition radars were up and ready. The hornet's nest was buzzing and we knew we could expect a warm welcome.

"Liberty has picture clean," said the controller from the E-2C Hawkeye who was monitoring the air warfare picture. This just meant that as far as he could tell, no enemy fighters had launched or were in the vicinity, based on the lack of electronic signature of their search radar.

"That's good to hear," I said as we flew into the ever-brightening morning.

"Two minutes to jammers on time," said Gucci.

"Roger that, we are good to go in the back," replied Skippy. I looked out to the left and right to find my two Hornet escorts above and behind me. We were on our timeline and heading to the outer point of our jamming orbit where at times approximately one minute apart we would launch our HARM missiles. The staggered shots would ensure blanket coverage of the target area during the strikers' most vulnerable time when they were closest to their targets. There was another Prowler/Hornet SEAD package to the south of our orbit position which would cover the strike package's egress route from the target with more jamming and HARM missiles.

"Master RAD switch is on, we are jamming," said Skippy. "All primary assignments look good. We've got good power out of all pods."

"Roger that," I said with a smile. It was comforting to know that the only thing the Iraqi radar operators were seeing now was some snow on their screens. We hit the outer orbit point on time and I pulled a sharp left turn to bring the jet around to a heading of 284 degrees and started to focus on the HARM launch. Since it was a preemptive launch we had preprogrammed the launch point and target site, so we simply needed to be at the right place at the right time in order to hit our target.

"Master Arm is on, ready for launch in a minute plus thirty," said Gucci. "Got some triple A off the nose, going hot mike."

"Roger, I'm jinking." I responded by yanking the stick in sporadic directions in order to make us an unpredictable target. "Shit. That flak is exploding above us. Going hot mike too." My labored and heavy breathing now filled the cockpit and I felt that my crew could also hear the sound of my heart beating in my throat. At nineteen thousand feet we knew we would be out of the range of the small-arms fire and we had expected to be out of the range of whatever AAA they could have located on the oil platforms below. It was clear we were wrong. The barrage fire from what must have been a 100mm cannon was creating harmless-looking black clouds of smoke slightly above our altitude. Any one of these little black clouds would have ruined our day if it had hit us. The small puffs started to become more frequent, and I began to feel that we were indeed in the hornet's nest.

"Just keep jinking. Forty-five seconds to our inner orbit launch point," said Gucci.

"Roger," I said. The Prowler was handling well and I was maneuvering it in an unpredictable manner as I attempted to avoid the flak. I knew that our jamming was most effective when I was able to fly with my wings level, so I was trying to balance the need to keep my wings level for jamming and yet at the same time use jinking maneuvers to avoid getting shot down.

"Weapon station number two is selected, you have your needles," said Gucci. I maneuvered the Prowler to the left as we closed on our launch point. The crosshair needles of my ADI slowly moved together to the center of the display. The INS digital range display flicked from one to zero and my trigger finger resolutely squeezed the trigger on the stick. Having never launched a HARM missile before I was a little unsure of what to expect. I knew there was going to be a brief delay, but after two seconds passed I knew something was wrong. I squeezed the trigger even harder and then yelled, "Shit! No launch—Gucci, check your switches!"

"The switches are good," said Gucci with indignation in his

voice. "Shit!—wait . . ." Every second we were late with the HARM shot was putting the strikers in jeopardy. If our missile was not launched in time its targeted radar might be able to launch and guide a SAM to kill one of our guys. We had also just entered an SA-2 envelope ourselves and we needed to turn around. Gucci flicked the switch again, redesignating the missile. My hand was still squeezing the trigger and as soon as the circuit was properly connected the missile's rocket motor ignited, and it was smoothly launched off the rail.

"Ironclaw, magnum," I called on the radio to warn my Hornet escorts that I had just launched our missile. I then slammed the stick to the left and pulled for all I was worth. The rapid onset of G's made me cough as I tried to breathe. Halfway through the turn I rolled wings level momentarily to scan for incoming SAMs. "No SAMs," I grunted and rolled aggressively back to my outbound heading. I couldn't believe that we had shot our HARM late. I prayed that the mistake had not cost someone his life. We continued to jam outbound from the target and completed one more orbit dodging the flak from the oil platform on the inbound leg. The computer tracked the estimated time to impact of our missile according to the preplanned profile it would fly. When the digital clock counting down the missile's time of light reached zero, Skippy's voice from the backseat said, "Signal's down on impact, call it a kill." The HARM had done its job. It had followed the radar signal to its source and, exploding on impact, destroyed the site.

Once the strikers had all called "feet wet" over the strike frequency we started to fly the specific return-to-force profile. I recognized Simba's voice making the "feet wet" call and realized that even if he didn't like being debriefed by LSOs, he was still a great pilot and strike lead. By flying at specific airspeeds, headings, and altitudes we were able to reassure our surface ships that we were good guys returning and not bad guys coming to sink them. We topped off with the air force airborne Texaco station and made our way back to Mother *Midway*.

When we got back to the ready room we soon learned that our late launch had not caused a problem and that all of our comrades had once again returned safely. Our crew breathed a collective sigh of relief as we headed to the wardroom to eat. Before leaving the ready room we each reminded the operations yeoman to log our flight time in our logbooks, using the traditional green ink denoting combat operations.

CHAPTER TWELVE
Night Strike

"Don't break my jet," shouted Beast as I walked out of the hatch to the flight deck. It had become a superstitious expression for Beast that seemed to keep his jets and aircrew coming back in one piece.

"I couldn't break it worse even if I tried," I said with more than a touch of sarcasm in my voice. Following the rest of my crew out, I slammed the hatch closed and pulled down the lever securing it. It was a black night, and I had just signed an acceptance sheet for a jet that had five major gripes on it from the crew that had just landed ten minutes ago. This was my first night strike and I had hoped that I would at least have an aircraft that was functioning properly for the flight. Beast had promised me that they were all problems that could be fixed prior to our launch, so the chain of trust began. I trusted Beast, who trusted Chief Rat, who trusted Clement, who trusted all of the young guys working on the jet. Holding the handrail I climbed the steep ladder up to the catwalk along the edge of the flight deck. The recovery had ended only a few minutes before and the deck was already filled with flashlights of different colors, adding to the scene an image of fireworks at eye level without the noise of explosions.

The jet was parked on Elevator One next to the island, so from where I had climbed up out of the port catwalk I had to cross the flight deck to the starboard side cautiously. The amber lights of the tower's superstructure shed light on the Prowler and I groaned audibly at the scene I saw. There were thirty minutes left until launch, and before me was a decrepit-looking jet jacked up without a right main-mount tire. The Prowler's cheek panels and engine bay doors were all open. Two or three men were inspecting inside each door, and other men were scurrying back and forth retrieving parts and replacement components from various maintenance shops below the flight deck. It was an ugly scene, but this was my jet and I was determined to take it flying, so I needed to be upbeat with the men.

Chief Rat greeted me. "Hiya, sir, I know it looks all hosed up, but we're gonna launch ya' on time."

"Roger that, Chief. What's the status on the INU?" I asked calmly, knowing that it was a black box that was critical to our inertial navigation solution.

"That's no problem. Clement and the ATs are replacing it," said the chief with confidence. He knew I trusted Clement and by mentioning his name in conjunction with the INU problem the chief knew I would feel more at ease with the situation. "Sir, the problem I'm worried about is low oil pressure. We're trying to fix it now but you're going to need to look at it closely on start-up."

"Got it, Chief, thanks. Tell the guys they're doing a great job." I met the plane captain at the front end of the jet and he followed me around as I did my preflight. These guys were really busting their butts to get me airborne. There must have been fifteen of them—some only a few years out of high school with grease baked onto their faces from a long day on the deck. But the enthusiasm for their work was evident. This is what they had signed up for, it was what we had all signed up for. We all felt like men with a purpose, taking part in something important. So no matter how hard the work, how low the pay, how bad the living conditions, these young men would keep going. They were wishing me well and hoping that their work would get me off the deck in time to join the strike.

My preflight was abbreviated because most of the important things on the aircraft were being inspected by the maintenance crew, and the panels would need to remain open during start-up. So I did a quick walk around and climbed up to my cockpit. Precariously perched on the small boarding platform I did my best to conduct an inspection of the ejection seat. I always figured it would be a flight like this when I was rushed and unable to check everything as well as I usually did that I would have a serious problem. Whenever I felt rushed I always tried to slow down and force myself to double-check my procedures. But we were now at war and some precautions would need to be forgone. I needed to trust the deck guys to button up everything tight and do all the checks correctly even though they were exhausted at the end of a long day on deck. What if one of them left his wrench in the engine bay? It could happen. It had happened. It was a mistake that could ruin my day. At the end of the catapult stroke such a wrench would tear through the aft end of the jet. Ejection would be likely if not inevitable. Shaking my head, I slid into my seat. I couldn't let myself think negatively. I needed to focus on the mission that lay ahead.

Our strike this night was to attack Shaibah Airfield and we would be flying a similar jamming orbit as we had earlier in the day located just off the Bubiyan peninsula. Our intelligence was that Shaibah was well defended by SAMs, so our role in the strike was critical. We would be jamming and shooting a HARM on a specific timeline; the only thing different was that it was now extremely dark.

Gucci was in the front seat with me again for our first night attack. I was somewhat relieved. I trusted Skippy and Wolfey, but I liked having Gucci's experience in the front seat. He was more aggressive, and his experience gave him better situational awareness. Until I had gotten a few missions under my belt I thought that his experience would benefit our crew more in the front seat than in the back. Both Skippy and Wolfey knew the backseat system cold and I knew they could handle the mission in terms of the jamming assignments. "Good-looking jet," said Gucci sarcastically as he slipped into his seat next to me.

"You bet'cha," I said, not knowing what else to say to seem more relaxed than I was feeling. When Gucci was ready for power to be connected, I signaled the plane captain, but the replacement of the INU was not yet complete, so the plane captain simply shook his head and held his fist in the air, which meant "hold on." While we were holding on, the other jets on the deck were starting up. A Hornet located across the deck was the first jet to taxi forward to the catapults.

"This is going to be a quick start," said Gucci. "We probably won't get a complete alignment." I just nodded, knowing that mistakes happened when things got rushed. After debriefing our morning strike and reviewing our HARM launching procedures in excruciating detail, I had gotten some sleep in the middle of the day. My mind and body felt alert now, but I knew that it was going to be a tough mission and I needed to stay alert throughout. On a night like this I thought about the old ready-room joke that said, "A night cat shot is the result of an inadequate preflight." This meant that if you looked hard enough, you could almost always find something you could down the jet for and not go flying on a really dark night. I was tempted to look for something, but these men were all working so hard to get me airborne it would be a real blow to them if I copped out and called the jet down for something insignificant. Without knowing it, these young guys were applying pressure on me to be a leader, to be tougher than I was; in short, to hack it.

The flight deck in front of our jet was now packed with jets nose to tail in a line for the catapult shot that would send them into the blackness where sea and sky merged and were indistinguishable to the eye. Finally the plane captain gave me the start signal, and our engines roared to life one after the other. During the start I closely watched the oil pressure and decided not to mention the fact that it was just slightly below the acceptable lower limit of forty pounds per square inch. That was a hard limit, but these guys wanted nothing more than to see this jet go flying and I wasn't going to be the guy to down it in a combat situation.

"My instruments all look good. I'm giving the chief a thumbs-up."

"How's the oil pressure look?" asked Gucci, who could barely see the small gauge by my left knee.

"It's right on the lower limit. But I say we go flying." The darkness made it difficult to give hand signals, but because we were so close to the island, ambient light from the superstructure helped improve visibility, so I gave Chief Rat a thumbs-up to signal that we were ready to go flying. In the muted light I saw him smile and raise his right hand slightly above his head. I couldn't quite understand the signal at first, but then I smiled and laughed. He was making an "Ironclaw" signal with his fingers spread and bent in a menacing clawlike pose. I nodded and mimicked his claw with my own right hand. The signal created a connection and feeling of teamwork and trust. Chief Rat continued to use his Ironclaw signal with me throughout the war.

The cat shot was a good stiff one and once my eyes were capable of refocusing on the instruments, I cleaned up the jet and climbed out on the assigned departure radial. After going through the standard departure comm drill Gucci said, "Fly about 330 until I can get an update for the nav." Without saying a word I rolled to a heading of 330 knowing that Gucci was working hard to get the nav system on track as quickly as possible. Accurate navigation was essential to our mission, and even though I was ready to back him up, Gucci, as the front rightseater, had primary responsibility for the navigation system. "I have a good lock on the Dharan TACAN and am doing an update to the system."

"Sounds good," I said.

"Steering is to the tanker track," said Gucci, sounding more relaxed and confident now that the nav was accurate. We both knew we would need to monitor it closely because of the uncertainty of the new INU the ground crew had just installed.

"What is the INS showing for winds?" I asked.

"260 at forty-five, close to forecast," said Gucci. "We're looking good."

The air wing had flown two smaller strikes during the day after our return from our morning mission, and miraculously, we still had not lost an aircraft to enemy fire. I knew as we looked around the ready room guys were thinking, *Who will be the first to go?* It was a creepy way to look at your friend over a meal, wondering if the next time you sit down to eat he won't be around to join you. I shook these thoughts out of my head. I needed to keep my mind in the cockpit until I was chocked and chained back on deck with my engines shut down at the end of the mission. The steering needle stayed steady and the computer indicated another fifteen miles to go to the nearest point on the tanker track. On this mission we were trying simply to rendezvous on the tanker instead of rendezvousing overhead the carrier and flying in formation to the tanker. There were pros and cons to both approaches and we would see how this new procedure would work out. Personally, I thought it made good sense and would make for a more expeditious strike.

My rendezvous on the tanker was solid, and I stabilized in-port observation while an A-6 completed its refueling. Tanking on the KC-135s was still a struggle for me and I did not look forward to it, but I now knew that I could do it. I plugged the basket on the first attempt, and even though I felt as if it were an exercise in torture, I completed the procedure without any unintentional disengagements. Once complete, I slid over to the tanker's right side, waiting for my fighter escort to finish his tanking.

The Hornet pilot got clearance to tank and maneuvered his jet into the proper position. He closed slowly but confidently on the basket. At the last instant before entering the basket the pilot got distracted and the tip of the Hornet's refueling probe caught the edge of the basket, which snapped down and slapped the nose cone of his jet. Startled by the missed attempt, the Hornet pilot backed off and stabilized again. The next attempt was much smoother than the first, but unfortunately, the damage had been done on the first approach. "Trout 12, Dragon 405 is plugged but showing no flow."

"Roger, Dragon 405, showing the same. Suggest you disengage and attempt again."

"Roger, Dragon 405, disengaging," said the annoyed Hornet pilot. He smoothly disengaged from the tanker and slid back a few feet and stabilized once again. After a few seconds of pause, the Hornet approached and plugged again. "Trout 12, Dragon 405, has negative flow."

"Roger, Dragon 405. Your system may have been damaged by your first approach."

"Trout 12, Dragon 405 disengaging. I'll try again after the A-6," said the Hornet pilot, who was obviously frustrated by his inability

to take on fuel. He slid below and behind the next A-6 in the gas
line off the tanker's left wing. Within a few minutes the last A-6
had completed his tanking and the Hornet was up again. The A-6
had no problem getting gas, so it was clear that if there was a
problem, it was with the Hornet, not with the tanker. The answer
was confirmed after another good plug in the basket resulted in no
fuel for the Hornet.

"Great, no fighter cover for us," said Gucci, verbalizing what
each of us was thinking.

"Ironclaw, Dragon 405, I'm down and returning to Mother. I'll
see if they can launch a spare."

"Roger, we're going to press," I said, knowing that all the spares
had shut down long ago on the *Midway*'s deck and that even if they
could launch one it would be too late to be any good by the time
it could catch up to us.

"Good luck, Ironclaw. Dragon 405 is detaching to the right."
The Hornet's bright fluorescent strips and red anticollision lights
faded quickly in the blackness of the night.

"Let's hope Liberty and AWACS are squared away tonight," I
said. The navy's E-2C Hawkeye and the air force's E-3 AWACS
were the only aircraft that would be able to provide us with warning
of approaching enemy fighters tonight. That was not a fact that
filled any of us with great confidence. The guys in the early-warning
aircraft quickly reached task saturation on these large, nighttime air
strikes, and threat warning quickly dropped a few notches on their
priority list. I was resigned to the fact that I would be the pilot of
a flying bull's-eye tonight. Our mission called for us to fly a predictable orbit over the oil platforms that might have comm capability with one of several fighter bases in Iraq. The thought did not
bring a smile to my face.

We separated from the tanker and flew a 350 heading toward our
jamming orbit. "Without an escort I think we should go without
our external lights," said Gucci.

"Definitely," I said as my left thumb flicked off the master switch,
allowing our jet to blend into the night. Our one advantage was
that we knew that at night Iraqi pilots were heavily dependent on
ground-controlled radar intercepts and we were also jamming

those. Such a radar intercept still demanded the pilot to acquire the target visually in the end game, so whatever we could do to reduce their ability to see us was to our advantage. With our lights out we headed north into enemy territory—alone and afraid.

"Liberty is picture clean," said the anonymous voice of the Hawkeye controller on the strike frequency. This night those words were going to be especially soothing. I couldn't help but feel that I was pilot in command of a flying target just waiting for an Iraqi fighter to thank me for making his first kill of the war so easy.

"Steering is to the outer point of our jamming orbit," said Gucci. "Two minutes to jammers on." Our jamming obscured the strike group from ground-based radars, but it clearly highlighted our general sector in the sky. All it would take is one aggressive fighter flying right down the jamming strobe to ruin our day.

"Guys in back, once you get the jammers set up, I need you to keep up a good lookout. Without an escort we are very vulnerable," I said with a clear tone of concern.

"Understood," said Wolfey, "we'll be looking."

"Jammers on," said Skippy. "We have good power out on two of our pods, but the third is hurting. We're trying to bring it back up."

"OK, let me know when you have it on line," said Gucci. "Tank, we're about one minute out from the first oil platform."

"Roger, I see triple A off the nose." The dark sky was being shredded by the bright lines of 57mm and 76mm AAA. "Look at those tracers. They're coming up to our altitude," I said.

"Break left, break left," said Gucci. I yanked the stick hard to the left and a stream of tracers lit up the sky where we had been only a second before. Training took over as I pulled hard into the break turn-away from the tracers. At that moment I saw a bright flash in my peripheral vision and felt the jet shudder around me. My immediate thought was, *Oh my God, we've been hit.* I reversed my break turn and pulled even harder. I pulled as hard as I could and saw another bright, blinding explosion aft near the tail section, and as I increased the pull I felt even more vibrations from the aircraft. My heart racing, I pushed the throttles as hard as I could and pulled on the stick even harder.

"Altitude," piped up Gucci.

"Got it," I said as I reduced the pull, leveled the wings, and tried to start climbing out of the hole I had fallen into. My maneuvering had been reckless and costly. We had lost five thousand feet in the various defensive maneuvers I had made and now we were flying in the very heart of the AAA fire that we had been trying to avoid. Climbing uphill the Prowler had about as much maneuverability as a Mack truck crossing the continental divide. My left arm was locked and the throttles were pressed to the stops as I tried to squeeze every ounce of thrust out of the Pratt & Whitney engines underneath me. We managed to avoid the AAA somehow, and when I finally got up to twenty thousand feet, I realized that I was behind on the timeline for the HARM launch for the mission. Maintaining max thrust we accelerated toward our launch point.

"Liberty is picture clean," came the voice of our eyes-in-the-sky broadcasting over strike frequency. We were glad to hear that there seemed to be no Iraqi fighter activity. My mind quickly shifted back from the tactical picture to flying my jet.

"The jet seems to be handling OK, but I thought we had been hit," I said.

"Me, too," said Gucci. "I released two chaff-and-flare programs to help us out," he said over the intercom as he continued to work on the navigation solution.

"You released two programs? Oh my God!" I said.

"What's wrong?" asked Gucci.

"What I thought was flak exploding near us was just you releasing chaff-and-flare programs without me knowing it." My inexperience and Gucci's nerves led us to the embarrassed realization that in the darkness and confusion of the night we had been trying to avoid our own chaff and flares. What had felt like explosions was airframe buffet attributable to the strength of my own pull. I had yanked the Prowler into heavy buffet dangerously close to stall speed.

"Hell, that's embarrassing," I said, realizing the mistake was now behind us. "But now we have to launch this missile on time."

"Steering is to the launch point and if we maintain this speed we will be five seconds late to our point," said Gucci.

My arm remained locked at the elbow as I tried to squeeze out all the thrust from our engines. It felt like the Prowler still had some acceleration left and I wanted to launch this HARM on time. My eyes darted back and forth from the steering needle, to the time to go on the computer, to the clock. All the parameters were closing in and coming to a climax.

"Missile on Station Two is designated. You have your needles," said Gucci. They were the same needles I referenced for night landings, but now they were linked to the HARM control panel. I pulled the jet around to the right and then back to the left once the needles had centered up. As the horizontal needle began to come down I prepared to pull the trigger. I judged the rate of movement of the horizontal bar and squeezed the trigger just prior to its meeting the horizon. I closed my eyes to avoid being blinded by the brilliance of the HARM's rocket motor in the darkness. As soon as the missile left the rail I keyed the mike and once again broadcast the warning to my fellow strikers: "Ironclaw magnum."

"Right on time," said Gucci. "Let's turn outbound." I pulled the Prowler around to a southeasterly heading and we continued our jamming as we headed outbound from the target.

"Liberty's picture clean," came the reassuring voice from the E-2C Hawkeye. A few minutes passed in silence, which was then broken by good news.

"Hammer flight feet wet," pronounced the Hornet strike lead.

"Thunder flight feet wet," echoed the Intruder lead. It appeared as though the Iraqis had missed everyone again. I couldn't believe it, but I relaxed and climbed to the RTF altitude and slowed to the RTF airspeed for the boring yet satisfying flight back to the ship.

We had recovered from our mistake and had salvaged the mission. After performing a death spiral into the heart of the oil platform's AAA envelope we had been able to speed up enough to hit our launch point on time. We were less optimistic that we had hit the target, however, because the signal had disappeared before the missile had impacted. That fact meant that it was more than likely that the HARM missile we had fired, no longer having a radar signal to home in on, had missed its intended target. This time the Iraqi radar operators had survived, but our mission was still successful because we had forced them to turn off their radar and without it, they were blind, with no way to shoot down our striking aircraft.

CHAPTER THIRTEEN

Coyotes
Airborne

The junior officers in the squadron started calling us *batboys* because Ren and I were getting assigned all the night strikes. Tonight was going to be my third night strike in a row and my fifth mission since the shooting started five days before. As Ren and I sat around the bunkroom waiting for our briefing to start, I put my good-luck pen to paper and wrote Alice my daily letter.

20 Jan 91

Dear Alice,

I'm plugged into my headphones listening to some classic Motown hits. Music soothes the savage beast. I think that's a famous quote. Even if it's not, it should be, because it's true. I am tired and hoping to get a few hours' sleep before my midnight briefing for a 3:00 A.M. launch.

It is better to strike at night. It is safer for us, and since our equipment is more sophisticated, we can attack quite successfully under the cover of darkness. Our initial attacks have been effective, yet I don't think this conflict will end anytime soon. . . .

What little free time I have when I'm not flying, planning, or trying to catch up on my sleep is spent daydreaming. I try to imagine where and when I will next see you. What will you be wearing? What will you say? What will you be thinking? I suppose I have an overactive imagi-

*nation, but it is a great help during times like this. You are in my
dreams.*

All my love, Sherm

I folded the letter neatly then placed it in an envelope which I
sealed and addressed. I put it in one of the myriad pockets in my
flight suit, which was hanging up along the wall at the foot of my
bed, then I tried to get some sleep before my wristwatch alarm set
for 2330 would beep me back to the war.

Unfortunately, it took the loud ring of the phone to wake me
up. Groaning angrily I grabbed my watch and pressed the button
that illuminated the face: 0003 flashed on the digital readout.
"Shit." I picked up the phone on the fourth or fifth ring and said,
"This is Tank, I'm on my way," and hung up without listening for
a response. In a semiconscious state I threw on my flight suit and
boots and ran down the passageways to the ready room to listen to
the brief already in progress. Coming in late to a brief was bad
enough but looking like you had just crawled out of the rack was
even worse, especially for a new guy who definitely needed to hear
every detail of every briefing. The looks that I got from the more
senior aviators said it all too clearly: *Very unprofessional.* I slunk
around the back of the room and was one of the first to disappear
as soon as the gaggle brief was over.

During the next hour and a half I had a chance to wake up and
get organized. I even remembered to dig out my letter to Alice
from the depths of my flight suit and mail it before putting on the
remainder of my flight gear. What cobwebs were left in my brain
from my hurried and late wake-up at midnight were wiped away by
another unnerving night catapult shot.

It was a beautifully clear night and Skippy was in the front seat
with me. Even though the concept of getting shot at was still a
relatively new experience, I now felt confident enough to have
Skippy and Wolfey up front. We had been one of the first jets to
the tanker tonight, so after completing our tanking we had to fly

formation on the tanker's starboard side and wait for all the other members of our SEAD element to finish tanking.

I remembered that Winston Churchill once said, "Nothing in life is so exhilarating as to be shot at without result." I didn't know if it was an accurate attribution to Sir Winston, but nonetheless, I thought it aptly described the mood in the air wing. Every pilot and flight officer in the air wing was walking around acting larger than life. The aviators had all started to develop what I called the "warrior's walk." Their chests stuck out a bit more, there was an extra strut in their step and an aura of invincibility that came from getting shot at and missed. I had caught myself in the "warrior's walk" more than once in the past few days, and had corrected myself quickly. I figured the second I let myself get cocky and complacent would be the time I'd wind up in an Iraqi prison camp.

We were only a few days into the fighting and I kept trying to maintain perspective by thinking of the naval aviators who had gone before me. Men who had faced worse, sacrificed more, and endured longer than I had. There were some real heros: men like President George Bush, my Commander in Chief, who had been shot down in the Pacific during World War II; Senator John McCain, who had survived and overcome the worst of the Vietnam POW camps; and Vice Admiral Jim Stockdale, who became the leader of all Americans at the Hanoi Hilton. Each of these pilots had been shot down, and the latter two had sacrificed many long and brutal years in POW camps serving their country. After five days of missions, I felt that I was just doing my job and trying hard not to get killed. Compared with the suffering and sacrifice that these men had undergone, I thought it was important to stay humble and remember those who had flown before us—the pioneers of naval aviation. I had succeeded in fully deflating my own warrior image by the time the last Hornet had completed refueling. It was important to find a balance between confidence and humility in order to survive.

We were flying to the northernmost jamming orbit over the oil platforms again this night. Now I had a section of Hornets for fighter escort. The last strike had reported the first really significant Iraqi night fighter activity so far, and I was glad to have the Hornets with us. We flew north in a loose formation, the fighters above and slightly behind us. This gave them the flexibility to make tactical turns, keeping us in sight and using their air-to-air radars to search the sky ahead of us. I felt bolder knowing that they were there somewhere above me like guardian angels.

"Steering's good to our outer orbit point," said Skippy. "We are ahead of time now, so we'll fly to the outer point first and then get alignment as we head inbound to the inner point."

"Sounds like a good plan," I said as I made some fine adjustments to the Prowler's trim, given our newly filled fuel tanks.

"Liberty's got two possible Coyotes airborne, on Bullseye's 010 at fifty." We all sat up a bit straighter in our seats after the voice of the Hawkeye controller was replaced by the cackle of an open circuit on the front radio. We all knew that Coyotes were bad, and Skippy confirmed that by checking his kneeboard cards to decipher the message.

"That's two Fulcrums fifty miles north of our target. No threat yet," said Skippy, knowing full well that if those MIG 29s were so inclined they could cover the one hundred miles that separated us within a matter of minutes. We all would be listening carefully to Liberty's calls tonight.

Even though we were carrying a HARM missile, it was planned to be used reactively, which meant that we would only fire if certain specific hostile radars acting as guidance for SA-2, SA-3, or SA-6 came up. Gucci and Wolfey would be scanning our backseat system carefully for any of the radars linked specifically to these SAM systems that might threaten our bombers. My main concern, however, was the presence of the Fulcrums and what I would do if they attacked. It was comforting to know that Liberty had a position on them, but I worried that if there were two that Liberty could see, then there might be more that Liberty was unable to see or too overtasked to see. My criteria for different maneuvers were well briefed with the fighter escort, and I just hoped that I would not be placed in a position without fighter cover.

The fighter guys in the air wing had not yet registered a kill and they were chomping at the bit to shoot down any aircraft that the Iraqis sent up. I was now in a situation that I had never encountered

in training but had been warned about by many Prowler veterans
in our squadron.

In the typical strike-training scenario, a Prowler's fighter escort
leaves the Prowler to shoot down an incoming threat aircraft, and
one of three things happens: The first possibility is that fighters
shoot down the bandits, and the good guys are happy; the second
is that bandits shoot down fighters and then shoot down the
Prowler, so the bandits are happy; the third is that fighters get
disoriented after leaving the Prowler, and in their zealous search to
get a kill they end up shooting down the Prowler in what is coldly
termed a blue-on-blue engagement. This final scenario happens all
too often in predeployment air wing training, which I had yet to
experience.

I could hear it in their voices on the radio; our fighter escorts
were starting to get pumped. The calm, cool comm turned to chatter, and the back radio circuit was filled with a quick repartee. The
voice of the lead pilot came through clearly on our back radio:
"Dragon flight, snap left."

"Two," acknowledged his wingman in response.

"Liberty, showing Coyotes tracking south. Currently on Bullseye's 020 at 40."

"Dragon lead, negative contact."

"Two's negative contact." The uneasiness in their voices was
clear; the fighters didn't want to be flying at our current speed of
420 knots if they entered an engagement against the two Fulcrums.
The Hornets wanted desperately to bump it up and tap their afterburners, but that meant committing to an engagement, and the
Coyotes were still too far away to threaten us. This was the hard
part for the fighters. Their mission was to protect us from threatening aircraft, not to go out and kill Iraqi aircraft that posed no
real threat.

"Liberty, Dragon flight holding hands with Ironclaw, waiting for
words." The Dragon lead was subtly looking for Liberty to unleash
him and allow him to try to chase down the enemy fighters.

"Dragon, Liberty, stand by for words," I moaned. It was clear-
cut at this point and Liberty was hesitating. The fighters needed to
stay with us until the Fulcrums made an aggressive approach. The

pause over the circuit was painful, and when the silence was broken I was relieved to hear, "Dragon, Liberty, words are to stay with Ironclaw. Coyotes are now tracking north." Our crew relaxed for a few seconds at the news of the receding threat.

As the steering needle rotated off to the side of the compass indicating our imminent arrival at our outer point, I shoved the stick to the left, steering toward a new course leading over the oil platforms and to our inner orbit point. As on my first night strike, the red tracers from the AAA started to come up to our altititude and track along with us through the sky. Tonight I kept my composure and continued to fly in the general direction of steering while I jinked at irregular intervals to foil the oil platform gunners who were trying to lock me up with their radars. We now were just three minutes out from our inner point and my own trigger finger was ready to fire a missile. "Any good targets showing up?" I asked, hopeful that we might have the opportunity to silence another Iraqi radar.

"Nothing—they seem to have shut down their acquisition radars," said Gucci. "They're getting smarter."

"Liberty shows two possible pop-up Coyotes over Bullseye tracking south speed, five hundred knots." My heart jumped to my throat. The comm turned again to chatter.

"Dragon flight's committing," said the curt aggressive voice of the Dragon lead.

"Two," acknowledged his wingman. Both Hornets highlighted themselves for a brief few seconds as they tapped their afterburners to get up to their optimum engagement speed.

"Liberty, Dragon flight needs a vector to bogeys."

"Liberty now showing possible Coyote contacts on Bullseye 210 at five tracking south. Good vector for Dragon flight is 020 range forty miles."

"Dragon lead showing two contacts off the nose at thirty-seven. Sorting now. Right target high, left low. Dragon flight tac left," directed the Dragon lead.

"Two," responded the wingman. The two Hornets were now out of sight and I needed to make some quick decisions. Our onboard computer showed just over two minutes to the inner jamming point of our orbit and these were the two most critical minutes of the strike for jamming. If I turned outbound before I reached the inner point then the SAM operators might have enough time without our jamming to fire a good shot at one of our bombers. If I continued on course and speed I could be an easy target for the oncoming Coyotes whose closure rate with us was now almost a thousand knots. I decided to trust our Hornets and hope for the best. If we all did our jobs then our bombers could return home safely.

"Liberty, Ironclaw is pressing to inner orbit point. Status on Coyotes," I said over the radio with as much confidence as I could drum up.

"Ironclaw, Liberty, stand by."

"Good call, Tank," said Gucci over the intercom. "Still nothing on the system."

"Roger, let us know," I said, glad to know that Gucci agreed with my decision. The fighters' comm was stacatto and professional; the closure rate was tremendous. I now estimate the bandits were only twenty-five miles from our current position.

"Forty-five seconds to the inner point," said Skippy. He continued in a nonchalant tone of voice, masking the severity of the situation. "Uhh, Tank, I recommend, uhh, I think we ought to break right. I got a SAM launch at . . ." The rest of the sentence was lost in the groan from Skippy's voice as I whipped the Prowler around in a tight right turn, pulling on the G forces at the edge of airframe buffet, trying to break the lock on an incoming missile that I had not yet seen. My left fingers instinctively pressed a chaff-and-flare program further highlighting us to any possible fighter threat, but I felt the risk was worth it. "It was at two o'clock, should be at nine now," said Skippy as I relaxed my pull on the jet and the G forces lightened their weight on our chests. Scanning the horizon for an incoming missile I saw the burning telephone pole off in the distance on a nonthreatening trajectory. Either my maneuvering had broken its lock or it was never really locked on us at all.

"Not a factor," I said. We would never know if it would have been without Skippy's call and my pull. I quickly reversed the jet back to the left in an effort to get back on course.

"Ten seconds to the inner point," said Skippy.

"Liberty, Dragon requests an updated vector on Coyotes."

"Dragon, showing Coyotes now tracking north of Bullseye."

"Liberty, Dragon flight is knocking it off, need good vector to Texaco."

"Dragon, Liberty, roger, stand by."

Once again I watched as the steering needle rotated around the compass indicating our passage over the point. I rolled quickly to the left and pulled hard for ninety degrees before easing my turn to take a look for possible threats.

"Belly's clear," said Skippy, reading my mind as does a good rightseater.

"Thanks," I said as I rolled again and turned to our RTF heading.

The Hornets had scared off the Fulcrums and our jamming had intimidated the SAM threat and rendered it ineffective. It was frustrating not to be able to get any battle-damage assessment from our missions. We didn't blow up buildings or bridges and when we did kill a radar we didn't have a visual confirmation, so we were never really sure. If the signal went down at missile impact then we assumed it was a good kill, but we never had the videotape. We couldn't know if our jamming was really rendering their radars useless or whether they were able to work around it. The only tangible proof of our success was when everyone returned home after the mission.

"Thumper flight feet wet, mission report Horseshoe." Skippy checked his kneeboard card to translate.

"*Horseshoe* means one-hundred-percent mission success," said Skippy as we flew southeast into the orange sky of the rising sun.

CHAPTER FOURTEEN

Prepare to Eject

We had now been flying combat missions for a week, and the three aircraft carriers in the Persian Gulf were churning out sorties at an impressive rate. The around-the-clock operational tempo was taking its toll not only on the pilots and deck crew, but also on men working in the bowels of the ship, the engineering spaces. People were still excited about putting their training to use, but we all were beginning to realize that this pace could continue for a long time. The initial combat euphoria was wearing off and what I saw happening around the squadron and air wing made me worry. We had so quickly established air supremacy that guys were beginning to get complacent. The arrogant "warrior walk" was becoming more and more prevalent in ready rooms among more and more junior aviators. As an air wing we still had not suffered any losses, but that was because up until now we had maintained excellent flight discipline. We had rendezvoused professionally, flown our timelines precisely, and struck our targets on time. Yet in the past twenty-four hours, some near-fatal mistakes had been made. Fortunately, there had been no losses to personnel or aircraft, but it was time to take a break. Now we were getting our first "night off" of the war.

Since the air wing was not flying, we were all expecting a night of movies and popcorn to relax after our first week of combat. A group of us had already gathered around the bunkroom television, watching a three-day-old CNN tape of the first few days of air strikes. We were each dressed in different stages of readiness. Skippy and I, having recently returned from a mission, were still in flight suits, but in order to give his feet a rest, Skippy had taken off his flight boots and slipped on his Birkenstock sandals. The rest of us thought they looked ridiculous, but Skippy certainly did relax when he put them on. The two of us were sitting on desk chairs toward the back of the small TV viewing area while Horse and Ren were sprawled out in a couple of low-slung beach chairs just in front of the refrigerator. Each was wearing nothing more than a T-shirt and boxer shorts to keep cool in the warmth of the crowded bunkroom. The banter was lively as we watched the news. It was exciting to sit there and see footage of our strikes, and it was great to learn that Americans were supportive of our troops in the Gulf. The TV screen flickered and then displayed a bomb's-eye view of a bridge. As the electro-optic smart weapon destroyed a bridge span somewhere near Baghdad we all let out a cheer.

Our celebration was interrupted by the sound of the bunkroom's door being slammed open. Our dreams of a relaxing evening vanished. "This is bullshit," said Kamper as he stormed into the room. "We've been busting our butts for a week now and the first night we get off, the skipper wants to have a damn meeting." Kamper went on to describe that on the white board in the ready room written in his standard blood-red ink were the words ALL AIRCREW MEETING TONIGHT AT 2100. The response in the bunkroom was predictable. A chorus of profanity followed Kamper's announcement.

"You would think we could have one night to ourselves if for nothing else than to catch up on the sleep we haven't been getting. I don't think I've had more than three consecutive hours in the past week. I'd be grounded if I were in the air force," said Ren with a chuckle. We all laughed. Cracking jokes about our sister service's strict rules regarding crew rest was one of our favorite pastimes. Navy rules seemed to be viewed more as guidelines once the shooting started. We all tried to adhere to the sleep requirements, but the navy culture was clear; combat mission requirements took priority, and we all felt that was the way it should be.

"What is this meeting about anyway?" I asked, feeling that I should know. It was clear though once the question had been asked that there were others in the room who didn't know either. There was a pause and then came the answer.

"Dawg and I nearly ran out of gas last night on our mission," said Arnie, whose voice emanated from his rack. "Dawg will tell you all about it at the meeting tonight. Alpha Charlie has already tasked me to write an article about the incident for *Approach*." Writing an article for *Approach* magazine meant you were either a hero for having displayed great airmanship that saved your aircraft from certain destruction, or you were one lucky sonuvabitch who displayed sufficiently poor judgment to put yourself, your crew, and your aircraft in grave danger but were somehow blessed enough to survive to tell the tale. Both kinds of aviators wrote articles for *Approach* in order to educate other aviators, in the hope that readers would mimic the heroes and learn from the mistakes of the lucky sonsuvbitches. Whether he liked it or not, Arnie knew that all of us were putting him in the lucky-sonuvabitch category, even though he was not the pilot of the jet.

"What the hell happened to you guys?" I asked. "I was flying on that mission last night. You joined up on the tanker just two jets behind us."

"Dawg will tell the story tonight," said Arnie hesitantly. No aviator worth his salt could pass up an opportunity to tell a good flying story involving danger. We all knew this, so we pressed him.

"Dawg's a suit. He'll sugarcoat it in front of the skipper. We want to hear *your* version," said Ren, referring to Dawg's rank as a lieutenant commander and squadron department head by calling him a "suit."

"Well, OK," said Arnie as he rolled out of his rack. He wore his flight suit unzipped from neck to waist with the sleeves gently tied at his waist, showing off the athletic frame he had developed by studying karate for years. He was an honest-to-God black belt. We all figured with a name like *Arnold* it was natural to learn karate when you were a kid. Despite his name, Arnie was the squadron's premier ladies' man, but he was also a damned good ECMO, and I wanted to hear how they had gotten into so much trouble in the air.

Haltingly, he started to tell his story to the small group of us gathered in the bunkroom. "Let me back up to the beginning of the mission because that is when the chain started," Arnie explained. The chain was often referred to in safety mishap reports as the chain of poor decisions and judgments that if broken at any point during flight could have stopped the mishap from happening. The US Navy's safety center even sent out little posters of safety propaganda that said, DON'T BE AFRAID TO BREAK THE CHAIN. Often junior aircrew could feel intimidated by a senior pilot or too comfortable with that pilot's judgment. This is what happened to Arnie. The words came easily to Arnie because the events were so fresh in his mind, as are most moments of true fear.

Arnie continued, "Dawg had a bout with vertigo on the pre-mission tanker, so we never got as much gas before the strike as we had planned. But I felt comfortable that there would be plenty of gas available at the end of the mission. So rather than wait for Dawg's vertigo to subside and get the amount of gas planned, we pressed on to keep on our timeline with the rest of the strike package." The group of bunkroom listeners all nodded, understanding the decision and agreeing with it. The atmosphere in the bunkroom was a mixture between a jury listening to a defense lawyer's plea and a group of priests listening to the confession of a sinner.

After taking a moment to have a swig of lemonade our storyteller continued. "We reached our southern jamming orbit on time with our jammers on, and as we approached our inner orbit point we saw the flash of a SAM launch a few miles off our nose. It was like a burning telephone pole, just as the SA-2 had been described to us. Dawg made a good move rolling inverted and breaking under the missile while hitting a program of chaff and flares. The SAM exploded above and behind us, but that aggressive move cost us more gas. By the time the strikers were feet wet we were well below our planned fuel ladder, but we had plenty of gas to get back to the tanker. To conserve what gas we had we flew to the tanker track at a slower airspeed than planned and as a result we were last in line at the pump. Just like Tank said, there were two Hornets between their jet and ours." I nodded in appreciation for his mentioning the accuracy of my comment.

I tried to recall what the radios had sounded like after that strike but realized that as soon as we had completed our tanking we switched off the tanker frequency and shortly thereafter, switched off the Hawkeye's frequency so we would not have heard any of their comm after that. So far I sensed that the jury felt Arnie's crew had made good decisions based on the difficulties that had confronted them. Arnie then continued to plead his case and the jury sat listening quietly. He began to get more animated as he related the following first-person account of the comm sequence as he remembered it.

"When the Hornet in front of us had plugged the basket the tanker pilot said, 'Mako 12 is bingo fuel after this customer. Repeat, Mako 12 is RTB after this customer.' I looked at my kneeboard card and sure enough, Mako 12 was the tanker at our altitude. After the Hornet finished tanking, the tanker raised its basket and turned to a southwesterly heading back to its base in Saudi Arabia. We needed to find a new gas station. The visibility was good and we were still not too worried. The other tankers designated for our mission had already left, but we knew there were other strikes inbound and other tanker assets airborne. We simply needed to find the oncoming tanker stack and we would be all set. We now had about 5500 pounds of gas. I checked our primary divert field and we had 4000 bingo to get there, so we still had a cushion. The comm sequence went something like this:

" 'Liberty, Ironclaw, our assigned mission tanker is RTB, request vector to Texaco.'

" 'Ironclaw, Liberty, negative radar contact, recycle your parrot.' I went through all the appropriate checks but the Prowler's IFF would not bit test correctly.

" 'Ironclaw, Liberty still negative radar contact, call your father.' I then relayed our position relative to the nearest TACAN station on the western shoreline of the Gulf.

" 'Copy, Ironclaw, from that position a good vector to Texaco is 145 for twenty.'

" 'Ironclaw copies 145 for twenty.' Dawg then turned the jet to the new heading, which took us farther from our nearest divert field thereby raising the bingo fuel we would need to get back. We now had five thousand pounds of gas and I was starting to worry. If we didn't get gas from this guy then we would be close to our bingo fuel for our divert. But Dawg seemed confident it would work out; it always had. Within a few minutes Dawg spotted traffic off the nose and we all relaxed; we had found the tanker. Dawg bumped up the throttles to close on the tanker and effect a quick rendezvous, but we soon realized as we got closer that we had misjudged the traffic's aspect and that it was in fact heading away from the tanker track.

" 'Liberty, Ironclaw, we have traffic off our nose, confirm tanker.'

" 'Negative, Ironclaw, tanker now bears one twenty at ten from your current position.'

" 'Understand you have radar contact with us now.'

" 'That's affirmative.' Dawg turned to the new heading even further away from our divert. None of us thought to question how Liberty had suddenly gotten radar contact; we just assumed that they did. We were now at forty-five hundred pounds and I was getting nervous, but I didn't say anything. We all wanted to believe it would work out. Another few minutes passed as we droned southeast scanning the horizon for our tanker. Our gas gauge was steadily dropping.

" 'Tanker in sight,' said Dawg as he swung the jet around to the right, and there off the nose was a Canadian 707 with wingtip tanker baskets. We had tanked off this unusual plane the night before, so I knew Dawg would feel comfortable. We all breathed a sigh of relief as we joined up on the port wing of this tanker. I switched up to the tanker frequency we had used the night before, and Dawg positioned us behind the basket. I made the standard voice call and we waited to be cleared in to plug. When we heard no response we figured that we were on the wrong frequency, so we decided to plug anyway. We were low on gas and it was becoming a safety-of-flight issue. Dawg plugged the basket on the 707 but we got a red light and no flow. After a second attempt we knew we were in trouble; we were now below our bingo fuel to our divert and we were currently heading away from that field.

" 'Ironclaw, Trout ten, say your position,' came a voice on the tanker frequency.

" 'We are joined on you now.' There was silence on the circuit, then . . . 'Negative, no one is joined on us,' said the tanker pilot. Great, we now realized we had joined on the wrong tanker and this one seemed to be unable to give us the gas we now needed so desperately.

" 'Liberty, Ironclaw, we need a good vector to Texaco and we need it now,' said Dawg, jumping onto the radios with a sense of urgency in his voice. Liberty must have given us that last vector without really having us under radar contact. It was another poor assumption, another mistake in the chain. Our calm-and-cool radio voices were beginning to crack and we were trying not to let it show. We disengaged from the 707's wing tip basket and turned back to the west.

" 'Ironclaw, Liberty, stand by,' said the controller in a hesitant voice. We realized now that Liberty was not going to be able to help us unless we made ourselves a higher priority and established definite radar contact. At two o'clock I saw a flight of two aircraft and pointed it out to Dawg.

" 'Trout ten, Ironclaw, we have a flight of two in sight.'

" 'Negative, Ironclaw, we are in a single.' That was it. I reached down and turned our IFF to emergency, which I knew would light up the Hawkeye's radar screens and probably make Dawg mad at me, but we needed some special attention and we needed it quickly. I had no interest in running out of gas above the shark-infested waters of the Persian Gulf.

" 'Ironclaw, Liberty has your emergency squawk, positive radar contact. Coordinating with Trout ten now. Stand by for an updated vector.' Squeaky wheel gets the grease, I guess. It was amazing how the level of service improved once we were squawking emergency. Our controller's voice changed and I could tell we were now talking to the senior man on the Hawkeye. It was embarrassing, but I'm glad I did it.

" 'Ironclaw, Liberty, your new vector to Trout ten is 200 for 15,' he is heading right at you now.' We were now at two thousand pounds, well below our bingo to our divert field. We had flown right into a nasty box out of which our only hope lay in Trout ten. We now were committed to finding this tanker. If we didn't

get gas from it we would have to eject because we now had no
other options.

" 'Ironclaw copies, heading 200.' All we could hope was that this
new heading would bring an end to this wild-goose chase. 'Ironclaw
has a tally on Trout ten,' I said. The problem was that we were
heading in opposite directions and the rendezvous was going to be
difficult. Dawg did a great job expediting the join-up, but the aggressive maneuvering ate up a lot of our gas. When we were finally
in position and ready to tank we were down to a thousand pounds
of gas. [We all knew that the Prowler's gas gauge was not very
reliable below a thousand pounds. It was not considered a problem
because you were never supposed to let the jet get that low on gas.]
A little quick calculation told us that at our current fuel flow we
had about six minutes left before our engines would flame out.

"I watched from the right seat as Dawg selected air refuel and
lowered his seat. He stabilized the jet behind the basket and the
tanker pilot told us we were cleared in. Dawg approached the basket
slowly and plugged very nicely on the very first attempt. We all
breathed a sigh of relief when we saw the green light come on in
the tanker.

" 'Dawg was working hard to keep the proper position maintaining the necessary bend in the KC-135's hose. I watched the fuel
gauge carefully but the only movement of the needle that I saw was
downward to eight hundred pounds.

" 'Dawg, you're in air refuel, right?' I asked him, knowing full
well that he had the switch selected properly.

" 'Affirmative, what's the problem?'

" 'We have no flow.'

" 'Shit!'

" 'Trout, Ironclaw has no flow. We need some suggestions now,'
said Dawg, his composure beginning to crack.

" 'Ironclaw, we have good indications on our console. Something
must have come unseated in the basket. We'll recycle the boom.
Recommend you try plugging again and hit the basket with more
closure.' "

Looking anxious as he remembered his emotions from that night, Arnie became more animated as he recounted the comms.

" 'Ironclaw copies. Disengaging now,' said Dawg. We were now down to six hundred pounds indicated and we all knew that we only had a few minutes to go. The tanker's basket retracted into the metal sleeve known as the boom and we waited for it to reappear. From the backseat Cave piped up that both backseaters were prepared for a controlled ejection after the flameout. It wasn't until then that the thought of ending up in the middle of the Persian Gulf had really struck me. But it did now and I removed my kneeboard and tightened my seat straps in preparation for ejection. I knew Dawg was feeling the pressure; this was our last chance. If we didn't get good flow on this plug, we would be getting wet. Dawg stabilized the jet about sixty feet behind the basket and then said, 'OK, everyone prepare to eject if this plug is unsuccessful.'

"I saw his left hand push the throttles forward and I watched his right hand twitching on the stick, making the myriad of minute corrections that would hopefully guide the jet's refueling probe into the basket. When I looked up I saw us closing quickly on the basket. Dawg was going to hit it hard. *Slam!* The probe rammed into the center of the basket, which made the hose gyrate wildly in the air and the impact of the contact made the entire jet shudder. My eyes shot down to the gas gauge which was now bobbing somewhere between five hundred and six hundred pounds. At first there was no movement, but then, almost imperceptibly, I saw the needle start to rise.

" 'Trout ten, Ironclaw, we've got good flow. Repeat, we've got good flow. Thanks for the help.'

" 'No problem. Glad you don't have to go swimming. How much would you like?' asked the tanker pilot.

" 'We'll take as much as you'll give us at this point.' "

Arnie smiled as he finished telling his story. "It was definitely the closest I've ever come to ejecting," he said.

*   *   *

The jury nodded and there were a few muttered "Wow, that was pretty close," and other comments to that effect. Even though we all tried to be understanding to Arnie, each of us was saying to ourselves there was no way we would let such a chain go unbroken in *our* jet. Would I have had the guts to divert to a strange and unfamiliar field? It was easy to say and tougher to do. In the end, we all laughed and Horse summed up the jury's mood by saying, "Arnie, the real moral of that story is that if something isn't working right, all you need to do is hit it harder."

Everyone laughed at Horse's comment, and the conversation shifted back to the upcoming meeting in the ready room. We continued to bad-mouth the skipper's decision to hold the meeting simply because that was what the group was doing. I remained quiet, thinking the story would prove valuable to other members of the squadron. Such a forum of public confession and humiliation was a technique that the skipper liked to use, and it was one that did not endear him to the junior officers. We all thought it was a terrible way to lead, but he certainly had us all scared, and that fear did motivate us to learn and think faster than we otherwise might have if we were not frightened. There were better ways to lead, but leadership through intimidation and fear seemed to be his style, and I knew now that if I could stay one step ahead of him, my chances of surviving this war would be good.

A few hours later in the ready room we all gathered to listen to Dawg's confession. It was a sad sight to witness a normally confident senior pilot expose his poor judgment to younger, less-experienced aviators, but he did it with the hope that nobody else would fall into the same trap. To his credit, Dawg gave an excellent accounting of the flight, and his tone was far more self-deprecating than I would have expected. The incident had obviously made a significant impression on him. Dawg knew that if his last stab at the basket had not worked, he would have been responsible for the loss of a seventy-million-dollar aircraft, the possible death or injury of his three crew members, and the ruination of his fifteen-year navy career in one grand stroke. As it stood now, it appeared it would just be another time that a navy pilot had cheated death and dishonor and had walked away unscathed. But the skipper insisted on having the last word.

He stood up in front of the assembled ready room as Dawg took his seat. Alpha Charlie rose to the occasion in rare form. "If any of you little shits make a mistake like that again I will rip the wings right off your chest and I guarantee you'll never fly again. There should be no question in your minds that bingo is bingo. I repeat: *bingo* is *bingo*. When your fuel indicator needle hits bingo fuel I expect all of you to divert according to standard operating procedures. I will not stand for any more hot-dog, shit-hot 'I'll get gas at the next tanker' attitudes in this squadron. Questions?"

Cave, being the resident expert on irreverence, could not pass up the opportunity. He raised his hand, unintimidated by the skipper's tirade.

"Yes, Cave," acknowledged the skipper.

"Sir, does that mean that bingo is bingo?" said Cave, trying to relieve the tension. The ready room chuckled quietly.

Alpha Charlie's eyes burned a hole into Cave's forehead, but Cave was too valuable to the squadron for the skipper to pull his wings, so Alpha Charlie let the obnoxious comment slide.

After the meeting I thought about Dawg's flight and the decisions he had made. What would my crew have done? Would I have been strong enough in the cockpit to tell Gucci that we needed to divert if he had suggested chasing the uncertain gas of a tanker? Both Gucci and I were strong willed. He was senior to me and the mission commander, but as the pilot, I was ultimately responsible for the aircraft and the safety of the crew. I hoped there would not come a time when we would be at each other's throats in the cockpit, but I knew that it could happen anytime.

CHAPTER FIFTEEN

Attention to Detail

"*Beeeast*," I bellowed as I slammed the watertight hatch closed, quickly suffocating the sounds of the flight deck behind me. "605 is a war machine, it flew great. Give me that one for my night mission tonight."

"What's it worth to you?" answered Beast, the salty mustang.

"The coldest San Miguel in the PI," I said, trying to seem more worldly than I was. I had only passed through the Philippines twice before and had only drunk a handful of San Miguel beers, but I had heard from Chief Rat that Beast had an affinity for the Philippine brew.

"In that case I'll see what I can do." He smiled and winked.

I felt great. We had just flown a low-altitude, armed reconnaissance mission over the Gulf on a short one-hour-and-ten-minute cycle. It was the first time in a long while that I had not worried about fuel consumption and had just enjoyed flying. We were teamed up with a section of A-6s and were looking for possible hostile naval targets. If we had found a hostile naval contact, we would have suppressed its acquisition radar by shooting a HARM missile down the radar's throat supported by jamming any other emitters on the ship's deck. This SEAD effort would have allowed the A-6s to roll in and lay a string of bombs on the confused ship. That was the mission, but unfortunately, we didn't find any targets. Instead we had a great time zooming around at low altitude. It was the lowest stress mission I had since the shooting started. My crew needed the flight. Wolfey was up front with me, and it was a good confidence builder for us as a team. The crew would now be rotating fairly regularly, so I would be flying with Wolfey up front more and more often.

Within minutes I had ripped off my flight gear, removed my Ruger and its two clips from my survival vest, crossed the passageway, and entered the ready room. I threw out a few hellos to the guys at the mailboxes shuffling paperwork, and gathered up my crew for a debrief.

"Great flight, Tank. I say we debrief it in the wardroom," suggested Gucci.

"Sounds good to me, unless you have something you want to cover here, Wolfey?"

"No, I'm starving. The wardroom sounds like a great idea."

"I'll let CVIC know what we did on the mission," said Skippy. "I'll catch up with you guys in the wardroom." We all turned around and left the ready room on our way to what would be a quick debrief followed by some idle chatter. On the way out I found four letters from Alice in my mailbox! I quickly devoured them while standing there, then hurried to catch up to the crew. I was smiling, knowing that I would reread them several times back in the bunkroom later in the day. It had been a fun, uneventful flight and Gucci made a good decision not to force a formal debrief on us when we had all performed well, and there were no real learning points to be stressed—not to mention, we were all going on a night strike together later, and we needed to focus on that.

After a quick lunch with my crew I walked back to the ready room. Once through the door and past the mailboxes I paused and hesitated, seeing the door to the vault was open a crack. I carefully pushed open the door to the Operations/Electronic Warfare vault, where we kept all our classified materials, our Rugers, and our ammunition under lock and key.

The operations yeoman, a young sailor named Bean, was seated at a small desk in the confines of this crowded little room. Even though it was packed with people, it was still nice and cool because this was the home of our tactical planning system, a large, high-speed computer that interfaced and shared data with our aircraft's HARM missile-targeting capability and our onboard jamming system.

Everything about it was classified, so we were all very careful to make sure that only authorized personnel had access to the vault. There was the usual crowd of TEAMS gurus sitting around the computer doing mission planning. Pez, Bhagwan, ET, and Zwickster were all discussing jamming tactics and I threw out the helpful suggestion, "Hey, guys, it's much easier just to shoot the damn radars."

They all looked at me with disdain and Bhagwan said, "Listen, you stupid stick ape [aka pilot], go grab a banana and then we'll talk."

"The wardroom is fresh out of bananas, Bhagwan, why don't you try standing up for a change." He already was standing, and he hated short jokes. He ended the discussion by flipping me the bird. I smiled and turned to the ops yeoman. The nuts and bolts of the jamming mission had never been my passion, so I had never really become a proficient TEAMS systems operator—none of the pilots were. I could do some basic flight planning on it, but the hard-core tactics and jamming techniques I left to the ECMOs. The young yeoman was tabulating the aircrews' flight time and various other flight statistics, such as arrested landings, night hours, instrument hours, and most important to all of the aircrew, combat hours. The black ink was for daytime, the red ink for nighttime. The combat hours were special, and they were logged in green ink to distinguish and set them apart in the aviator's flight log. Now this stuff I found more interesting.

"Congratulations, Lieutenant; you just completed your tenth combat mission last night. Only a few more to go for your first air medal." Apparently we needed to fly fifteen missions to earn a strike-flight air medal.

"Well, I'll just keep flying the missions," I said.

"Yes, sir," said the beefy young sailor, disappointed at my low-key reaction. I picked up my logbook and turned through the pages. It was a small, hardcover book, four by six inches and about three quarters of an inch thick. It had a rugged, blue-leather cover embossed with gold lettering in all capital letters: AVIATOR'S LOGBOOK. I had only one. The more senior pilots and ECMOs in the squadron had several that were glued together and then bound neatly with a leather jacket constructed by the squadron's parachute rigger. I looked at my logbook and felt like the new kid with the brand-new white sneakers who desperately wants to scuff them up a bit so that they look well worn. My logbook was so thin and new compared with all the more senior guys' books.

As I flipped randomly through the book memories came back: my first carrier landing in a T-2 Buckeye, on the USS *Lexington* in the Gulf of Mexico; my carrier qualification landings in the A-4 Skyhawk, also on the *Lexington;* and my first night traps in a Prowler on the *Nimitz;* I shuddered at that memory. My fingers turned a few more pages and there it was; green ink. It seemed to jump off the page and shout: THIS GUY IS A COMBAT-PROVEN NAVAL AVIATOR. I smiled, and in a moment of selfish delight I thought about all the guys I had gone through training with who would give anything to be where I was standing right now, holding their logbook with green ink in it. The medals sure would look good on my uniform underneath my wings of gold. My eyes moved down each column of numbers and checked them against my memory of my most recent missions. Something looked wrong.

"Seaman Bean, I don't think you copied down my instrument hours correctly for my last mission."

"Sir?"

"I believe I logged point four hours of instrument time on my last mission, and I don't see it in my logbook." Bean nervously shuffled through some papers on the desk in front of him and found the original yellow sheet that I had filled out after the mission in question.

"Sorry, sir. I guess I just missed it. I'll correct it right away," said the young sailor, embarrassed by the omission.

"Thanks for taking care of it. Those instrument hours are important for my qualifications."

"Yes, sir, I know," he said.

I handed him my logbook so that he could make the correction, and left the vault thinking how important it was to pay attention to details, just as Staff Sergeant Massey had taught me in Pensacola.

As I walked back into the hustle and bustle of the ready room I realized that in many ways I had never felt more a part of a team than I did right now. I had played sports all my life, had been a member of many teams, even the captain of several, but this was different. In a small way, I felt that we were actually shaping history and it was compelling to be caught up in something much bigger than the individuals involved. It was exciting to be at the center of an event that the entire world was focused on. I looked around the room at the faces: Gucci, Dawg, Ren, Horse, Skippy, Pez, Bhagwan, ET, Wolfey, Sushi, Zwickster, Face, Cave, Arnie, Lawboy, and others making up the collage of personalities that was our squadron. I had flown ten combat missions with this team, and I knew it was a milestone.

I sat down in my ready-room chair and remembered a study I had read about the Vietnam War that described the ten-mission milestone. The report found that a significant number of our pilots were lost before their tenth mission. But if a pilot was able to come through his early missions, his odds of survival greatly improved. I guess they figured that most guys made their stupid mistakes the first ten times out, and in combat, a stupid mistake usually means you get shot down. I had been lucky, and I knew I would never repeat some of the mistakes that I had already made.

Aviators, like athletes, can be quite superstitious and I was no exception. When I was very young and played Little League and Babe Ruth League baseball, if I had a hitting streak going I would wear the same socks and T-shirt under my uniform until the streak was broken. Luckily for everyone's nostrils in the bunkroom, I had outgrown that habit a long time ago. In some ways I figured that not getting shot down for ten consecutive missions was also a streak of sorts, but the fact that the *Midway* did our laundry only twice a week made the thought of wearing the same socks and T-shirt a very unpleasant proposition. So as a substitute I developed a ritual, spanning from the time I would leave the bunkroom before a mission to when I would man up the jet and start its engines. I had not focused on it consciously, but as I sat there in the ready room, I realized such a ritual existed and that I had better keep doing it the same way if I wanted to continue my streak of having as many arrested landings as I had catapult launches on the *Midway*.

There were a few hours to kill before my night-strike briefing at 2100. I had been up late the night before working with the A-6 and Hornet guys on the timeline for the SEAD portion of the strike. The plan had looked solid to me, and Gucci had promised to touch base with them this afternoon. I needed some quiet time to collect my thoughts before the brief, so I decided to go back to the bunkroom to begin my preflight ritual.

The bunkroom was like a cocoon, the only place where we could get some privacy. In order to do that I needed to get in my bed and close a blue cotton curtain that covered the length of my individual rack. As usual, the room was dark except for the faint red glow of the one or two overhead lights that still worked. I heard the rough sound of snoring from one row of bunks, probably Ren, I thought to myself as I walked gently toward the last row where my rack was located. I had by now mastered the gymnastic feat of jumping into the top rack, and I did so with little effort, quickly closing the curtain behind me. The darkness was almost complete, so I pressed the light on my digital watch to look at the time. Two hours until my brief; I could get an hour nap and then check on the planning cell to see if all was under control. After setting my alarm I tried in vain to fall asleep.

Will the Flankers and Fulcrums be flying tonight? Will tonight be the night they'll actually come after us? Will someone get shot down tonight? Who will it be? These were the questions that soaked up the energy in my mind. I tried not to dwell on them, but they were questions of the nagging variety. Whenever I didn't keep my mind occupied I found myself looking at a friend, thinking, *Will this be the last time we laugh at a joke together?* As a result, I felt myself maintaining an artificial distance from my friends in the squadron. We were all close, yet not so close to crush us if one of the group disappeared. Thoughts like these tend to make time evaporate. Sooner than expected my alarm was beeping at me, and I hadn't even closed my eyes. In the blackness, I had just been staring at the plastic sheet. I couldn't even see it as I lay listening to water drip from the steam pipe above.

I kept telling myself that these thoughts were natural. But they were also somewhat paralyzing. It was hard to make myself jump right out of bed when my mind focused on the possibility that I might never come back. I had yet to figure out what had made men get up in the middle of the night and go off to battle. Was it love of country? Was it belief in a cause? Was it fear of cowardice? Was it a longing for personal glory? For me, I believe it was a combination of such feelings that made me go flying over Iraq every night. For everyone it must be different.

A hollowness sat in the center of my stomach as I zipped my flight suit and laced up my boots, the hollowness caused by a natural fear of the unknown. I had grown accustomed to the feeling, and once I got airborne the feeling went away. In the air I was just too busy to think anymore. I just got the job done. But between now and the catapult launch my body needed to put on a good act to cover up the fear I felt.

Realizing that I had survived ten missions made me even more determined to keep my preflight ritual the same for every mission. I slipped my dog tags on over my neck, took a last look at Alice's picture on a shelf at the head of my bed, and turned to leave the bunkroom. As I closed the door behind me I heard one last snore and wondered when Ren's next mission was going to be. It would be soon, probably as soon as I landed from the mission I was about to fly. But before I could get to the catapult and lose the hollow feeling in my stomach there were briefs to attend. Tonight's gaggle brief was in the Eagles' ready room, right next door to ours. Gucci and I picked up our kneeboard cards of the day then walked next door, arriving a few minutes early in order to find seats.

The Eagles' skipper, the strike lead for this night's mission, was the picture-perfect attack pilot. His short, scrappy, athletic frame supported a chiseled face that was partially covered by a bushy black mustache. Both his hair and mustache were sprinkled with white hairs for each one of his many night landings. As a result of their coloring, which apparently had been that way for years, his call sign was Pepper. His confidence and poise permeated the ready room atmosphere. His junior officers worked away at preparing his brief and consulting with him on the presentation of details. Somehow it was different from our ready room. It seemed that the Eagles' skipper treated his men like men and believed in their capabilities. His junior officers bustled around the ready room doing last-minute chores as the skipper just sat there confident in the end result. As each overhead was completed and handed to Pepper he would inspect it quickly and nod approval. The ready room began to fill with crews from each squadron and was soon standing-room only.

At exactly 2100 the Eagle SDO turned on the ready-room television to the *Midway*'s intelligence center channel and the face of the Eagles' young intelligence officer filled the screen.

"Hank, Hank," shouted the Eagles' junior officers. *Hank* was his nickname and the ready room was showing their support for their squadron's intelligence officer.

"Good evening, Air Wing Five, and welcome to the event eight cyclic ops brief...." Hank went through the latest intelligence, highlighted by several late-breaking revisions to the Electronic Order of Battle. Most of the EOB pertinent to the air wing was supplied by our squadron as we used our sophisticated electronic surveillance measures equipment to precisely map locations of Iraqi surface-to-air-missile sites. Every SAM had an envelope of effectiveness displayed on a chart as a threat ring. Many overlapping threat rings, each with a different radius, made Iraq something of a headache to fly around. After a few minutes of updates and standard brief reminders Hank said, "That concludes the event eight cyclic ops brief. Good luck, and let's get our bombs on target on time."

The strike plan was a good one because it was simple and its premise was clear: Carry out an attack against the targeted ammunitions dump near Basra while minimizing the time that strikers would be flying through any overlapping SAM envelopes. As he briefed from the overhead projector Pepper described a detailed timeline that coordinated the actions of various mission elements, such as a MIG sweep consisting of a division of Hornets, a strike package of a division of Intruders and division of Hornets, and the SEAD package of a section of Prowlers and a section of Hornets. The timeline on the overhead projector helped every pilot to develop situational awareness for what the other elements of the strike were doing. When Pepper got to the part of the SEAD mission he looked at me and said, "When the strike package enters the SAM envelope here," pointing to one of the first set of overlapping rings, "we will be counting on the Prowlers to eliminate the associated acquisition radars of SAM systems so that we can ingress and egress safely." I nodded to the Eagle skipper, acknowledging our responsibility, and realized that if we did not do our job some of these A-6 crews might not come back. "Once again, the Prowlers are a go, no-go criteria for the strike. No

Prowler means no strike," said Pepper. I swelled with pride on the outside at this comment, but at the same time I cringed on the inside. Talk about pressure; if I didn't get my jet airborne, the entire mission would be scrubbed. I prayed that everything would be in good shape with my jet. So far, with no casualties on the *Midway*, we were on a roll and had no intention of stopping the streak. Our strikes were taking a toll on Saddam's soldiers and we were eager to press the attack. After forty-five minutes of excruciating details the gaggle brief broke up and the crews went back to their ready rooms to go over even more specific briefs and review their emergency procedures.

Gucci and I walked out the door that connected to our ready room. Skippy and Wolfey had seen Hank's brief, and I passed on to them the highlights of Pepper's brief. They had a jammer game plan developed for the mission that would make the most efficient use of the Prowler's onboard jamming system during critical times of the strike. I still felt an anxious hollowness in my stomach, and I hoped that we would again bring everyone home.

Once our crew brief was completed we each went our own way. I stayed in the corner of the ready room and organized my kneeboard for the flight. I placed the chart I would refer to inflight under my kneeboard clip beneath the card of the day, which gave all the important code words. I noted that on this night the Flankers would be called *panthers* and the Fulcrums, *cheetahs*. The timeline set for the strike would force us to burn a significant amount of gas, so the post-mission tanker rendezvous would be critical. We reminded ourselves in our crew brief about the refueling adventures of Dawg's crew. We had no desire to repeat their mistakes.

After a quick head call I went to maintenance control to see if Beast would take care of me tonight and give me 605, the jet that had flown so well for me earlier in the day. The usual cloud of cigarette smoke hung in the air over the maintenance control space when I leaned over and asked Beast, "So am I going to get 605?"

"Yeah, but remember, you'll owe me a couple of cold ones."

"Thanks, Beast, I love this jet," I said as I flipped the pages through the Aircraft Discrepancy Book. I had seen it all just a few hours before and the jet had not flown since. I quickly signed the acceptance sheet and returned to the ready room to collect my Ruger, radio, and kneeboard, and with them in hand, went to the para-closet and started to get dressed in the midst of the seven other men going on this mission. I always read the ADB before getting into my flight gear because it seemed that most guys in the squadron did the opposite. This way I could get out on the flight deck sooner without having to wait in line at maintenance control to review the book.

It was another dark night, but at least there was a sliver of moon that might help illuminate the otherwise overcast and hazy sky. As soon as I climbed to the flight deck Chief Rat came bounding up to me. "Sir, the yellowshirts are respotting the deck. They're pulling 605 aft to the fantail. It'll be TOW—Tail Over Water," which meant the jet would be parked with its tail hanging over the edge of the deck making it impossible to complete a close visual inspection of tail section.

"No problem, Chief," I said as the Prowler was slowly towed past us. I decided to do a quick, abbreviated preflight before the jet reached its intended fantail parking spot. Starting as I always did at the left engine intake I rapidly spotted things I could check while the jet was slowly moving aft: the general integrity of the intakes, the antennas on the nose, the hydraulic lines to the brakes, and so on. The preflight checklist took up four pages in the flight manual and it was now all ingrained in my brain. Within three minutes I was back at the tail section inspecting the engines' tailpipes. The right one looked good, but when I ducked under the jet's fuselage and made my way around to the left tailpipe, something felt wrong.

Preflighting an aircraft becomes rote after a while, but you learn that if you feel something is wrong, there usually *is* something wrong. The feeling is triggered subconsciously when you notice the presence or absence of something that usually is there or not there. The yellowshirts were positioning the jet to push it back over the fantail to its parking spot. In a matter of seconds I would lose the opportunity to check the tail section. I hadn't seen anything wrong, yet I felt that there was something out of place. I walked up to the yellowshirt in charge and said, "Just give me a minute to check the tail section again."

"Sir, we gotta park this bird now." I could have let him talk me out of my feeling, but I didn't.

"Look, one minute, that's all I ask."

"OK, sir, one minute," said the impatient yellowshirt looking at his watch. I raced to the tailpipes again with my flashlight, hoping to convince myself that I was imagining things. First I stuck my head in the port tailpipe and moved the light in a circular motion, checking the engine's heat shield and the retaining bolt. Everything looked normal. I heard the yellowshirts whistle and the jet started to move backward.

Damn, that was a fast minute, I said to myself as I ducked under the jet to look at the other side. The starboard engine heat shroud looked fine, but there was no retaining bolt! I hadn't noticed it before because it wasn't there! There was nothing holding the engine's tailpipe to the fuselage!

"*Stop the tractor*," I yelled as I ran toward the yellowshirt. "This jet is down, we need to get a structures mechanic to take a look. Don't move it." Chief Rat saw what was happening and ran up to the tailpipe.

"Jesus, sir, good catch," he said, reaching into the tailpipe and picking out the eight-inch-long bolt that had snapped and was lying alongside the tailpipe's casing. "That might have ruined your day."

"No shit, Chief," I said, upset by how close I had come to taking the catapult with a broken engine. "We need another jet now, or else this entire mission is going to be scrubbed," I said, recalling the words of the Eagles' skipper in the strike brief. Chief Rat turned his shoulder away from the wind and talked on his headset microphone to maintenance control.

"Sir, we're going to put you in 606. It has been having some electrical problems, but it's the only jet we've got right now."

"All right, where is it? Let's go."

CHAPTER SIXTEEN

Close Call

The broken retaining rod had shaken my confidence. I had flown 605 earlier in the day and just couldn't get over the fact that perhaps that retaining rod had broken while I was flying and I was lucky to have made it back to the ship without a catastrophic engine failure. I felt like preflighting 606 quite carefully, but of course now we were running late and our start sequence was going to be rushed. It did not fill me with great faith to learn that our newly assigned jet was parked on the elevator TOW. I would have no way of checking its tailpipes and their retaining rods. This would be one of the many times that I put my faith in our squadron's maintenance department. The bottom line was that Chief Rat said it was good to go and that was good enough for me.

Clement had run down to maintenance control to get the Aircraft Discrepancy Book for 606, which I had to read standing next to the jet while other jet engines around us were howling, each one seeming more impatient than the one next to it to launch into the night. The *Midway* turned into the wind for the launch as I stood there next to my jet leaning into the wind, now over thirty knots. The looseleaf pages of the ADB were snapping and crackling in the wind, making it next to impossible to read what the actual gripes were. There was a stack of pink gripes, meaning maintenance had not yet had a chance to fix them. The wind was making the cloth of Clement's trousers snap the way a flag does on a flagpole. My eye caught something on one of the sheets about the trim system, but I couldn't make out what it said. The other gripes did not look as if they affected any critical parts of the jet, so I signed the acceptance sheet, using Clement's back as a stand-up table. I had not been able to do a complete preflight. I had not looked closely at the ADB. I felt uncertain, rushed, and overloaded. I had a mission to do. This was combat.

Gucci, Skippy, and Wolfey were all strapped in by the time I climbed into my seat. Power was already on the jet and the dim red lights of the cockpit made me feel more at home. I started to relax. Now I was in my element; I was ready to go flying. My left hand started checking the switches on the left side and I worked my way around the cockpit making sure that everything was in its proper position. Satisfied with what I touched and saw, my left hand went out to its familiar place on the throttles and my right hand slid comfortably around the stick. To put the electric trim at the proper setting for the launch my thumb reached to the top of the stick. "*Ahhhgh! Yeeow!*" I shouted as I yanked my right hand off the stick and shook it in the air, trying to lose the pain that seared through it.

"What happened?" asked Gucci.

"I just figured out what one of the unreadable pink gripes on this jet is. The trim button just shocked me," I said, my hand still stinging from the moderate electrocution I had just experienced.

"Are you OK?"

"Yeah, but I've got to fix this thing before we go flying." The trim button allows the pilot to make minor adjustments to the configuration of the wings so that he can balance the aircraft in flight. It needed constant adjustment throughout every flight, depending on the airspeed, altitude, and attitude of the jet. I could not possibly fly the mission while getting electrocuted throughout the flight. It was a low-voltage shock, but there was a warning in the Prowler's flight manual that noted the voltage provided enough electricity to incapacitate some pilots. I was hoping that I would not be one of the "some pilots" who would become incapacitated. One of my first flight instructors had told me to always carry a strip of duct tape on my kneeboard in case of an emergency. I had never really understood what good it would do, but tonight I thanked him because I finally had a use for it. I ripped the tape off my kneeboard and wrapped it around the trim button, covering up the exposed wire that was shocking me. The thick cloth tape provided enough protection so that the button was still functional, but I no longer got the Frankenstein treatment every time I touched it.

"Is that gonna work?" asked Gucci, concerned that my brains might melt down during the flight.

"Yeah, I think it will hold up. If smoke starts coming out from my helmet, just yank my hand off the stick," I said. Gucci laughed at the image.

We lowered the canopies, started our engines, and soon we were ready to launch. The line for the catapult was disappearing into the night, and since a jet was being shot off the *Midway*'s bow every thirty seconds, our turn came up quickly. We taxied forward while going through our take-off checklist. The yellowshirt directed my every control input. *Clunk-dunk* was the sound I heard when we felt the coupling of the Prowler's launch bar to the catapult shuttle. My left arm was locked at the elbow with my left hand grasping the throttles and catapult grip as the Prowler's engines roared and rumbled, spewing exhaust into the jet blast deflector. My left thumb flicked the external lights switch, and our jet transformed into a war machine, glowing and flashing with light. As the catapult officer touched the deck, my head slammed into the seatback. The familiar pressure on my chest and the rattling and speeding along the catapult's track made me smile. It was another good cat shot.

"Ironclaw 606, airborne," said Gucci, making the mandatory radio call. *He is solid,* I said to myself, *so solid. He never misses a call and is always a few seconds ahead of the jet and usually ahead of me. I'm very lucky to have him in my crew.*

We soon switched up to strike frequency and got vectors to the tanker from Liberty. Our squadron definitely held the E-2C Hawkeye guys partially responsible for Dawg's near flame-out, so we now carefully considered any advice that they passed to us by radio. We considered their calls more advisory than mandatory. But the vector they gave us to the tanker made sense and was in line with its prebriefed location, so I turned to the recommended heading and flew into the darkness.

As we climbed out on the departure heading I kept scanning the horizon, looking for possible traffic. There were now four carriers in the Persian Gulf: USS *America*, USS *Theodore Roosevelt*, USS *Ranger*, and USS *Midway*. USS *America* had recently left the Red Sea and joined us in the Persian Gulf. That meant that there were a lot of jets flying around in the same small piece of sky. In the big picture the carriers were coordinated in terms of target selection and times on target so as not to conflict with one another, but I was not willing to rely on the big-picture planners to keep me from running into another jet. We did not have enough radios to monitor all the other frequencies used by other air wings, so we were not exactly sure if their departure and arrival traffic patterns would be in conflict with our own. For example, the *Ranger*'s aircraft might be in a recovery stack that could interfere with our departure. The thought that I might be flying right through the marshal stack of twenty aircraft from another carrier made me grip the stick even tighter. I was determined that if I were to die out here in the Gulf, it would at least be in a glorious fireball initiated by the guns of an enemy; in short, a warrior's death. I refused to be taken out ignominiously by a midair collision with another American jet.

The feeling of hollowness in my stomach that was present earlier had now disappeared only to be replaced by a gut-wrenching sense of anxiety. I constantly felt as if someone were chasing me, so I kept looking behind to the left and right for potential threats. The tanker track had moved farther north as had all the battle groups. As our attacks continued to pound Iraqi defenses, every day we felt more and more confident with our ability to control events in the Gulf. We had established air superiority at the outset of hostilities, and now we had air supremacy. Nothing seemed to be flying except for coalition aircraft.

We leveled off at our assigned tanker altitude and started to look intently for the moving, bright-white strobe light that would mark the tanker as being different from a star. It was hard to tell the difference. I regularly made the initial movements to rendezvous on stars until it became clear that it was going to take an awfully long time to join up. Even though I had grown accustomed to a mass rendezvous on the tanker, I still felt that it had the safety and organization of a swarm of bees coming across a flying honeypot. Jets would swoop in on the tanker with a singleness of purpose that was frightening. The Hornet guys were especially bad. They would swoop down to the tanker, concentrating only on the join-up, disregarding what other aircraft might be in the way. By the time we arrived at the tanker, the swarm was in progress and we watched as the bees attacked the honeypot. It was like jockeying for position on a three-dimensional on-ramp to a highway. There was no real protocol, because all the jets were arriving from different angles and different directions so it was a massive free-for-all. If the Prowler had been equipped with a horn I would have been leaning on it. In the end, I joined up on the left wing of our tanker and waited patiently for my turn.

As with any task, practice had made me more confident in my tanking ability. Tonight I poked the basket on the first plug and retracted so smoothly that the basket did not even noticeably move. With a full bag of gas, once again we were off to battle. The skipper was flying the other Prowler, and he had already left the tanker track with his fighter escort by the time we pulled off. Our Hornets were waiting for us and they joined up above and behind us as we headed off to our jamming orbit.

"Let's go through our combat checklist," said Gucci. "Stow all loose gear."

"Set here," I responded.

"Back's good," said Skippy from the backseat.

"O2 on and visor down," said Gucci.

"Set here," I said, followed by "Back's good," from Skippy. The checklist was familiar enough by now that it developed a cadence in the cockpit. I anticipated Gucci's challenges and replied with short, staccato answers that avoided any confusion. Our crew was really coming together. I smiled under my oxygen mask. This was what I had hoped for in combat—feeling part of a close-knit team that developed synergies, making us a greater force as a crew than the sum of our individual talents. We knew one another's habits in the cockpit and knew one another's responsibilities. Within two minutes the checklist was complete and we were checking our timing to ensure that we arrived at our outer jamming point on time and with alignment to the strike package.

"Looks ugly ahead," said Gucci, his head buried into the radar boot.

"You mean the weather?" I asked.

"Yeah, there are some major thunderstorms ahead. Looks like they're right over our orbit."

"Great," I said sarcastically. "We need to stay at this altitude for our mission profile. They didn't have anything in the forecast about storms."

"I know. We'll have to just wait and see how bad it is when we get there," said Gucci.

At night it was difficult to tell visually where a thunderstorm began and where it ended. Now the dark shadows of the night were only illuminated by the sliver of a moon that provided just enough light to differentiate between the emptiness of the night sky and the presence of even darker storm clouds, which rose up until my eyes could no longer separate the two shades of darkness. It was impossible to tell how thick or dangerous thunderstorms inside dark storm clouds might be. I just knew that if we altered our mission profile, it could have a negative impact on the strike. We needed to be jamming in just the right place at just the right time or else some of our A-6 friends might never make it home. Visibility was decreasing as we flew north, a fact that made us all grow increasingly tense. I remembered the piercing look in Pepper's eyes. He was counting on us to protect him from the SAM threat.

So far during the first ten days of the war the weather had not played a major factor. Tonight that was changing. One of the most important things to do while flying in a threat area is to maintain visual flight conditions so that you stand a fighting chance at avoiding the threat by using evasive maneuvers. If you can't see it then you can't possibly maneuver to avoid it. Flying in clouds is not the smart way to go when in a SAM environment. We would once again be flying over oil platforms that had been firing at us since our first strike.

"I've just done a radar update on Failaka Island. Nav is tight. Just over five minutes to go to our outer orbit point," said Gucci.

"Roger that."

"Liberty shows picture clean," said the Hawkeye controller, who was looking for enemy fighter activity.

"We'd better start climbing to stay out of this storm," said Gucci.

"We've got to maintain this altitude at least for our inbound leg as the strikers are making their ingress to the target," I said.

"If we fly into the heart of this storm we won't be able to see anything that is shot at us. We need to stay visual."

"The A-6 guys who are dropping the bombs on the target will have the same problems."

The light-orange digital display on the INS in the cockpit's center panel showed that we were quickly approaching our point. "Look, our guys are about to drop bombs on an important target," I said. "We need to be where they are expecting us to be. Let's stick to our plan inbound and we can climb out of the storm on the outbound leg while the strikers are egressing." I could tell Gucci didn't like the idea of flying blind. But it was what the mission required and, more important, I couldn't stand the thought of an A-6 getting shot down because we flew a different profile. It was the right thing to do.

"Thirty seconds to jammers on," said Skippy from the back. "Let's jam 'em." Somehow, his soft but insistent Montana voice combined with his aggressive choice of words eased the tension between me and Gucci.

"All right, we'll maintain our altitude on the inbound, but we'll climb to get visual on the outbound leg."

"Roger," I said, pleased that we were going to stick to the plan. The two Hornets providing our fighter escort were not about to follow us through the goo. They could provide better coverage for us by flying high above the storm and scanning with their radar for potential fighter threats.

So far, I had not gotten zapped by the trim button and hoped that I could make it for the rest of the flight without being incapacitated. Like all the other warnings in the Prowler's manual, it was a warning that had been written in the blood of naval

aviators who had paid the ultimate sacrifice for something as ig-
nominious as a trim button. The duct tape seemed to be doing the
trick, and I was purposely not trimming the jet nearly as much as
I normally would. My gloves were moist with sweat now, which I
knew might promote the conductivity of electricity. My thumb was
just a big lightning rod and my body was not grounded. I rolled
the Prowler to the left to intercept our outer orbit point and start
the critical three-minute inbound run toward the target on a heading of 320.

"Jammers on," said Skippy as we rolled wings level to maximize
our jamming effectiveness.

"It just looks like layers to me," I said, trying to be as optimistic
as possible in describing the weather, knowing that layers were still
bad because they would still obstruct our view to the potential
threat. A SAM could pop through the layer below us at any moment
and I would not have time to avoid it. My discomfort grew as the
layer below us quickly turned into the thicker moisture of a large
storm cloud. After another minute of flying we were completely
swallowed by the cloud. Visibility was poor and we were relying
solely on our INS and ground-mapping radar to tell us when we
had reached our inner point of Bubiyan island. The strikers should
be within the heart of the SAM envelope now, so our jamming
effectiveness was crucial; we were hoping it was degrading the Iraqi
targeting solution on our A-6 bombers.

"Anything unexpected on the system?" I asked, hoping that if a
good HARM target radar popped up we would be able to launch
our missile.

"Nothing," said Wolfey. It seemed the Iraqis had learned quickly
that if they radiated certain radars during a strike, they would be
destroyed. As a result our crew had not shot a missile in the past
four days. My hand was holding the stick firmly because of the
storm's turbulence as my eyes scanned the instruments in the cockpit, checking everything for normal indications. The Prowler felt
small compared with the storm that surrounded us. We now had
just over two minutes left to fly inbound. I strained my eyes as if
to see through the clouds, but it was not possible. Somehow I knew
that there was not a SAM meant for my jet nor was there antiair-

craft artillery that would find us. I felt naively protected by the clouds that had surrounded our jet, hiding us from our enemy's eye. I watched the secondhand on the small analog clock in the center of the cockpit tick tirelessly toward our turnaround point. I decided to fly jinking maneuvers in case the gunners on the oil platforms opted to try to lock us up with their radar-guided AAA. Since I couldn't see it coming, I didn't know for sure whether or not it was in the air. The cockpit was silent and I knew that everyone was just looking at the clock for the outbound turn. Right now we were a "grape." Even though I was jinking every few seconds, we were still flying in a predictable direction and were vulnerable to both ground and air threats. I began to feel guilty about pressing Gucci to maintain our flight profile. The analog clock moved slowly around the face and the digital clock counted down toward zero when we would be on top of our turn point.

"Ten seconds to go," said Gucci. We had made it this far and I was determined to keep up our jamming until the very end of our inbound run. When the digital clock turned to zero I slammed the stick to the left, rammed the throttles to the stops, and locked my eyes onto the instruments. The attitude gyro rolled to ninety degrees of bank as I pulled the Prowler through the turn as rapidly as I could. The Gs felt good on my body and I kept the pull on until we had reached the reciprocal heading of 140. Leaving the throttles at full military-rated thrust I held down the Prowler's nose and let the jet accelerate to Mach .7, and we started the climb-out to visual conditions.

"Liberty has two cheetahs airborne, twenty-five north of Bullseye. Heading south at angels 30, five hundred knots. I repeat, two cheetahs north of Bullseye heading south." This was bad. We were climbing slowly through the clouds of the storm, trying to get to visual conditions, and there were two enemy fighters heading our way. I felt like a grape on the vine waiting to be picked, but we needed to keep jamming and keep our heading if we were going to offer any protection to the A-6s now egressing from the target area. I wanted to tell everyone to keep an eye out, but it was useless because we were flying in the middle of a cloud. If we descended, we would be lowering ourselves into the SAM and AAA threat, and if I kept climbing, I faced the possibility of being a target for an Iraqi fighter pilot flying his Russian-built Fulcrum.

"We've got to keep climbing to get to visual conditions," I said.

"Concur," was all that Gucci said. Passing through twenty-five thousand feet there was no let-up in the thickness of the clouds and I began to wonder how high up this storm would reach.

"Liberty shows two cheetahs ten miles north of Bullseye, heading south." Passing thirty thousand feet we finally saw some stars, and the cloud cover of the storm began to dissolve. As soon as I had broken free from the bonds of the storm, I leveled off at thirty-two thousand feet and started to kick my rudder pedals from side to side so that I could expand my field of view in my rearview mirror to look for any hostile jet on the horizon. First I hit the right pedal and gave Gucci a look out of the right side of the jet, then I jammed my left foot against the pedal thereby swinging the Prowler's tail to the right, allowing an unobstructed view of my six o'clock. Nothing was there. I turned back to face front, and off to the left at about three quarters of a mile at high speed I saw an F-14 with just its wingtip lights on traveling at engagement speed. "Traffic ten o'clock, friendly fighter," I said. My eyes strained and flicked back and forth. That fighter should have a wingman. The fact that I didn't see the wingman off to the left concerned me. "Where's his damn wingman?" I said over the intercom in a quiet but anxious voice, my eyes swinging to the right.

"I don't see—" the rest of Gucci's sentence was rendered unintelligible because I shoved the stick forward as hard as I could, empowered by the sheer terror I felt. The Prowler's G meter jumped up to negative 2.3 Gs. The second F-14 flew over the top of our canopy within a matter of feet, almost handing our crew an ugly death. My heart was in my throat as the Prowler hit a nosedive back into the clouds from which we had just emerged. "Damn, F-14s," I said. Gucci simply nodded, visibly shaken from the near miss.

"Liberty shows two cheetahs now ten miles south of Bullseye, tracking south."

The fighters were still coming, but the F-14s were now being vectored onto them, so my first concern was to get out of the clouds and back to visual conditions where I would stand a better chance at defending myself if I could see the attack coming. The Prowler's ground-seeking nose was buried in a dive and it took a good hard pull to redirect the jet's downward vector initiated by the last-ditch avoidance maneuver that I had just accomplished. A nose-low, unusual attitude in the clouds was not a great place to be, but it was better than having run into that F-14. I leveled the wings and pulled the nose to the horizon, using the attitude gyro in the cockpit. After a few seconds with a climbing vector we were once again out of the goo. As soon as we were free of clouds I kicked in both rudders, allowing us to get a good look at our six o'clock to check it was clear.

"Liberty shows two cheetahs turning cold and tracking north."

"That was a close one," I said.

"Yeah, I don't think that F-14 was very friendly after all," said Gucci.

"Liberty, Thumper flight feet wet. Mission status: starstruck."

"Thumper, Liberty, roger, copy starstruck." Gucci checked his kneeboard card and *starstruck* translated to 100 percent mission success. The strike package had completed its mission and once again all of our guys made it out all right. We had made the right choice to stick to our profile. The strike was a success and nobody could second-guess us now. Gucci plugged in the first point on the RTF profile and we turned to the south skimming along the tops of clouds toward the RTF window.

I switched on the autopilot and relaxed. My mind began to drift now that we were safely south of the Iraqi threat. I felt like the guy on a basketball team who pulls up for the three-point shot from downtown and everybody in the crowd cringes because he is a rookie and not much of a three-point shooter. The coach shouts, "No! No!" just as he releases the ball. But then when the ball flies through the basket, touching nothing but net, the crowd cheers wildly and the coach shouts, "Good shot, good shot!" We had made it through the mission without getting shot down, and as a result, everyone would praise our crew's aggressive decision. If we had gotten hit—well, let's just say I wouldn't be as popular.

Tonight had not been a good night. First it was the retaining rod on the engine, then the electric shock, culminating in the near midair collision with the F-14. I was certain that the A-6 crews probably had more frightening tales to tell, but as for me, I had cheated death more than enough for one day. On the flight back to the ship I flew the RTF profile as prescribed, pulling the throttles back to conserve fuel so that we wouldn't need to stop for gas at the tanker.

I realized that either event, the retaining rod or the F-14, could easily have been the end for me, and it reinforced a feeling I had from the beginning that I could in no way rationalize or justify— but somehow, I knew I would get through this war unscathed. Perhaps Alice's prayers were making a difference. I don't really know where the feeling came from, but somehow I felt protected. I convinced myself that Alice and I were meant for each other and that we would spend the rest of our lives together.

I flew a solid night approach and smiled when I parked without having to do the bow dance with the yellowshirts. When I got back to the ready room there were no fewer than *seven* letters from Alice in my box. Thank God I survived the flight if for no other reason than to read her heavenly, handwritten letters. That night I relished life and thought about the future with the woman I would marry.

CHAPTER SEVENTEEN

Time-out

It was now the second week of February and after four weeks of constant air operations the Allied Coalition had clearly established air supremacy in the Gulf. The *Midway*'s aircrews as well as the ship's officers and sailors were all on the brink of exhaustion. The *Midway* was working extremely hard to keep up the same pace as the larger, more modern nuclear-powered carriers which each had more deck space, more catapults, and more aircraft. To her credit, the *Midway*, amazingly, was doing just that. But the fast pace had taken its toll on the ship's flight deck, which had become more hazardous than could be considered reasonable even for a wartime environment. It would have been a tremendous black eye on our battle group had the *Midway*'s first loss of the war been right on its own deck, and it looked like that might happen any day now.

We were flying a daytime armed reconnaissance flight with Wolfey in the right seat and Gucci and Skippy in the back. The mission had been uneventful, since it seemed that by now what was left of the Iraqi fleet was either on the bottom of the Persian Gulf or tied up in port serving as stationary targets for coalition aircraft. But there was always someone in the intelligence center who demanded reconnaissance for possible surface threats to the carrier, and today was our day to fly the mission. Being the only Prowler in the recovery I joined a section of A-6s overhead and we flew into the break as a tight, three-plane formation. I took special pride in flying in tight formation around the carrier, knowing that a nice tight formation always drew approving nods from the LSOs on the deck below as pilots entered the break.

The lead A-6 did a good job of guiding us into the break smoothly, allowing me, in the dash-three position, to maintain the six feet of wingtip clearance that I was working to keep on dash two. As we leveled our wings at 800 feet and 400 knots, my left and right hands continued to make the constant corrections needed to stay in position while we flew over the *Midway*'s wake. Passing over the carrier's island the lead A-6 broke sharply to the left. The Intruder's wings were ninety degrees to the depths of the Gulf as the pilot pulled his jet through the humid air. I bet it was humid enough that there were visible vapors forming on the upper surface of our wings. Seventeen seconds later dash two broke, then I broke.

I grunted with the onset of the Gs to ensure that I wouldn't gray out as the blood tried to drain from my head under five times the force of gravity. When the jet slowed to 250 knots I dropped the landing gear, the flaps, and the tailhook as I struggled to make a smooth transition to the landing configuration. "Gear one, two, three down and locked, flaps thirty, stab shifted slats are out. . . ." I blurted out almost unintelligibly as I attempted to focus on flying the jet.

Rolling gently off the 180-degree position about a quarter mile abeam the *Midway*'s LSO platform, I kept my eyes inside the cockpit, monitoring my angle of bank, my airspeed, and my rate of descent. I was shooting for 450 feet after 90 degrees of turn and I hit my altitude but was four knots fast, a speed discrepancy not noticeable to most state troopers but enough to cause our jet to bolter. Reducing power as I trimmed nose up corrected for that error and as I rolled into the groove I was on and on. This was a good start. I just needed to concentrate and keep scanning to fly an OK pass. My eyes darted back and forth from the meatball, which was just cresting high above the green horizontal datum lights, to the centerline. But there wasn't any centerline. The painted centerline had been scraped off the deck by the last month of around-the-clock operations. I kept making small corrections to keep me on what I thought was centerline as I sped toward the massive hunk of floating steel.

"Right for lineup," said the LSO. I responded immediately with a wing dip to the right, but was slow to add the necessary power to maintain the proper rate of descent. *Slam! Screech!* The hook grabbed the second wire and my body was thrown forward toward the instrument panel with the rapid deceleration. Just as I slammed into the deck I saw the meatball sagging below the datum lights. With luck the LSOs would not notice that I went a little low at the ramp.

The sea state was high today and the *Midway* was acting up, delivering her infamous Dutch roll and making the deck a treacherous place. The last-second "right for lineup" call from the LSOs had been a good one because even after the correction I had a strong left drift in at the end of my approach. The *Midway* rolled to the left as I was landing and that roll combined with the slippery deck meant that after our roll-out I was looking right over the edge of the deck into the port catwalk—a place where you did not want to be. The flight deck was slippery because of the constant punishing torture it had absorbed during the past month. Continual flight operations had worn down the deck surface to bare steel. When a flight deck is in good shape it's covered with a nonskid surface applied as pavement on top of the steel deck. It offers jets as well as yellow gear tractors traction on the deck's surface. The controlled crashes in the landing area had begun to create cracks in the nonskid surface and soon large chunks of surface material were flying around the deck. Part of the danger was from loose debris on deck, but the other part of the problem was the lack of traction that the bare steel presented to jets trying to maneuver on the flight deck. Tires on the jets were inflated to rock-hard pressures. So when such tires on a Prowler tried to taxi across a pitching steel deck covered with oil and hydraulic fluid, the result is an out-of-control sixty-thousand-pound warhorse with no way to stop other than to crash into another jet or to go over the side.

Going over the side in any jet is a frightening thought, but going over the side in a Prowler would be a nightmare. Since there were four crew members to get out of the jet, the decision to eject had to be made early. If, for example, the nosewheel went over the edge of the deck, the aircrew would be instantly outside of the safe ejection envelope and would not all survive. So you either needed to eject before the nosewheel left the surface of the deck or you needed to take your chances and see what happened. Sometimes the jet might get hung up in the catwalk and the flight-deck crew might be able to hook a crane to the jet before it fell into the water, but there were no guarantees that it wouldn't simply roll off the deck and keep going into the drink. If that happened, the crew was faced with underwater ejection which is something that has never been attempted in the Prowler. The bottom line was that there were no good options for going over the side.

With this in the back of my mind I waited for the *Midway* to roll back to the right until adding power to taxi. As the deck had gotten progressively worse during the past week, I had learned to anticipate an expected slide across the slick deck and to use it to my advantage. I followed the yellowshirt's directions as best I could and maneuvered the Prowler out of the landing area. When the yellowshirt signaled me to stop, I locked my brakes and my momentum kept the Prowler skidding for another few feet. Since we were the largest and heaviest type of jet on the *Midway*'s small deck, we were skidding less than the Hornets and Intruders. Within a few minutes we were parked near the fantail on the port side, and the blueshirts were chaining us down to the deck.

We watched the flight-deck crew battle the elements and laws of gravity in order to get the jets neatly parked for the next launch. After dropping their bombs, the Hornets and Intruders were even lighter than when they had taken off and as such, they were sliding even more. I watched as a Hornet started taxiing aft down the center of the deck. The *Midway* rolled to port and the Hornet picked up a rightward vector in its taxi. The wheels were sliding across the steel and not gripping at all. The Hornet taxied slowly and when the *Midway* rolled back to the starboard side, the Hornet drifted back toward the aisle in the middle of the deck. Unfortunately, that was where everyone landed, so the deck was at its worst where the Hornet now taxied.

The yellowshirt was moving his arms together quickly to indicate to the pilot that he should pick up the pace of his taxiing. His signal demanded a speed greater than the pilot felt was appropriate, so the Hornet was creeping slowly across the slick steel deck. The yellowshirt was insistent though and as the starboard side of the ship dipped down toward the sea he continued to give the pilot a "hurry up" signal. Finally, the pilot—against his better judgment—came up on the power just as the deck rolled to port, and his fate was sealed. The combination of the boost of power and the roll to port sent the Hornet sliding across the deck directly at our jet's nose.

I thought about making a radio call, but there was nothing to say. The Hornet pilot locked his brakes in an effort to stop the jet's momentum, but it kept coming. The long, thin, bulletlike nose of the Hornet seemed to turn into a battering ram that was drawn to the bulbous nose of my jet as if it were steel to a magnet. The Hornet pilot dropped his tailhook, but there was nothing for it to grab.

"He's going to hit us," I said, feeling completely helpless as the Hornet continued to slide across the deck. But a young blueshirt carrying a chain ran up and without hesitation crawled under the sliding aircraft and latched one of the chain's hooks to the Hornet's belly-hold point and then took the other end of the chain and secured it to a pad eye in the deck's surface. The Hornet kept sliding until it came to the end of its leash. It then stopped abruptly just about a foot away from our nose cone. The young man in blue had just saved two jets from millions of dollars of damage that would have grounded them for a long time. His supervisor patted him on the back, and judging by the smile on his face, that pat on the back was reward enough. The flight-deck crew then reacted quickly as they chained down the Hornet tightly to the deck, ensuring it wouldn't move any closer to our Prowler. Seeing the situation stabilized I decided to climb out of the cockpit and get off this three-acre ice rink, back to the comfort and safety of the ready room.

Once through the hatch to maintenance control I exclaimed, "Beast, we nearly got rammed by a Hornet that was sliding while it was taxiing. That deck has got to be fixed."

"Well, you obviously parked in the wrong place. Would have been your fault if our jet got dinged," he said unsympathetically.

"Right. What was I thinking, parking there? Sorry," I laughed.

"Anyway, that is our last event. They just canceled the rest of the day's events because of the deck," said Dawg, who was now the squadron's maintenance officer. "We're going to sail south and spend a few days at anchor in order to resurface and repair the deck, then we'll get right back into it."

"Probably a good idea," I said after what I had just witnessed. A quick debrief followed and I felt a sense of relief and more relaxed than I had in a month, knowing that I would have a few days off from the rigors of flying constant combat operations.

Once back in the bunkroom I knew where my focus would be for the next few days: mail. During the past two weeks the *Midway* had been receiving literally several tons of mail per day. Many letters were from friends and family of the men on the *Midway*, but even more were letters from Americans writing to "Any Sailor, Any Marine, or Any Naval Officer." One hopeful young woman addressed a letter to "Any Single Navy Pilot." A friend of mine in one of the Hornet squadrons got the opportunity to respond to that one. It felt wonderful to see the support we were receiving on the homefront. Teachers had their entire classrooms write these "Any Sailor" letters, and the ship's mailroom kept busy trying to divide them up fairly among the ship's divisions and squadrons.

My favorite story was told to our ready room by the admiral of the battle group who came to speak to us one day during our one-week layoff from flight ops. He said he had heard of an "Any Sailor" letter written by a popular country and western singer who, wanting to do a good deed for an American fighting man, had enclosed a check for one hundred dollars to the sailor who opened the letter. The sailor replied to the singer and returned the check, writing something along the lines of:

> *Dear Sir,*
>
> *I am not on this ship serving my country for the money. I am proud to be doing what I am doing and so are all of my shipmates. We believe*

it to be the right thing to do, and we thank you for your support, but I
want to give you back your check. If you really want to do something nice
for me you could give my parents tickets to your next concert. They're
big fans of your music.

The singer did just that, and the parents were thrilled by the invitation and excellent seats. This was the type of attitude that abounded on the *Midway*. Everyone was walking tall after a month of combat operations in which we had taken it to our enemy and had not lost any of our own. In many ways it seemed almost artificial. The operation had gone exactly according to plan. I had been frightened several times, but we had not had to deal with the regular deaths of squadron mates or the routine occurrence of losing a few aircraft during a night strike over enemy territory that aviators during Vietnam, Korea, or World War II had had to deal with. I knew that it was still a war, and my heart went out to those we lost on other ships and to our air force brethren who were shot down, but the weaponry was now so advanced and the killing so removed that it felt almost sterile. I suppose it has always felt that way for aviators to some degree. Flying into combat is definitely different from walking into it. It will always remain different. For the aviator, the enemy is usually represented by an inanimate target, a bridge, a factory, a radar, or an ammunitions dump, so it is far easier to make the killing seem impersonal, and even when you are bombing people, they are so small they don't seem human.

I often thought about my comrades in the desert, the soldiers waiting in trenches while we bombed the enemy; waiting in constant fear of a chemical or biological weapon attack that could cause them to die a sickly death. These men would be the heroes, for it was they who would actually remove Iraqi troops from Kuwait. I only hoped that our attack from the air would make their job easier and would save lives of the coalition's "Any Soldiers" living in the desert waiting for the order to attack.

The letters on my desk had formed a huge pile and I pulled out some stationery and started to write to each and every one of the many people who had written to me. Some of my friends from high school and college were now teachers and they had gotten their classes to write to me. It was overwhelming and it felt great. I wanted each one of those kids to know how much his or her letter meant to me and how important it was for all of us fighting the war to know that our friends and families back home appreciated us and what we were doing.

There were letters from friends of my parents, friends of my grandparents, friends of my brother, and friends and family of Alice. General Eisenhower once said, "An army will fight as hard as the pressure of public opinion behind it. In the end, it is public opinion that wins wars." I believed that he was right, and for that reason I believed that this war would be over soon.

CHAPTER EIGHTEEN

Lonely on
the Platform

"I'm gonna rip somebody's head off if we don't get under way soon," growled Chief Rat as his red face puffed away on yet another cigarette.

"That might make a good article for the base newspaper," I said. "The headline could read NAVY CHIEF REMOVES MIDWAY SAILOR'S HEAD."

"Everyone would think I was going around the ship stealing the crappers," chuckled Chief Rat, reminding me that in navy lingo a *head* is the word for a toilet.

Maintenance control was filled with smoke, and all of the chiefs were in a fairly bad mood. I realized that everyone was much happier working eighteen to twenty hours a day because it didn't give them time to think about home and get depressed. Six days at anchor in the southern end of the Persian Gulf passed slowly for the air wing. We were all eager to get back in the air and contribute to the campaign. Rumors were rampant on the mess decks that the ground war would start any day now and none of us wanted to miss out on the action. The day before I had passed two young marines talking in excited tones about how they were pushing to get transferred to a unit on the front lines where they would see some real action. As I walked by I heard one of them say, "I wanna be there when the marines land . . . ready to kick some butt . . . before this war ends." I smiled at his naive enthusiasm and knew that his parents were very happy to know that their son was on the *Midway* and not on one of the amphibs preparing for an assault.

Resurfacing the deck was a slow process and required a lot of hot hard work by members of the flight-deck crew. The problem was that heat here in the middle of the day was too intense for the new nonskid surface to set properly. It was laid down as a hot, tarlike pavement on top of the steel deck which itself was so hot that the nonskid remained soft, tarry, and unsuitable for flight operations. Finally by the end of the sixth day the captain of the ship felt that repairs were about as good as we were going to get them and he ordered the *Midway* under way.

My crew spent most of the six days catching up on sleep and planning strikes against new targets that would support the ground campaign that we knew was around the corner. The three other carriers in the Persian Gulf had continued their operations while we were at anchor and had maintained air supremacy. As it turned out, the first day of flying after the layoff was my duty day as Landing Signals Officer. I had finally been assigned to a team on a regular rotation and was really enjoying learning to be an LSO. One of the finer points involves understanding all of the different regulations regarding pilot qualification for day and night carrier landings. Once qualified at night a pilot needed to get a night trap every seven days to stay qualified. If the time between night traps was greater than seven days, the pilot needed to get a day trap on the same day of the next night trap. Since the *Midway* had spent six days at anchor many of the pilots in the air wing had lost their night qualification and many others were on the last night of theirs. After six days of inactivity all of the air wing's pilots would be rusty, a fact that would be more evident at night than during the day.

As we expected, the daytime landings were not great, but they were safe. It was the first night recovery where we started to see some colorful approaches. I had been the controlling LSO at night only twice before, so Regbo, our team leader, and Mad Dog, the CAG LSO, wanted me to write for the first few night recoveries before I took control of the radio and pickle switch. Writing was purely secretarial duty, but it helped me to learn and to calibrate my eye. As approaches were flown the controlling LSO would call

out the grade and comments and I would diligently record everything he said in a form of LSO shorthand that appeared like hiero-
glyphics to the uninitiated. But to LSOs, the small scribbles would
tell of everything that a pilot did from the beginning of the approach to the landing. At night the carrier approaches were straight
in to the ship's centerline, unlike the daytime when approaches were
much more dynamic. What night approaches lacked in dynamic
flight profiles they more than made up for in the sheer terror involved when darkness robbed pilots of all their normal visual cues.

The first recovery of the night was rough. I could tell not only
by watching jets coming down the final approach path but also by
watching the nervous expression on Mad Dog's face. He always
wore a serious face, but this night there was something more in the
thinness of his lips and tightness of his jaw. On each jet he concentrated completely, and it appeared as if he believed he could will
the pilots to fly good approaches, but that was not the case. The
pilots one after another seemed to be flying low, barely clearing the
ramp and not making the early aggressive power corrections necessary to get back up on the proper glide slope. LSOs hated approaches like these because if given the call for power in close, many
pilots would go high and bolter. The LSO's mission was defined
as coordinating the safe and expeditious recovery of aircraft. There
was a fine line between what was expeditious and what was safe. If
the LSO only accepted perfection, then recoveries would never end.
But if LSOs accepted too many poorly flown approaches, then
someone would crash on the ramp and kill not only himself, but
some of the deck crew as well.

The air boss kept up a running dialogue with the LSO platform
in the hopes of pressing the edge of the expeditious envelope, often
seeming to favor it over safety. On one approach, for example, a
member of my team had given a power call to an incoming Hornet
and the Hornet pilot added too much power and boltered. The
telephone on the LSO platform would ring and Mad Dog would
pick it up and say a lot of "Yessirs," and then hang up the phone
and resume calling the recovery as he saw fit. He'd say, "It's easy
for *him* sitting in that damn glass booth to question our power calls
when it's *us* down here who will get swallowed by the fireball if one

of these jets smacks into the ramp." It was like this all night long. The boss would press for a more expeditious recovery; the LSOs would do their best to keep all the pilots off the ramp and on centerline.

Finally, before the last recovery, Mad Dog said, "Hey, Tank, why don't you wave this one?"

"Sure," I said, feeling quite worn out by the long night of recoveries, but always looking for a challenge.

"There will be eleven aircraft: four Hornets, four Intruders, a Prowler, a tanker, and a Hawkeye. Think you can handle it?"

"Eleven passes, eleven traps," I said with a false sense of confidence.

"Yeah, we'll see," came Mad Dog's reply. "Regbo, you back him up."

"All right, Mad Dog, I got it," said Regbo.

We were all tired after the long day of breathing in hot jet exhaust, hearing the shrill screams of jet engines at full power roaring only a few feet away from our heads and looking into bright sun throughout the day. Now at least the sun was gone, but my face felt windburned and I was ready to call it a day. I fervently hoped that all the pilots in this last recovery would cooperate by flying good, safe approaches.

As we waited for the recovery to start I stepped off the LSO platform, out from behind the windscreen, and was greeted by a Gulf wind over the deck that carried the distinct scent of a mixture of JP-5, hydraulic fluid, and oil. It was impossible to avoid it when you breathed in, so your lungs just got accustomed to it. The steam swirled out of the catapult tracks on the bow, and that steam wafted by us on the LSO platform like ghosts of pilots past, reminding us how important our job was tonight. These were the ghosts of pilots whom every naval aviator knew. We all had friends who had learned the hard way that naval aviation was an unforgiving business. If we didn't do our jobs well tonight perhaps there would be a new flight-deck ghost living in the steam of the catapults on the *Midway*.

Two members of our team leaned up against the windscreen behind us while Regbo, Mad Dog, and I prepared for the recovery. The LSO PLAT display was dimmed appropriately as was the Fres-

nel lens so that pilots would get good visual definition of the meatball as they flew in close and across the ramp. If lights were too
bright then the meatball would blossom in the darkness, growing
distorted and giving the pilot a less accurate indication of his position on the glide slope. Once we had adjusted all of the lighting
carefully, we got our radio checks.

"Tower, Paddles, radio check on button sixteen," I said.

"Loud and clear, Paddles."

"I have you same. Tower, Paddles, radio check on eighteen."

"Loud and clear, Paddles."

"Roger, I have you same," I said. Regbo then checked out his
radio on both control frequencies and we both checked our waveoff lights by squeezing our pickle switches. The lights checked
good. We were ready to go.

"Paddles, first jet is Dragon 305 at five miles," said the controller
on button sixteen.

"Paddles, copies," I said. The first four jets down the pipe would
be the Hornets because they were always the lowest on gas. Each
aircraft had a different light configuration and was distinguishable
in different ways at night. The Hornet was very distinctive. Its two
huge vertical stabilizers each had a red anticollision light on the tip
which was barely visible above the wings when the Hornet was in
landing configuration. For the LSO to tell if the Hornet was maintaining a good flight attitude, its wingtip lights needed to form a
straight line with the small approach light on the nosewheel landing
gear door. The first Hornet started out as a faint blinking light,
and three miles behind it was another flickering light. Spaced one
minute apart these eleven jets would fly their approaches in the
hope of getting aboard safely on their first attempt.

"Dragon 305, three quarters of a mile, call the ball," said the
controller, whose voice I heard loud and clear in my handset on
button sixteen.

"Dragon 305, Hornet ball 4.5," blurted the pilot.

"Roger ball, Hornet. Twenty-five knots," I said in as calm a voice
as I could muster. "We've got a clear deck," I proclaimed to the
rest of the LSO team, bringing down my right hand to my side
with the pickle switch. The Hornet came barreling down the glide

slope mezmerizingly steady. In the middle, the pilot failed to detect a left drift and since I was primarily focused on glide slope, neither did I.

"Right for lineup," said Regbo calmly. The Hornet's wings dipped to the right, responding instantly to the call.

"Power," I called, since I had not heard the Hornet's engine roar increase with the wing dip. I knew he would go low if he didn't add more power with the lineup correction. The jet screamed past us and the tailhook cleared the ramp by about seven feet and slapped the deck just short of the *Midway*'s first wire. The engines then howled at full power until the Hornet had come to a complete stop near the edge of the angled deck. Once the pilot pulled back on the throttles, the large General Electric engines relaxed and spooled down to idle. Within seconds Dragon 305 had cleared the landing area and we were ready for the next jet.

"Fair pass. Little high start to in the middle, not enough power on drift left in close, low on lineup at the ramp," I said, pleased with how quickly I had been able to make the call with confidence. The next two Hornets flew solid passes that did not need any radio calls and I decided to give them both OK grades. The last Hornet started off a little high and lined up left and his troubles only got worse.

"Chippy 402, three quarters of a mile, call the ball," said the controller.

"Chippy 402, Hornet ball, 4.6," said the pilot quickly under what was clearly heavy breathing.

"Roger ball, Hornet, twenty-five knots. You're lined up left."

"I'm watching his lineup, Tank," said Regbo, "you just keep him off the ramp."

"Roger," I said as I watched the incoming jet search for the proper lineup. The pilot had a big correction to make, since he was already lined up left and the ship's angle driving away from him tended to amplify a left drift in almost every approach and it was no exception on this one. The Hornet drifted back to the right, trying to establish itself on centerline, but it overshot the centerline and now was lined up right with only a few seconds remaining.

"Come left," said Regbo, which was a good call, but this time instead of hearing a power addition I heard the power being reduced and the engine spooling down. The pilot set up too great a correction and Regbo was forced to give him another call, "Right for lineup." The Hornet was underpowered for this maneuver, though, and I did not hesitate.

"Waveoff, waveoff," I said with authority in my voice while holding down the button on the pickle switch that turned on the bright red flashing lights behind the Fresnel lens. The Hornet was now dangerously low after making the right for lineup correction and the pilot went to full power when he saw the wave-off lights and heard my voice. Within an instant his vector changed from one which might have taken him to an untimely end to one which would give him another chance at the approach in a few minutes after he flew a gentle lap around the night landing pattern, regrouping his nerves and rebuilding his confidence.

"Good call, Tank," said Regbo. "He needed it."

"Yeah, that was pretty ugly. I hope he can get his act together on the next one."

"Call the pass," said Mad Dog, angry that the Hornet had done so poorly.

"Waveoff, high lined up left start, not enough power on left to right in the middle. Not enough power on lineup at the ramp," I said. As I looked up, the first Intruder had just reached three quarters of a mile. The Intruder pilot flew a fair pass to be followed by another Intruder and then Chippy 402 would get another chance. As I called out the grade and the comments for the second Intruder I watched Chippy 402 close on the *Midway*. This time he was working toward a better start. At a mile and a half out he was on course and on glide path. I stood there with the phone to my left ear and the pickle switch in my right hand raised above my head waiting for the Intruder that had just landed to clear the deck.

"*Foul deck!*" screamed one of the other LSOs from the windscreen.

"Foul deck, gear and lens set for a Hornet," I responded still holding my right hand in the air so as not to forget that the Intruder was still working to get off the deck, but when I turned to look, it could not move its tailhook off the surface of the deck.

"Chippy 402, three quarters of a mile, call the ball," said the controller.

"Chippy 402, Hornet ball, 3.7," said the anxious voice of the pilot. He was really working hard making little corrections all the way down the pipe. My right arm was still raised though, and we were reaching dangerously close to the decision point.

"Intruder's hook is now up and it's starting to taxi!" yelled the other LSOs in the back. "*Foul deck!*" one of them screamed. The Hornet was flying a great approach and I couldn't bear to ruin it, but there could never be an exception for a foul deck.

"Waveoff, foul deck," I said into the phone once again pressing the pickle switch and sending the young Hornet pilot off into the night yet again.

"Chippy 402, approach, your signal is tank. Tanker should be hawking you at two o'clock and angels two," said the controller. Finally the Intruder was clear of the landing area and we once again had a clear deck for the next Intruder. Within the next five minutes we recovered an Intruder, a Prowler, and an E-2C Hawkeye. All that was left was the tanker and Chippy 402.

"Who's flying 402?" I asked.

"Flounder," said Regbo, "he's a nugget, and he's been struggling a bit at night." I was a nugget and could relate easily to how Flounder must be feeling. It was a dark night and he was all alone. I knew how alone he felt. Mad Dog sensed it, too.

"Paddles, Chippy 402 is tank complete at five miles," said the controller.

"402, Paddles," said Mad Dog.

"Go ahead, Paddles," Flounder's voice sounded a bit shaky.

"Your last approach looked good all the way. Just get a good start and do the same thing. We'll have a clear deck for you this time."

"Roger that," said Flounder with what I thought was a weary tone to his voice. Was it weary or determined? I couldn't quite make it out. He was now at three miles and I felt that I needed to be really alert. Flounder was probably mad at himself for screwing up his first pass and then angry at the Intruder for causing a foul deck. He would be looking to get aboard on this pass. A few more seconds passed as the Hornet approached, blinking in the darkness.

"Clear deck," shouted Regbo.

"Roger, clear deck, gear and lens set for a Hornet," I responded.

"Chippy 402, three quarters of a mile, call the ball."

"Chippy 402, Hornet ball, 4.5," said Flounder. He had a good start and was working to keep it. I could imagine him in the jet sweating, breathing heavily, and concentrating more intensely than he had ever thought possible. But in the middle, he started to sink.

"Little power," I said very gently over the radio to get him to make the correction. In his nervous state he added too much power and started to go high in close. "Easy with it," I said and then at the ramp without warning Flounder made a poor correction; he simply pushed the Hornet's nose down and reduced his power.

"Power! Power! *Power! Power! Power! Jeeesuuuus Chriiiist!*" I screamed into the radio. I heard the power come back to the jet engines and the Hornet's afterburners each spouted a burst of flame ten feet long. The aircraft seemed to climb from a position below the deck. The Hornet's wheels barely cleared the ramp and the jet's tailhook slapped the roundown of the fantail's edge. The new non-skid surface made for excellent fireworks as the tailhook dragged along the deck, sending a magnificent plume of sparks arcing into the night sky. When the tailhook, exhausted from its fiery trip across the deck, finally reached the first wire, the Hornet rolled to a stop. My mouth was open and my heart was thumping against my rib cage. Another few inches lower and the jet would have exploded only one hundred feet from where I was standing. The life of a young pilot had been spared. I turned around to commiserate with my LSO brethren, but there was nobody on the platform. They had all wisely jumped into the LSO safety net.

Mad Dog was the first one back up on deck. "Tank, I can't believe you stood there for that," he said as he strode up to me.

"I don't know why I did. I was just yelling *Power!* in the phone. I guess I should have dropped it and jumped."

"Yeah, I didn't think he was going to make it. Nothing you could have done differently though. He just dove for the deck." My knees started trembling in a delayed reaction to the fear that I should have felt a minute earlier.

Fortunately, the tanker flew a solid pass and the recovery was complete. Flounder had flown a cut pass, which meant it had been unsafe. We later learned that no damage was done to the jet, but Flounder would go before a performance review board. Boards occurred every now and then. They were an unpleasant but necessary part of naval aviation. Perhaps Flounder did not belong in "the show"; not everyone did.

CHAPTER NINETEEN

The Inferno

Our air strikes now had a new focus: destroying the Republican Guard of Saddam Hussein. Viewed by many as the backbone of the Iraqi Army, the Republican Guard units now often became our primary targets. Intelligence officers and high-level joint planners in Riyadh created a grid system for organizing the systematic destruction of these core units. At the operator level on the *Midway* we called the grids "kill boxes." As I helped to plan these missions I thought of our comrades in arms in the desert. I hoped that our work would make their work easier. Coalition troops had spent the past several months waiting and waiting and waiting. They were living the lives of soldiers; eating dried food out of packages and sleeping in the desert on the front line. During the past five weeks the coalition's air campaign had relentlessly bombed Iraqi positions, but it was clear that air power alone would not expel Iraqi forces from their deep trenches. Now it was time for our Allied armies to face the terror that they had been anticipating for months in their nightmares. On February 24, 1991, the ground war began as coalition forces attacked the entrenched Iraqi Army.

A scheduling conflict had forced a crew change and I was going to be flying this day's mission with the XO, Odie, and Shoe. I had flown with each of them separately only a few times, so I was a bit apprehensive about our crew coordination for this mission. The XO would be in my right seat, which was fine, but I knew that I would miss the smooth working relationship that I had developed over the past month with Gucci. Like me, both Odie and Shoe were on their first cruise and I knew they were capable of making the same type of stupid mistakes that I had, so I knew I would need to be extra-alert.

In preparation for this mission I talked to Ren about flying with the XO. Ren didn't enjoy flying with him, but said he found him to be professional and competent in the cockpit. The now-underground UMPQUA group had taken to calling the XO *Nitro*, because he had a very low flash point and was viewed by many of us to be unstable and highly explosive. It was not a very original call sign, seeing as another skipper in one of the A-6 squadrons was also nicknamed Nitro, but it was nevertheless appropriate. His most positive trait was that he did not seem to hold a grudge. He could blow up at you one minute and then act as if he were your best buddy the next. I got the feeling that he loved being at war.

Today, in support of the ground offensive, the air wing was striking deeper into enemy territory than we had ever struck before. We believed that destroying the Republican Guard would be the most effective way to eliminate the greatest number of Iraqi assets in the shortest period of time. Attacking the Republican Guard was a great idea, but it was a close air support mission and the Prowler's system and armaments were not designed to effectively support this type of engagement. As a result, our mission this day was fleet protection. We called it a "Wormburner" mission because our job was to neutralize with jamming and/or HARM missiles any Silkworm missile site along the coastline that posed a threat to the coalition's naval forces. In the event of a Silkworm attack, the Prowler would position itself optimally and use its jamming and HARM missile system in order to deny, degrade, and possibly destroy the Silkworm's threat to the fleet.

It became obvious right away that the unusual makeup of our crew was going to lead to some minor confrontations in the cockpit. When you are a lieutenant junior grade and are flying with the XO of your squadron, those are confrontations that you lose. So if there were any differences in habit patterns, I would be the one having to make the necessary adjustments. The tone of the mission was set during the brief when I reviewed my emergency procedures with the crew. As I had been saying for over a month, "If we have a brake failure on the flight deck, I will select the auxiliary brakes, make a radio call—"

"I'll handle the radios, Tank," said Nitro.

"Ahh—yes, sir. Well, in that case, I would select auxiliary brakes, the XO would make the radio call, I would apply the brakes, use nosewheel steering, drop the tailhook—"

"I'll get the hook," interrupted Nitro.

"Ahh—yes, sir. OK, where was I? . . ." Eventually we made it through the brief of Nitro's new and improved emergency procedures. The XO had said that he was going to do so many things if we had an emergency that I actually was hoping we would have one just to see him in action.

When we finished the brief we each went our own way to complete our individual preflight rituals. Just as I had done every day for the past thirty-eight days and nights, I went to the head, checked the ADB, signed the acceptance sheet, picked up my survival radio and Ruger, got dressed in my forty-plus pounds of flight gear, and waved to all the chiefs and Beast in maintenance control as I walked out of the hatch into the warm Gulf air.

I was the first one from our crew on the flight deck. The start of the ground war was exciting news, and I could see that it was having an impact on the *Midway*'s men. Everyone on the flight deck seemed to have a renewed sense of fighting spirit, and we all believed that our ground attack was a telltale sign that the war was moving rapidly toward a conclusion. We were confident that our thirty-eight-day-long bombing campaign had made a big difference in softening up Iraqi defenses, and now we would be able to see to what extent it had really worked. The redshirted ordies were writing all kinds of creative messages on the weapons about to be delivered against the Republican Guard. One note that I remember from a politically motivated crewman was inscribed on a cluster bomb that read, "From one Republican to another."

The preflight, startup, and launch went smoothly. Chief Rat had his men working efficiently and happily. They were all excited about the prospects of the war ending soon. On the mess decks, the young sailors were all speculating about when we would leave the Persian Gulf and how soon we would have a port visit in Thailand to relax and celebrate the successful completion of a combat deployment. As I taxied up to the catapult I looked at Chief Rat, standing there surrounded by his men. He held his right arm up and formed the "Ironclaw" salute with his hand. I returned the salute with my own version of the menacing "Ironclaw," my fingers spread and muscles taut like a cat's paw poised to strike. Even though most of his face was covered by the large goggles he wore, I could see Chief Rat's smile and I knew that we had a good jet.

It was a standard daytime launch and we flew at five hundred feet until reaching the seven-mile arc from the carrier, then I pulled sharply back on the stick and we commenced our climb to the tanker. During the climb-out to the northwest we were confronted by an evil surprise, something that none of us had expected and all of us had a hard time believing. We saw in the distance, rising from the sands of Kuwait, a large, menacing black cloud.

As we flew north toward the tanker track I stared at the rising, billowing blackness of the cloud. For a few moments I was baffled as to what could have caused such a cloud. I thought maybe a nuclear, chemical, or biological weapon had been used by the Iraqis as a last-ditch retaliation to stop our relentless assault. The prospect that we were flying toward a cloud of potentially toxic, irradiated, or biologically contaminated air made me far more scared than facing their biggest guns and missiles. As we got closer I saw the bright orange flames leaping up from oil wells on the desert floor. There were hundreds, perhaps thousands of these orange lights amid the smoke. This must have been planned and executed by Saddam's army. The fires raged, and to see them from above fifteen thousand feet impressed upon us the severity of the situation. The damage to innocent human life, animal life, the environment, and property was going to be astronomical. This was not an act of war in which there exists a code of honor; this was a criminal act.

The blackness of the smoke dissipated only insignificantly as it rose into the sky a sinister black and at altitude became a sickly dark gray cloud. In its appearance and purpose the smoke embodied pure evil. It turned day into night, and it seemed to have a life of its own as it drifted south looking to intercept any inbound coalition aircraft. "What a disaster," I said into the mike as I prepared to get into position to tank from the KC-135.

"I can't believe it," said Shoe. "I have never seen anything like it. It is a tragedy. Saddam is one sick sonuvabitch."

The cloud was billowing in the wind and it seemed that as we watched there were more and more oil fires starting in the desert, adding to the blackness of the cloud. Seeing the oil fires and random, wanton destruction they represented filled me with a renewed conviction to strike at our enemy and defeat him. Soon the cloud of toxic oil fires would be drifting toward the tanker track and it would degrade visibility significantly as long as these fires raged. Perhaps that was the intent. Perhaps it was a tactical move. If it was a tactic, it was ineffective and was having the wrong result because it only served to infuriate our coalition forces. Everyone became more determined than ever to defeat Iraq swiftly, end the war, and remove the Iraqi Army from Kuwait. It was necessary not only to repatriate Kuwait, but also to put out the fires that now were destroying the land and natural resources of Kuwait.

Once we were topped off with gas we detached from the tanker and began our flight to the northwest corner of the Gulf. Perhaps we were overconfident, but we flew with the attitude that there was no more air threat to us, and the AAA and SAM threat, while still significant, was pocketed in specific locations. After thirty-eight days of similar missions we felt we knew where the threats were located. We were confident that the SA-2s and SA-3s had been silenced along the coastline and that our only real threat for a low altitude "wormburner" patrol was from small-arms fire and AAA.

"Nav's tight and we're on time," said the XO, who was busy cross-checking everything in the cockpit to make sure that we were fully operational. "Let's start our descent to get under this oil fire smoke. I don't want to be a 'grape' in the clouds," he said. I agreed it would be far better to see what threat might be coming at us so that we might have a chance of avoiding it.

"Yes, sir," I said as I pulled the throttles to idle and allowed the

Prowler's enormous blunt nose to seek the earth. Our current heading took us right toward the base of the oil fires sprouting up from the desert landscape. As we descended I could not help but think that we were descending into hell's inferno. The black smoke rising from the desert varied in intensity. The lower we got, the darker it was. At the darkest part where the fire was burning brightly and the smoke was the blackest—this was the place where the Republican Guard was living. Saddam's elite fighters were located throughout the area and our air wing's mission now was to destroy them.

Knowing that my buddies in the Intruder and Hornet squadrons were flying above me dropping ordnance on the Republican Guard positions, I felt a strong desire to be with them instead of patrolling the coast in defense of a fleet that had already won the war on the waters of the Persian Gulf. We passed through 5,000 feet and the radar altimeter started beeping.

"Radalt reset to three thousand feet," I said as I adjusted the altitude bug on the instrument's face to beep again at 3,000 feet. The tone went off again at 3,000 feet and still we were in the black smog created by the oil fire smoke.

"Radalt reset to a thousand feet," I said, following procedures to the letter. The steady *beep-beep-beep* came on again as the jet descended through 1,000 feet above the ocean. Now I slowed my rate of descent and began to concentrate a bit more. The numbers on the radalt were now marked in hundreds of feet. "Radalt is now set at five hundred feet," I said, hoping we would not have to go much lower than that. My eyes watched the needle as it moved past 900, 800, 700, 600, and 500. *Beep-beep-beep*, sounded the warning tone. "Radalt now set at two hundred feet," I said. Slowly I began to get more visibility as we descended the final 300 feet.

"Let's keep it above two hundred fifty feet, and let's take it in close to the coast. I want to check out the oil damage," said Nitro.

"Yes, sir," I said as I leveled off at 250 feet and 300 knots. Our ground-mapping radar showed the coast about five miles away and we kept flying ever closer to the coastline that we now assumed was safe and under our coalition control.

"Are you picking up any signals in the back?" asked Nitro.

"Nothing," said Shoe confidently. His voice eased my mind about the possibility of some new SAMs that could have come to the area under cover of confusion caused by the coalition's ground attack. Below me the water's surface was smooth. It was probably because of all the oil that was being dumped into the Gulf from pipelines that had also been opened along the coastline. It was a depressing sight and I shook my head in disgust. It was as if the Iraqi Army had stabbed Kuwait multiple times and held the country to the ground as it bled slowly to death. The pollution seeping into the Gulf caused a black slick of infection that was slowly spreading. The inferno's black smoke now blocked the light of the sun, making it seem as if evening had arrived. We flew over coalition ships and several small islands until we were within a mile of the coast. I turned to the north and followed the coastline as Odie and Shoe listened for any signs of Silkworm activity.

As we flew north along the coastline I kept scanning the shore, looking for anything that signaled hostility. I was definitely nervous, feeling once again like a very vulnerable "grape." The beaches looked ugly and tarry due to the oil that they had absorbed. My scan came back inside the cockpit to check the instruments. Everything looked normal.

"Tank, ten o'clock low on the water," said Odie from the back-seat. As my eyes shot in that direction I immediately saw what Odie was describing. The water was being churned up in a line moving toward us. A quick glance to the left confirmed my fears as I spotted the muzzle flashes of an AAA emplacement. The gunner was aimed low, and his bullets were hitting the water two hundred yards closer to shore than we were flying. The gunner started to adjust his fire, and the line of bullets hitting the water began to walk toward our jet. My left hand shot forward gripping the throttles, and my right hand buried the stick in my thigh as I turned sharply away from the bullets now hitting the water below us. Our climbing right turn exposed the Prowler's belly to the gunner, giving him a huge target, but somehow he was not able to adjust his fire quickly enough and we soon entered the black smoky haze of the oil fires, without being hit.

"Any radar activity?" Nitro asked the backseat.

"Still nothing up," said Shoe.

"Damn, I thought these radars would come up, with all of these ships so close to the shore," said Nitro. The visibility was terrible. I could barely see the port wingtip of our jet during the initial stage of the climb. We had flown a mission profile that made me feel like a live worm wiggling on the end of a hook. The fish had come after us, but fortunately, had not swum fast enough to catch us.

My concern quickly turned from bullets to jets, other American jets from the other air wings on other carriers. Once again I was flying blind and I hated the feeling. I nearly had had a midair collision once in the northern Gulf, and I knew that it could easily happen again.

The time and maneuvering at low altitude had depleted our fuel more quickly than anticipated, so now it was time to head for the tanker. The climb-out through the blackness of oil smoke was unnerving, but within minutes we had risen above it and I leveled off at twenty-five thousand feet en route to the tanker, to be followed by a zip-lip recovery on the *Midway*. It was a relaxed daytime return flight and it gave me time to think about the mission we had just flown.

The inferno on the ground had added a new element of risk to our missions. As smoke rose into the atmosphere it created a haze that was in some ways worse than the smoke itself. At least when you flew in thick clouds of smoke you *knew* you couldn't see anything, but the haze it created on its fringes was more deceptive; you *believed* you could see more than you actually could. The next day the haze would be worse; Odie might not be able to see the bullets hitting the water; I might not be able to see the muzzle flashes that I had seen today. And tomorrow the gunner might adjust more quickly, so then we might not be flying our jet back to the *Midway*.

These were not constructive thoughts. I knew they were natural, but I couldn't stop myself from thinking about all the "what-ifs." *What if I hadn't been so lucky today? What if I am not so lucky tomorrow?* I could sense that the fighting would soon be finished, but would it end soon enough? Now more than ever before, what I wanted most was simply to survive.

CHAPTER TWENTY

Mission Complete

"*Beep-beep . . . beep-beep . . . beep-beep . . .*" chirped the annoying sound of my wristwatch alarm. I reached over in the dark, grabbed it, and pushed each of four buttons until the intolerable noise stopped. It was time for an early-morning brief. I had set the watch to give me just enough time to roll out of bed, shave, and make it to the 0500 brief. Even though I had been awake planning the upcoming mission late into the night, I had gone to bed ready to go flying. I was wearing the shirt and shorts that I needed, and my socks were prepositioned in my flight boots, which sat on the floor. Above the boots hung my favorite flight suit.

I slid out of bed as quietly as possible in the dim red glow of light and took my shaving kit to the bathroom. I no longer noticed the smell of JP-5 in the water as I shaved and brushed my teeth. The smell had become a part of an existence that I really hoped would end soon so that I could get home to Alice and my family. Even though I no longer smelled JP-5, I still felt it sting my freshly shaven face as I rinsed off the shaving cream. I always wondered what would happen if there was a fire and I tried to put it out using this sink water. I was convinced that it would make the fire worse.

A hollowness was there again in my stomach, which felt tight. I knew I should try to eat something before this long mission, but I didn't think anything in the wardroom would really appeal to me. Above all, I needed to stay hydrated and I knew that I would take along enough water for that. The bright white light from the bath-room had temporarily blinded me, and as I left the sink and reen-tered the dimly lit bunkroom I was groping clumsily. I nearly ran into Skippy, who was on his way to shave. We exchanged quiet good-morning grunts. Skippy would be late, but he was in the back-seat and the overview brief wasn't as important for backseaters. Tiptoeing back through the dark room using my hands as a blind man would, I found my flight suit and boots and put them on. My eyes started to adjust to the darkness as I dressed by feel and then made my way out to the passageway.

The brief was scheduled to start two minutes later in the Eagles' ready room, which was adjacent to ours, so I planned to pass through our ready room, pick up our cards of the day as well as a blank kneeboard card, and go right to the brief. I made my way quickly through the passageway, ducking under bundles of cables and stepping over the kneeknockers. It was a form of exercise that helped to get my blood flowing on the way to our ready room. As I walked, a new feeling joined the hollowness in my stomach—the horrible feeling of having forgotten something. My mind started ticking off the critical items I needed for the mission. I had given the strike lead our SEAD plan briefing sheet the night before, with a specific description of the aircraft and weapons load-out of the jets involved, so I was confident it wasn't something necessary for the mission brief, but it was *something*: What was it?

When I reached the ready room door I was still deep in thought. What was it that I had forgotten? It would drive me mad until I remembered. I glanced at the mailboxes, which were all clear be-cause it was early and only crews flying in this event were awake. My box was empty, but then it hit me: *mail!* I had forgotten to bring the letter I'd written to Alice late the night before, and as a result, I had also left my good-luck pen in my stationery box. My right hand made the familiar reach to my left-shoulder pen pocket in my flight suit, and there was nothing. I had never forgotten my pen before a mission. This was not a good sign. Not only would I be late for the brief because I would need to go back to the bunk-room, but now my habit pattern and ritual had been broken. An uneasy anxiety started to crawl over my body. Maybe today would be the day I would get—

"Hey, Tank, come and look at this," yelled Wolfey, who was standing in the middle of the ready room. I broke out of what must have appeared to be a nightmarish trance and walked down the aisle between the ready-room chairs. Wolfey pointed at the closed-circuit TV. Big white block letters were printed across the black screen. The message read:

**TERMINATE OPERATION WOLFPACK.
REJOICE, WE ARE VICTORIOUS.**

My eyes locked on Wolfey's and we both smiled as we walked toward each other with our right hands extended. After forty-three days of fighting, the war was over. Gucci and Skippy came into the ready room and started whooping when they saw the message. "We did it! It's over. We're going home," I said, filled with a sense of pride and relief. The smiles were broad on all the men's faces. We started shaking hands and pounding each other on backs and shoulders. We didn't really know what to say, but our mutual joy shared in the moment of victory was clearly understood.

There would be no more dark nights worrying about coyotes and cheetahs sneaking up behind us; no more looking at friends wondering whether or not this would be the last time I would eat a meal with them; and no more flying through Iraqi bullets. My squadron mates could rip up the letters that they had written to their wives in case they were shot down. There would be no more catnaps between missions and no more need to call on your body and spirit to do more than was reasonable to ask of them. There would be no more prayers for the poor grunts in the desert. The feeling of relief was tangible in the ready room. I imagine my face showed the same.

In that small ready room on the *Midway* my crew felt a sense of accomplishment and shared a moment of fulfillment with all those people who had participated in Operation Desert Storm. Our sense of pride was wrapped in the belief that this was an historic moment.

President George Bush had said, "This will not stand," and we had taken his words to heart. For our crew, our squadron, our air wing, and our ship it was one of life's moments that gets engraved forever in one's memory. The coalition built during the Gulf War represented a display of international will unlike any seen since World War II, and it made me appreciate even more the sacrifices and hardships that the world had suffered through fifty years before. Ours was but a small sip from glory's cup compared to the grim sacrifices of the allied soldiers, sailors, airmen, and marines who fought so nobly for so long; but our small sip set a country free.

While voices of my squadron mates chattered around me I stood back and looked at all the happy faces in the ready room. Wolfey was calling all of the staterooms and bunkrooms in the squadron to pass the word that victory was ours. At that moment, I realized how thankful I was that we hadn't lost anyone in our squadron to this war. Even though UMPQUA hated him, Alpha Charlie deserved some credit, I believed. He did not lead us the way we wanted to be led, but perhaps he led us the way we had to be led. In the final analysis, it was hard to argue with the fact that we all survived and performed our mission so well that all the rest of our air wing survived. I suppose I would rather follow a mean sonuvabitch in combat who could keep me alive than a nice guy who might get me killed.

I soon left the ready room and went back to the bunkroom to retrieve my pen and write a letter to Alice, the person with whom I most wanted to share this moment.

28 Feb 91

> *Dear Alice,*
>
> *The war is over. Soon we will be heading home, and soon we will be together again. I am incredibly happy and relieved. I really can't believe how great you are to me. Yesterday I received four letters from you. I read each one several times. In one of them you wrote, "You're stuck with me." Well then, I guess we're stuck with each other.*
>
> *Given my geographically undesirable status and the extreme unpre-*

dictability of my job I hope that you will agree we need to make the most
of any opportunity we have to see each other. . . . I expect that I will be
able to get leave in conjunction with LSO school sometime in July or
August, but there is no way that I can wait that long to see you, so I
suggest that you visit me in Japan after your exams. . . . You can con-
sider the airline ticket a birthday present to a law student on a budget
from someone whose income is derived directly from your tax dollars. . . .

In one of your letters you wrote that you feel you really know me well
in some ways but not at all in others. I believe that we know each other
incredibly intimately in all of the ways that are truly important, such as
character, integrity, and loyalty. The other small things are things to be
excited about learning about each other. I know that when I write the
words I love you, *they mean exactly the same emotions to you as they*
do to me. We share common values and beliefs. This is why we write to
each other every day and find that to be the best part of our day. Let's
make it all happen, Alice; all of the things we have both been dreaming
about since we met each other. You will be in my dreams.

All my Love, Sherm

The *Midway* stayed in the Persian Gulf for another ten days as
the air wing flew missions monitoring a no-fly zone that was established by the surrender agreement. I was then offered a great opportunity when I was picked by our XO to be his right-hand man
for making arrangements for the battle group's port visit to Pattaya
Beach, Thailand. Nitro had been selected as the senior shore patrol
officer, and he selected me to be his assistant. We flew off the
Midway in a COD a few days after the Iraqi surrender in order to
set up for the arrival of almost ten thousand American sailors at a
small beach town on the coast of Thailand's best deep-water bay.

Nitro and I spent the next two weeks meeting with local business
leaders and government officials in order to reserve blocks of hotel
rooms and to convince local establishments to treat our sailors well.
As senior shore patrol officer, Nitro had the authority to recommend or not recommend any establishment based on his own judgment. If he believed it was not a good place for our sailors to visit,

he could even make it "off limits." The local businessmen took this threat seriously and were extremely friendly to us during our two weeks of advance work. The *Midway* and her men had fought in the "mother of all battles," as Saddam had called it, and now it was our job to ensure our sailors got to experience the "mother of all parties." After more than one hundred consecutive days at sea, we knew that the sailors were going to need to let off some steam. It was our mission to make sure they could have fun and do it safely.

Our two weeks of advance work with local businesses and government officials paid off, because after the battle group had spent five days in Pattaya Beach, no one had died. A few sailors came close though. One was found floating face down in a pool, but he was rescued and revived in time. Another sailor had helium balloons tied to his neck when someone near him flicked his Bic lighter, making the balloons explode. He survived, but was badly burned. Another sailor came to the shore patrol office extremely drunk and tried to convince us that he was James Bond. We had several hotel rooms set up for the James Bond types whom we promptly restrained and encouraged to sleep it off.

The next stop was Hong Kong, which was quite tame compared to Thailand. After a few days there, the *Midway* turned toward Japan and sailed for her homeport.

Ten days later I woke up for the last time in the new-guy rack with the plastic hanging over it to protect me from the constant dripping of hot water from the steam pipe. I realized that I was the last new guy who would sleep in this rack on an operational deployment. Who had some of the previous new guys been? I wondered if there was a great navy hero who had slept in this rack when he was a lieutenant junior grade. If so, he was probably now an admiral, more than likely already retired. The *Midway* had served nobly for many years and it was time for her to haul down her colors. In a few months' time the *Midway* would sail back to the United States to be decommissioned and scrapped. It was sad to see so great a ship with so much history be reduced to razor blades, but she was past her prime and her time had come and gone.

Now we were about to pull into Yokosuka, Japan, our homeport. Somehow the *Midway* was bringing home everyone who had left on the deployment in September 1990, seven months earlier. I felt unbelievably fortunate not to have lost anyone close to me. The captain and the CAG deserved great credit for that and at least, in my mind, so did Alpha Charlie. Our skipper knew he was not liked by the junior officers in our squadron, but he believed he had saved our lives by being tough on us throughout the deployment. I cannot argue that point because it is true; nobody was killed in combat. The only problem was that what he considered tough, we found degrading and intimidating. He had commanded the squadron in his own way, and on paper we had been successful. Our mission was to ensure that all strike aircraft were protected from the Iraqi air defense threat, and we had accomplished that mission to perfection. I would have led our squadron differently, but perhaps my results would not have looked so good on paper. I suppose for that reason being in Alpha Charlie's squadron was educational. It was a valuable lesson for me in terms of what I view as important in a leader.

Without having faced the loss of a close friend the war experience seemed somewhat surreal to me. I was glad that was the case, but it was finally brought close to home when I learned of friends on other carriers who had lost squadron mates. One friend of mine from high school, a Hornet pilot on the *Saratoga*, lost his wingman on the first night strike over Baghdad. I understood his pain, and yet found it difficult to empathize because I had not experienced such a loss. The feelings must be horrible; the hollowness and sense of loss combined with wondering, *What if I had been in his jet? What if I could have made a radio call to warn him of the incoming missile, or just in general, what could I have done differently?* I was so thankful that nobody I knew well had made the ultimate sacrifice. For those who did lose loved ones, the war was even more real.

*   *   *

Two days earlier, all of the carrier's aircraft had taken part in the longstanding tradition of the air wing fly-off. The fly-off was always dramatic and made for a glorious homecoming for the more senior aviators in the air wing. Many lieutenants and almost all lieutenant junior grades, myself included, were left behind to ride the boat to the pier. As a member of the air wing, I thought I should be with the air wing when they flew off, and I felt terribly out of place on an aircraft carrier without aircraft. Representative aircraft from each squadron flew over the airfield in Atsugi, Japan, in a dramatic diamond formation. It would have been great fun to participate, but I was just too junior. At the time of the fly-off I was quite depressed, but after all the senior guys had left, the ship took on an enjoyable and relaxed atmosphere. For forty-eight hours a few of us enjoyed life without Alpha Charlie and Nitro. There were, of course, a few unlucky senior officers left onboard to supervise the "underlings" who remained behind. The night before, I had learned that I was on the list of officers required to "man the rail" for the *Midway*'s homecoming. This meant that I needed to get dressed in a formal uniform and stand on the edge of the flight deck for the final two hours of the *Midway*'s last deployment while tugboats guided her to the pier.

The uniform I needed to wear was called service-dress blue. Just like all my classmates, I had bought a well-tailored version of the uniform when I completed Aviation Officer Candidate School in Pensacola. The double-breasted jacket was highlighted by gold striping on the sleeves, below an embroidered gold star. Each of six gold buttons had an eagle embossed on it that gleamed even in the dim red light of the bunkroom. I checked each eagle carefully to make sure it was "flying"—that is, upright in relation to the ground. I wore my wings of gold over my heart so that the bottom tip of the anchor at the center was just exactly one quarter of an inch above my pocket. I didn't have any medals or ribbons yet, but I was excited to think that would be changing soon. My hat, or my cover (according to navyspeak), had been sitting in my locker since my arrival onboard in December, so it looked a bit crumpled. Yet with a little bit of care and attention I stretched the wrinkles out of the white fabric. As I prepared my uniform, I remembered doing the same thing for uniform inspections with Staff Sergeant Massey United States Marine Corps. As I got dressed, I attempted to inspect my own uniform with the same degree of attention to detail with which Staff Sergeant Massey had inspected it over two years before.

"I can't believe I have to man the rails this morning," I said to Pokey as I prepared my uniform.

"Well, I'm sure you could skip it if you wanted to," said Pokey from behind the curtain of his rack. Being a relatively senior lieutenant, Pokey had not been asked to man the rails.

"Yeah, I suppose nobody would notice," I responded hesitantly.

"Even if they do notice, what are they going to do—take the time to find you and ball you out? I doubt it." I knew that for all practical purposes Pokey was right, but I just felt obliged to follow through. I put on my uniform, polished my shoes, and grabbed my cover.

"Pokey, I'll let you know how it goes. I'm going to go up to the flight deck." I heard some incomprehensible grunt from Pokey's bed, and I was out of the room before I could hear his comment.

The service-dress blue uniform felt very strange, since I had worn nothing but flight suits for the past four months. The necktie and tight, polyester-blend shirt chafed my neck as I walked through the passageways toward the squadron spaces and the hatch, where I planned to access the flight deck.

"Hiya, Beast," I said as I breezed past the maintenance control office.

"Hello, Tank," said Beast with an approving nod that told me I was looking sharp. Not that it really mattered though, I thought to myself; there was nobody here in Japan who was going to be waiting for me or waving a sign that said, WELCOME HOME, TANK. Alice was back in the United States eagerly awaiting my return, but the fantasy of seeing her in the crowd put a little spring in my step. I wondered what her banner might say if she could have been here? However, I knew she would *not* be here because she was in the middle of her law-school final exams, but it was still fun to dream.

Once on the flight deck my stride was filled with a mixture of enthusiasm and caution. I walked carefully, trying to avoid the slickest parts of the deck. The flight deck was a sea of activity. Everyone was smiling and cheerful. The sailors all looked sharp in their service-dress blue uniforms with the "crackerjack" flaps on their backs flapping happily in the spring breeze. The starboard rail, which would be facing the pier as the *Midway* was backed in by tugboats, was already packed with eager sailors. I walked over to the starboard side and tried to squeeze in to the crescendoing crowd. It took some effort to wedge myself into the front row, but being an officer helped, as the young sailors showed me more deference than perhaps I deserved.

I realized that standing there shoulder to shoulder amid these sailors would be the ideal medicine for any American cynic. Their faces radiated so many positive emotions. I saw happiness, friendship, self-confidence, and above all, I saw pride. These young men were bursting with pride in their ship, their US Navy, and their country. It was an electrically exciting scene to witness. These were not sailors from my squadron, I did not recognize any of them, and yet we were sharing this moment. I made eye contact with one of the young men, who looked no more than eighteen. Instead of looking away, he met my eyes and smiled. "Hello, sir. Great day to be alive!" he said. The energy in his eyes could probably have powered up his hometown for a week.

"It certainly is," I replied as I offered him my hand. We shook hands for just a moment and then returned to our own little worlds each searching on the pier. It was unrealistic for me to even look for or hope to see Alice, but I knew that others around me were also searching and hoping. As we came within sight of the pier the sailors around me got more and more excited. I was glad I was with these young men at this moment. We were now standing at parade rest with our hands behind our backs and our feet spread shoulder-width apart. My chest was out, my shoulders back, my stomach in; their pride had inspired me. My eyes kept scanning the crowd.

The tugboats worked hard, their engines churning up water and creating a frothy wake. Hundreds of sailors and officers lined the starboard edge of the ship as the *Midway* closed in on the pier. There were thousands of people, both American and Japanese, waving American flags and also displaying welcome-home banners. I started to look with interest at the signs and faces in the crowd as we got closer. First-time dads were looking for their "cruise babies." CONGRATULATIONS DAD, IT'S A BOY! or IT'S A GIRL! signs were prevalent as were signs with big red hearts in between two names. Most of the signs were on large white sheets so that they could be visible to the flight deck. My eyes wished that there would be one that said ALICE & SHERM. I looked at the sailor next to me, who simply said, "There she is!" as his smile broadened and his eyes remained locked on his love. I felt a fleeting sense of jealousy, and then I shared in his happiness. He too had probably been writing to her every day, dreaming of her at night, and now he was practically jumping out of his skin to hold her in his arms. I tried to pick out who she was on the pier, but there were just too many faces.

For me, watching this scene reminded me of sitting on top of a mountain boulder, viewing the exciting point where two powerful tributaries join forces to become a mighty river. Soon the brow would go down and sailors would rush off the ship in search of their families. Within minutes the two crowds would be swirling, bubbling, and gurgling together just like an eddy formed at the point of confluence in a river of emotion. The power of the moment lay in the anticipation of it, as if the brow were a floodgate holding back and separating the two tributaries. But no physical barrier could truly keep these two groups apart. The interaction of the currents had been happening for the previous seven months and was happening in the space between the ship and the pier. It was truly a magical atmosphere where hope, fear, pride, and love swirled around powerfully, making it a uniquely human moment.

There was a band on the pier playing martial music. The trumpets' sound filled the still morning air. Every single one of the faces on the pier was elated. The worries and fears of the past seven months were now gone, washed away by a torrent of joy. I felt drenched by feelings emanating from the pier. It was like nothing I had ever experienced, for it was indiscriminate love and affection washing over all of us on the *Midway*. It was the most genuine and powerful homecoming that I have ever and probably will ever experience.

The loudspeaker on the flight deck boomed, "Attention on deck. Hand salute." Officers and sailors snapped to attention and saluted a large American flag on the pier that was waving easily in the breeze. The band on the pier then started to play the national anthem while we all stood at the rail with our right arms bent at the elbow, our hands raised to our brows. I checked my positioning to make sure that it was just the way that Staff Sergeant Massey United States Marine Corps had taught me to salute. Up my spine shot the familiar tingle that I feel every time I hear the national anthem. Its familiar notes offered each of us a homecoming. My eyes wandered to the left and right along the long line of men. I caught glimpses of sailors singing the words we all knew by heart. For me, the mission was now complete.

In several of my letters from the *Midway* I had invited Alice to spend the upcoming summer with me in Japan between her second and third years at law school. Realizing that we had only actually spent seventy-two hours together, Alice wisely suggested that I first come home to Connecticut for a few weeks of vacation, before we made a decision about the summer. I agreed that made sense and arranged to take three weeks' leave from the squadron in May, hoping to convince Alice to come back with me to Japan in June for a visit. It was clearly a test, but having just won a war, I felt up to the challenge. It was a test for both of us, to see how we would enjoy each other's company over a period of time longer than the wonderful memory of our Thanksgiving weekend together five months earlier.

I arrived at LaGuardia Airport in New York on May 14, 1991, and Alice was there to meet me. It was a hot day and she was wearing a white cotton shirt and pink shorts that accentuated her tanned arms and legs. Even though five and a half months had gone by since we had last seen each other, we both knew right away that the spark in our relationship was not only still there, but had ignited a fire. We had said so much to each other in our letters that when we first saw each other we didn't talk much, not knowing where to start. It was as if we wanted to say it all again in person, but we both knew that was not necessary. At the arrival gate we kissed briefly and nervously, the way you kiss when you are just a little bit embarrassed and excited.

Alice and I spent every waking moment together seeing friends and family, going to welcome-home parties, and even sneaking away for a few days to the Adirondacks. My parents hosted an especially large welcome-home party in my honor. The reception that I received was overwhelming. I had heard on CNN that America had really come together behind the Gulf troops, but to see it, feel it, and shake the hands of people who were thankful for what we had done made it real for me. I felt incredibly proud to have taken part in something that I believed was good for America's soul as a nation. I believe that the Gulf War helped rekindle the love between our nation and its military, and since I loved both of them, I could not possibly have been happier. The three weeks went by too quickly, but after many long walks, long talks, and late nights, Alice decided to visit Japan.

We flew back to Japan together in June, and one month later we took a trip to Kyoto over the Fourth of July long weekend. On a moonlit night on the shore of Lake Biwa, I got down on one knee and asked Alice to marry me, and she said yes. We soon set a date for the end of September 1992, fourteen months away. The wedding would be after her graduation from law school, her passing the bar exam, and my return from my next six-month deployment.

The Operation Desert Storm deployment was the *Midway*'s last operational cruise, so sadly, our air wing needed to find a new aircraft carrier. The navy decided that the *Independence* would replace the *Midway* as America's forward deployed carrier based in Japan. So, in September 1991, with Air Wing Five embarked, the *Midway* sailed out of Yokosuka Harbor for the last time on its way to Pearl Harbor. There we met the *Independence* and its air wing and we swapped carriers. Air Wing Five retained its name, but its composition of aircraft was completely different. We had lost one of our Intruder squadrons and one of our Hornet squadrons; and we gained two F-14 Tomcat squadrons and an S-3 Viking squadron. For those of us who had served on the *Midway* during Desert Storm, it was a difficult transition. In our minds, no carrier could possibly replace *Midway*'s magic.

Even though it had been difficult to land on, the *Midway* had an indomitable spirit. Sailors who had served on her were aware of the magic that existed onboard this great warship, which infused sailors and aviators with a belief that we could do anything we set our minds to, whether it was clearing the deck for an emergency aircraft in less than six minutes or resurfacing the flight deck in only five days. No challenge was too great for the *Midway* and her men. The carrier left Pearl Harbor and sailed toward America's west coast where she would be decommissioned and eventually scrapped.

The following spring I returned to the Persian Gulf with my squadron and the new Air Wing Five now embarked on the *Independence*. We flew missions in support of Operation Southern Watch, enforcing the no-fly zone that had been established immediately after the Iraqi surrender. It was more green-ink time in my logbook, since the area was still considered a combat zone. The missions were much more of a cat-and-mouse game than the directed definitive strikes that we had flown during Desert Storm. However, the constant threat of SAMs always kept the flying interesting.

Of course, Iraq's attempts to defy the no-fly zone brought tensions to a head just as we had planned to leave the Persian Gulf in August. As a result, we were extended into September, and I began to get nervous about missing our wedding. The wedding was scheduled for September 26; we had reserved the church and reception place more than a year in advance. As days went by I began to become more distracted about not getting off the carrier than I was about getting shot at by an Iraqi SAM. At the last possible moment the *Independence* was finally relieved by another carrier, and I left and flew out of the Middle East just six days before our wedding. It was a close-run schedule, but I arrived home just in time for all the parties. It was truly a beautiful wedding and magnificent reception in lovely New Canaan, Connecticut. Alice and I were married at last, and our two families were inseparably joined.

At this writing, I have decided to leave the navy and pursue a graduate degree, with plans to enter business. Alice and I have just celebrated our third wedding anniversary, and we have a wonderful twenty-month-old son named Henry.

My service in the United States Navy will always be a high point in my life. It has truly been an honor and privilege to serve with such a dedicated, loyal, and patriotic group of men and women. In my mind, the United States Navy is America's first line of defense, and naval aviation will always be at the tip of America's sword.

GLOSSARY OF NAVAL

AVIATION

ACRONYMS AND TERMS

AAA Antiaircraft artillery.

ACLS Automatic Carrier Landing System. A system that links the aircraft to the carrier and provides azimuth and glide-slope information to the pilot for night carrier landings. Its fully automatic feature, which allows aircraft to land without pilot control inputs, was unavailable to the Prowlers flying off USS *Midway*.

ADB Aircraft Discrepancy Book. A binder kept by the squadron's maintenance department to track past discrepancies, known as "gripes," with a jet's systems.

AFCS Automatic Flight-Control System.

angels Altitude in thousands of feet: angels 12 = 12,000 feet.

AOA Angle of Attack. Aerodynamic term for airspeed in terms of the nose attitude of an aircraft. A nose-up attitude gives a higher angle of attack and lower airspeed. A lower nose attitude offers the opposite.

AOCS   Aviation Officer Candidate School.

bandit   A confirmed enemy aircraft.

BDA   Battle Damage Assessment. A military intelligence term meaning post-strike evaluation of damage caused to the intended target.

bingo   The predetermined amount of fuel that when reached will force an aircrew to divert to a suitable direct airfield ashore.

BK   A bunkroom on a ship for junior officers, which would normally house six to ten men.

BN   Bombardier/navigator.

bogey   An unidentified aircraft.

break   The break is the entry point into the carrier daytime landing pattern. The purpose of the break, a 180-degree hairpin turn overhead the carrier, is to bleed airspeed so that the pilot can safely lower the landing gear, flaps, and slats transitioning to the landing configuration.

CAG   Commander of the Air Group. The acronym has been maintained even though now the job is officially called Commander of the Air Wing. The job is held by a navy captain.

CAP   Combat Air Patrol. A defensive mission performed by fighter aircraft protecting either another aircraft or possibly the aircraft carrier itself.

CO   Commanding Officer.

COD   C-2 Greyhound aircraft designed for Carrier On-
              board Delivery.

CVIC   The *Midway*'s hull number was CV-41. The let-
              ters *CV* indicated aircraft carrier in the navy's ship
              designation system. As a result, CVIC stood for a
              Carrier's Intelligence Center.

division   Formation of four aircraft.

DME   Digital Measuring Equipment. A digital readout
              in miles, indicating the distance between the air-
              craft and the TACAN (Tactical Air Navigation)
              ground or ship station selected by the pilot in the
              cockpit.

ECMO   Electronic Countermeasures Officer. There are
              three ECMOs in a Prowler's crew. One sits beside
              the pilot and focuses on navigation, while the
              other two sit beside each other in the backseat and
              concentrate on the radar-jamming mission.

EOB   Electronic Order of Battle. The EOB details the
              location and characteristics of Surface-to-Air Mis-
              sile (SAM) sites, early-warning, and acquisition ra-
              dars.

ESM   Electronic Surveillance Measures. ESM entails
              passive electronic signal collection used to develop
              an EOB.

G force   One G is equal to the force of gravity. As you walk
              around on the street, you are under the force of
              one G. In an accelerated state in the air (i.e. a
              sharp turn), you can multiply the force of gravity.

For example, a 200-pound man executing a 5-G turn weighs in effect 1,000 pounds.

go dirty   Expression used to mean transitioning the aircraft to the takeoff/landing configuration. The aircraft is "dirty" when the landing gear, flaps, and slats are all extended, and "clean" when they are all retracted.

gouge   Navy slang for advice or wisdom passed from senior to junior aviators.

HARM   High-speed Anti-Radiation Missile. The missile homes in on selected radar frequencies and destroys the radar site emitting the signal.

Hawkeye   Type of aircraft. E-2C Hawkeye command and control aircraft.

head   Navy term for toilet.

Hornet   Type of aircraft. F/A-18 Hornet strike-fighter.

hot mike   Cockpit intercom setting which means that the microphone is on constantly, not just when keyed. It allows the entire crew to hear not only the pilot speaking but also his labored and stressful breathing.

HVU   High Value Unit. The Prowler is an HVU because its replacement cost is close to seventy million dollars. There were only four Prowlers in the *Midway*'s air wing.

ICS   Internal Communications System on an aircraft.

IFF   Identification Friend or Foe. A coded device that emits a discrete signal from an aircraft that allows battle group assets to identify friendly aircraft.

ILS   Instrument Landing System. ILS is a backup system to the ACLS. It provides slightly less accurate azimuth and glide-slope information to the pilot.

INS   Inertial Navigation System.

Intruder   Type of aircraft. A-6 Intruder.

INU   Inertial Navigation Unit.

JO   Junior Officer. Typically considered to be lieutenants, lieutenant junior grades, and ensigns, the three lowest officer ranks in the navy.

JOPA   Junior Officer Protection Association.

LSO   Landing Signals Officer.

marshal   The stack of aircraft waiting to make night or bad-weather approaches for landing on the aircraft carrier. The stack is staggered by altitude and distance from the carrier, the lowest in the stack being the closest and the highest being the farthest.

meatball   The Fresnel optical landing system on the deck of the aircraft carrier displays visual glideslope information to the pilot on final approach.

nugget   A navy carrier pilot on his first deployment.

pass   A synonym for approach.

PLAT   Pilot Landing-Aid Television. The PLAT view is broadcast throughout the aircraft carrier's closed-circuit TV system from a camera flush mounted on the centerline of the flight deck's landing area.

Prowler   EA-6B Prowler electronic attack aircraft.

RTB   Return to base.

RTF   Return to force. Used in place of RTB when at sea.

SAM   Surface-to-Air Missile.

SDO   Squadron Duty Officer.

SEAD   Suppression of Enemy Air Defenses. SEAD is the Prowler's primary mission. The Prowler accomplishes the mission by employing HARM missiles for a "hard" kill on radars or jamming for a "soft" kill.

section   Two-aircraft formation.

skipper   Naval aviation term for commanding officer.

strike   Area of control within a fifty-mile radius of the aircraft carrier.

TACAN   Tactical Air Navigation. A cockpit instrument that displays azimuth and distance information to the selected ground or ship station.

TEAMS   Tactical Electronic Attack Mission System.

Tomcats   Type of aircraft. F-14 Tomcat fighter aircraft.

TOW   Tail Over Water. Refers to jets parked on the flight deck edge so that the tail section of the aircraft is actually hanging over the edge.

trap   Arrested landing on ship or shore where the aircraft's tailhook grabs a steel cable that stops the aircraft.

UMPQUA   Underprivileged Minions Perpetually Questioning Unlimited Authority. Title of VAQ136's JOPA.

UNREP   Underway Replenishment. UNREPs are conducted while at sea to replenish the carrier with everything from beans to bullets.

Viking   S-3B Viking anti-submarine warfare aircraft.

XO   Executive officer. The XO is the second in command after the CO.